The Early Modern Englishwoman:
A Facsimile Library of Essential Works

Series III

Essential Works for the Study of
Early Modern Women: Part 2

Volume 7

Women and Witchcraft in Popular Literature,
*c.*1560–1715

Selected and Introduced by
Marion Gibson

General Editors
Betty S. Travitsky and Anne Lake Prescott

ASHGATE

The Introductory Note copyright © Marion Gibson 2007

All rights reserved. No part of this publication may be reproduced, stored in a retrieval system, or transmitted in any form or by any means, electronic, mechanical, photocopying, recording, or otherwise without the prior permission of the publisher.

Published by
Ashgate Publishing Ltd
Gower House
Croft Road
Aldershot
Hants GU11 3HR
England

Ashgate Publishing Company
Suite 420
101 Cherry Street
Burlington, VT 05401-4405
USA

Ashgate website: http://www.ashgate.com

British Library Cataloguing-in-Publication Data
Women and witchcraft in popular literature, c.1560–1715. – (The early modern Englishwoman : a facsimile library of essential works. Series III, Essential works for the study of early modern women, Part 2 ; v. 7)
  1. Witches – England – History – 16th century – Sources 2. Witches – England – History – 17th century – Sources 3. Trials (Witchcraft) – England – History – 16th century – Sources 4. Trials (Witchcraft) – England – History – 17th century – Sources 5. Women – England – Social conditions – 16th century – Sources 6. Women – England – Social conditions – 17th century – Sources
  I. Gibson, Marion II. Travitsky, Betty S. III. Prescott, Anne Lake
  306.4

Library of Congress Cataloging-in-Publication Data
The early modern englishwoman: a facsimile library of essential works. Series III, Essential works for the study of early modern women, Part 2 / general editors, Betty S. Travitsky and Anne Lake Prescott.

Women and witchcraft in popular literature, c. 1560–1715 / selected and introduced by Marion Gibson.
    p. cm. — (The early modern Englishwoman. Series III, Essential works for the study of early modern women. Part 2 ; v. 7
  Includes bibliographic references.
  ISBN 978-0-7546-4136-0 (alk. paper)
   1. Witchcraft—England—History—Sources. 2. Women—England—History—Sources. I. Gibson, Marion, 1970–
  II. Series.

BF1581.W63 2006
133.4'309420903—dc22

2006045879

The image reproduced on the cover is part of an emblem from *A Collection of Emblemes*, Book 3, p. 178, by George Wither, 1635. *STC* 25900c. Reproduced by permission of the Folger Shakespeare Library, Washington DC.

ISBN 978-0-7546-4136-0

Printed and bound in Great Britain by Antony Rowe Ltd, Chippenham, Wiltshire

CONTENTS

Preface by the General Editors

Introductory Note

The Examination and Confession of certaine Wytches at Chensforde (1566)

A Detection of damnable driftes, practized by three Witches arraigned at Chelmisforde (1579)

W.W.
   A true and iust Recorde of the Information, Examination and Confession (1582)

G.B.
   A MOST WICKED worke of a wretched Witch (1592)

A. Ri. [James Balmford?]
   'A Report Contayning a brief Narration', pp. 92–103 in *The Triall of Maist. Dorrell* (1600)

Witches Apprehended, Examined and Executed (1613)

Damnable Practises Of three Lincolne-shire Witches (1619)

Henry Goodcole
   The wonderfull discouerie of ELIZABETH SAWYER a Witch (1621)

A MOST Certain, Strange, and true Discovery of a WITCH (1643)

THE EXAMINATION, CONFESSION, TRIALL, AND EXECUTION, Of Joane Williford, Joan Cariden, and Jane Hott (1645)

Mary Moore
   Wonderfull News from the North (1650)

Francis Bragge
   WITCHCRAFT Farther Display'd (1712)

PREFACE
BY THE GENERAL EDITORS

Until very recently, scholars of the early modern period have assumed that there were no Judith Shakespeares in early modern England. Much of the energy of the current generation of scholars has been devoted to constructing a history of early modern England that takes into account what women actually wrote, what women actually read, and what women actually did. In so doing, contemporary scholars have revised the traditional representation of early modern women as constructed both in their own time and in ours. The study of early modern women has thus become one of the most important – indeed perhaps the most important – means for the rewriting of early modern history.

The Early Modern Englishwoman: A Facsimile Library of Essential Works is one of the developments of this energetic reappraisal of the period. As the names on our advisory board and our list of editors testify, it has been the beneficiary of scholarship in the field, and we hope it will also be an essential part of that scholarship's continuing momentum.

The Early Modern Englishwoman is designed to make available a comprehensive and focused collection of writings in English from 1500 to 1750, both by women and for and about them. The three series of *Printed Writings* (1500–1640, 1641–1700, and 1701–1750) provide a comprehensive if not entirely complete collection of the separately published writings by women. In reprinting these writings we intend to remedy one of the major obstacles to the advancement of feminist criticism of the early modern period, namely the limited availability of the very texts upon which the field is based. The volumes in the facsimile library reproduce carefully chosen copies of these texts, incorporating significant variants (usually in the appendices). Each text is preceded by a short introduction providing an overview of the life and work of a writer along with a survey of important scholarship. These works, we strongly believe, deserve a large readership – of historians, literary critics, feminist critics, and non-specialist readers.

The Early Modern Englishwoman also includes separate facsimile series of *Essential Works for the Study of Early Modern Women* and of *Manuscript Writings*. These facsimile series are complemented by *The Early Modern Englishwoman 1500–1750: Contemporary Editions*. Also under our general editorship, this series includes both old-spelling and modernized editions of works by and about women and gender in early modern England.

New York City
2007

INTRODUCTORY NOTE

In late 1581, as icy winds blew in from the marshes and the North Sea and the east coastal communities shivered through another winter, two neighbours fell out in the small English village of St. Osyth, Essex. This must have been an everyday occurrence, when resources were scarce and tempers proportionately short. But in this case it would lead to the death of one of the female antagonists and the imprisonment of the other. One of the women, Ursley Kempe, later told how her friend Ales Newman had come to her house and called her a witch. Ales had further said that she would take away the instruments of Ursley's witchcraft and show them to the local magistrate. Surprisingly, Ursley did not take the accusation seriously – she thought Ales 'did not meane it'. Yet witchcraft was a serious crime, defined as such under the Witchcraft Acts of 1542 and 1563 (and later 1604). The 1563 Act then in force stated that anyone proven in court to have invoked evil spirits, or to have used witchcraft leading to someone's death, would be executed. Even if such witchcraft led only to its victim becoming ill or losing goods or money, the convicted witch would be imprisoned for a year and forced to stand in the pillory four times during her sentence. Given the unhealthiness of Elizabethan gaols, this often amounted to a death sentence. Ursley should have taken the accusation seriously.

But after their quarrel, a strange thing happened – according to Ursley. She and Ales resolved their differences, and instead of Ales taking Ursley's 'witcherie' to the magistrate, Ursley allowed Ales to take it to her own home. Her 'witcherie' turned out to be several familiar spirits, demonic creatures that witches were thought to keep, often in the shape of talking toads, cats or other animals. Familiars symbolized the witch's supposed pact with Satan and assisted her in harming others. Ursley was admitting that she was indeed a witch. But what she was offering Ales was the chance to obtain her magical instruments. Perhaps Ales would be reassured if she knew where Ursley's spirits were – at least they were not attacking Ales. Or perhaps she was being offered a share in Ursley's power. Either way, shortly thereafter Ursley went to Ales and asked if she would mind sending Ursley's familiars to Grace Thorlowe. Grace was a servant with whom Ursley had quarrelled over a payment of cheese in exchange for a healing spell. Ursley wanted to punish her, and Ales sent a spirit to make her ill. When it returned it told Ursley that it had attacked Grace's knee. Ursley rewarded it with a drink of blood, which familiar spirits were thought to suck from witches, and the spirit went home to Ales.

This is a story that begins plausibly, in a recognizable landscape of poverty and neighbourhood tensions, but soon stretches the limits of our trust. Once we realize, from the pamphlet reproduced in this volume, that the story is actually Ursley's response to examination by the magistrate, to whom she was eventually denounced as a witch by Grace Thorlowe, several issues become pressing. How far can we believe Ursley? Do we stop once her story involves magic and talking cats? Or do we question its very basis – her relationship with Ales and the strange cooperation following the quarrel? Was this a shared fantasy of empowerment? Did it happen at all? Ursley is apparently trying to shift the blame for sending her spirit onto Ales. Yet she also implicates herself in something most modern readers will think impossible. Why would she claim a witch's power and thus risk her life? Why would she call the magistrate back and offer three separate confessions, each more detailed and fantastic than the last? Ursley was executed for witchcraft in 1582, having pleaded guilty at her trial and having implicated several other women.

Meanwhile, an unusual fate befell Ales Newman. When questioned, she said that she remembered quarrelling with Ursley and thinking her a witch, but she objected to everything else that Ursley said, despite the magistrate's attempt to trick her. She stoutly denied she was a witch. Why was Ales able to resist the suggestion that she was an omnipotent magician, a devilish sinner, when Ursley could not? Why did she speak hardly at all, whereas Ursley filled pages of the scribe's paper with stories of spells and revenge? Ales did all the right things to avoid conviction, but she was charged jointly with Ursley with causing the deaths of three people by witchcraft and both were found guilty. Yet whilst Ursley went to the gallows, Ales was reprieved and imprisoned. This was not, however, the one-year penalty imposed by the statute for lesser witchcraft offences. Ales was still guilty of a triple murder, and Elizabethan gaols were not easy to leave – alive, at least – if one was poor and could not afford fees. Several other witches imprisoned with Ales died within weeks of each other in 1583, possibly of gaol fever. But Ales survived and continued to wait. And in 1588, the year of the Spanish Armada, she was pardoned in a general pardon and released.

Between the 1563 Witchcraft Act, which facilitated the prosecution of witchcraft in the Elizabethan assize courts, and the repeal of the laws in the 1736 Witchcraft Act, around 90 per cent of those we know were indicted for the crime in England were female. Witchcraft was regarded as *crimen exceptum* (an exceptional crime), since it was difficult to produce hard evidence of it, but from 1563 it was indictable. There are significant problems with the figure of 90 per cent female accused, however, not least because it is based only on *surviving* records. The best survival rate of English assize court documents is that of the records of the home circuit, the judicial district covering the five southeastern English counties: Essex, Hertfordshire, Sussex, Surrey and Kent. Here, there are just under 800 cases where an indictment for witchcraft survives, or one is known about from other sources, but there are many reasons why these records are not fully representative.

First, about a quarter of these assize records from the time of Elizabeth and James I are missing. Second, despite the cultural importance of the area, a sample based only on the counties surrounding the capital cannot compensate for lost records elsewhere. England's counties were unequal in size and status, their administration also complicated by ancestral judicial rights and exemptions, but each judicial unit would have produced records of prosecution. These might have shown important regional differences in, say, the conception of witches' power, or in the sex of suspects. Scholars have been at work on regional judicial records, but documentation simply does not survive in any bulk for the pre-Civil War period in the North, West or Midlands, so that in these areas a complete survey from 1563 will never be possible. Estimates of prosecutions and executions are only guesses; James Sharpe's *Instruments of Darkness* only reluctantly offers a figure of about 500 executions. Published works are often our only evidence: Goodcole's *Wonderfull Discoverie* (1621), for example, or Moore's *Wonderfull News* (1650), both reprinted below.

Third, records of accusations rejected before the trial or resulting in acquittal were supposed to be discarded. This was often not done, apparently, for many such records remain, yet we do not know how many others succumbed to correct procedure. Fourth, many cases never reached the courts. This could happen for a variety of reasons. Witchcraft prosecutions usually began with a magistrate taking statements from the parties involved – informations from accusers and examinations from suspects – which he was then obliged, because witchcraft was a serious crime or felony, to forward to the assizes along with the suspected witch whom he must commit to gaol. But if, for example, a quarter session (or its equivalent meeting of local magistrates to judge non-felony cases) occurred between the committal and the assize, the witchcraft case might be heard by a grand jury there so as to determine if it should progress, at which point it might be thrown out and lost forever. Similarly, if the suspect died in gaol no trial would be held. No one knows how many cases were lost to the archives in these ways.

Finally, despite the Elizabethan government's determination to bring witchcraft prosecutions under the jurisdiction of the secular, criminal courts, many cases continued to be brought to church courts, as had been traditional, or were dealt with informally – for example, by recourse to counter-magic. Although the 1563 law and its 1604 successor provided for prosecutions for a range of witchcraft crimes other than those causing injury or death to animals and humans, there seems to have been great reluctance to address these lesser crimes in the assize courts. Raising spirits to assist in treasure hunting, or practising sorcery to provoke unlawful love were both forbidden, but there are only a few surviving home circuit indictments for the former, and none for the latter. The Jacobean Act was even more wide-ranging: as well as restating previous provisions, it added that conjuration of, covenant with or feeding of evil spirits was punishable by death, as was the use of any part of a dead body in witchcraft activity no matter what the result. Yet there is no evidence that such provisions resulted in a rush of prosecutions, and lesser witchcraft matters, as well as some that concerned felonious activities, continued to be dealt with by the Church's legal system.

The one known exception is the Palatinate Court of Great Sessions at Chester, the local equivalent of the assize. Here, the high proportion of male accused is matched by the many accusations of conjuration and medical magic, suggesting that men were quite readily suspected of witchcraft. But the kind of witchcraft of which they were more likely to be accused was less often brought to the criminal court than was the *maleficium* (harming and killing) more usually attributed to women (see Sharpe 1996). Scholars who have worked on ecclesiastical records in the South East, South West and North have discovered substantial numbers of witches, male and female, not present in the total given for assize prosecutions. Since these totals are themselves limited by the date and type of record survival, it is clear that there are major problems in the discussion of witches' gender as well as of other statistical data. Nevertheless, women are an overwhelming majority in each series of records, and the association between women and witchcraft is evident throughout the printed works.

Why were so many women thought to be witches, guilty of an impossible crime? The question is a broad one, for people across Europe from Russia to Portugal shared similar beliefs, as did most other societies (and as some do today). But the question must also be a specific one, for not all early modern European societies believed that most witches are women (Ankarloo and Henningsen). In Finland, the sex of accused witches varied over the period of its witch trials: in the sixteenth century about 60 per cent of the accused were men, whereas this was reversed during the 1660s and 1670s during the peak of prosecutions. In Estonia, 60 per cent of defendants were male. In Iceland, with few prosecutions, they were overwhelmingly male with only 10 out of 120 cases made against women. Although other European nations and the American colonies believed that witches were usually female, they differed as to how they thought witches behaved.

In England, female witches were more likely to be held responsible for *maleficium* than for conjuration. They were more likely to bewitch by private mutterings than to raise storms at 'sabbaths' with several hundred other witches. There is evidence of sabbath beliefs in Scotland, where political turmoil and Catholic–Calvinist conflict appear to have lent credibility to fears of massed covenantings with Satan, but even in the later English period there is little that reminds us of Continental gatherings. Clearly, English images of largely female and largely solitary witches were distinctive, even if closely related to assumptions elsewhere. England's accusatorial court system may have played a part in creating this distinct stereotype: typical stories led to secure convictions. But England's social structures, political history and moderate Protestant Church surely helped predispose accusers, questioners and readers of pamphlets to expect witches to be women, and women represented in a certain way.

The economics of early modern England, with its hard-pressed agricultural communities, also helped intensify the fear of witches. Late Elizabethan England, caught in agricultural depression, was torn between old and new understandings of what to do about the poor. Should beggars and persistently needy neighbours be offered charity (according to the model of mutual dependency idealized by Catholic feudalism) or driven away as work-shy and undeserving (a model growing out of early capitalism's Protestant work ethic)? In the late 1960s, Keith Thomas and Alan Macfarlane concluded that economic marginality was a major factor in the accusation of witchcraft because of this confusion. Deprived of the charitable provision by Catholic institutions and of the old official injunction to give alms, they argued, English Protestant society hardened its attitudes to the poor with new poor laws. Women were particularly vulnerable economically: more likely to be reduced to begging, they were open to accusations of witchcraft when refused charity. A classic situation has a witch who, denied help by a neighbour, goes away murmuring to herself, and then the neighbour's cattle or family fall ill or die. In identifying this story, both Keith Thomas and Alan Macfarlane draw on contemporary documents, especially those of the Kentish gentleman Reginald Scot. In 1584, Scot wrote:

> May it please you to waie what accusations and crimes they laie to their charge, namelie: She was at my house of late, she would have had a pot of milke, she departed in a chafe bicause she had it not, she railed, she curssed, she mumbled and whispered, and finallie she said she would be even with me: and soone after my child, my cow, my sow, or my pullet died, or was strangelie taken.

Scot regards this as a foolish rationalization of unconnected events, but he also specifies the refusal of charity – a source of witchcraft stories (Macfarlane; Thomas).

Why do women in the pamphlets so often seem unproblematically to accept their identity as witches who have killed their neighbours, husbands and children? It has been suggested that women claimed medical or sacred power as witches because to claim power of any kind satisfied a deep need in a misogynist society. They were seldom invited to speak at length about themselves, especially assertively, and what we read in the accounts of witches (and their female accusers) is often just such unusual assertion (Gibson, 1999; Ginzburg; Purkiss, 1996), sometimes against other women. Examining the home circuit records, James Sharpe found that almost as many women as men were called as witnesses at witch trials from 1600 to 1702. In some cases, there were more women than men, and in one case all the witnesses were women. This is made remarkable by the finding that, for example, in all felony cases from 1610–19 in one county there were twelve male witnesses to every one female. Women were apparently much more likely to give evidence at a witch trial than in any other felony case. Did a magical realm allow them space to speak and act, albeit constrained by man-made legal discourse and laws, even if doing so against each other? Was there a satisfaction in creating a text with self-assertion that might even see print?

Witchcraft in the pamphlets does appear as a crime committed or imagined in hotly-competitive female space. As Sharpe says, 'witchcraft accusations ... reveal a social arena where channels of female force, female power, and female action could run' (1994). The stories told by witches and accusers often involve home baking, brewing, spinning or child-rearing – all activities in which women took the lead. Other women who came to the door to beg or to borrow household resources were thus a threat. For Diane Purkiss, this was true both in actuality (resources were precious in a world where accuser and accused might quarrel over one dish, or two eggs) and symbolically (Purkiss, 1996). The woman at the door who seemed later to have cursed the beer, functioned for the accuser as an 'antihousewife, her own dark Other', because she had brought pollution and disorder to the victim's house. This explains why women fell out even in cases where charity was granted – where an item had been lent, or a resource freely given, yet where the witch was still thought to have attacked, invading her victim's precious home. This is a fantasy world in which female competition can be read as resentment of a fetishized mother figure (Willis; Roper). Here the pamphlets' female voices appear self-possessed, deploying the stories that we read as weapons in a battle over women's space.

Witchcraft as a belief and a literary topic fulfilled many cultural and social functions. Belief in witchcraft did not end neatly – it persists without legal reinforcement to this day in some quarters – and it did not end because of the dawns of feminism or the Age of Reason. As Stuart Clark has pointed out, it was still possible to construct a rational defence of witchcraft belief, as demonologists had long done, by assuming an implicitly binary universe in which the existence of God and his ministers argues for the existence of Satan and his. For Clark, belief in witchcraft (and its focus on women) was likewise a matter of oppositions and inversions. That which was other than the dominant (female, for example) could be seen only in terms of the dominant (male, for example), and thus as oppositional or wickedly parodic. As feminists know, such thinking has not ended, and neither has belief in witchcraft. Why, then, was its prosecution ended in 1736? Ian Bostridge suggests that hatred and fear of witches, imagined as the opposite of a unified and politically neutral state, made no sense in a new age of parties: if the state is no longer sacral, and if enemies are not devils but Whigs or Tories, what place does witchcraft have? We shall see that pamphlets on the Jane Wenham case in 1712 offer a case study of the decline of witchcraft belief.

Texts on Witchcraft

The story of Ursley Kempe and Ales Newman is one of many that became the subject of ephemeral literature from the mid-Elizabethan period until the birth of the newspaper industry in the eighteenth century. The works reprinted in chronological order below are selected from topical literature representing the prosecution of English women for witchcraft between 1566 and 1712. Each story is unique, full of questions, anomalies and confusing details, and these texts appeared in great enough numbers to show that they were fascinating to a public that included both the literate and those who could listen to others read. The term 'popular' indicates the pamphlets' usual cheapness (although longer ones would have been prohibitively expensive for the 'lower sort'), their ephemeral nature, and/or sometimes crude and hastily produced content, as well as their attempt to publicize and widen understanding of their subject (Watt). Although the pamphlet concerning Ursley and Ales (*A true and iust Recorde* [1582]) is long, most were brief and available for a few pennies. There is little direct evidence of readership, but – for example – a witchcraft pamphlet of 1593, *Most strange and admirable discoverie*, was owned by a church clerk in Nottingham and read or lent to friends as far apart socially as a musician's apprentice and a minister (Harsnett).

Men were also prosecuted for witchcraft, but this anthology concentrates on women as accusers, witnesses, authors and suspects. The materials here represent all the ways in which women's activities as witches were represented in popular literature. Demonologies (the formal theoretical texts on witchcraft) and the texts of plays and poems are omitted here because they were aimed primarily at a more leisured and literate readership who could afford such items. The first pamphlet reproduced here was the first to publicize a prosecution for witchcraft, which it took as its exclusive theme, showing the subject's prominence in public consciousness after the Witchcraft Act of 1563. This thorough and comparatively lavish compilation, with its two poems, transcriptions of pre-trial documents, court report, scaffold speech and multiple woodcuts, was published in 1566 in several parts, indicating a belief in a good market. It was followed by a range of other pamphlets on supernatural themes (before 1736), some 35 to 40 of which can be said to feature a witchcraft trial or witchcraft events. Mostly anonymous, they varied from a few gatherings of leaves to several hundred pages: seven more are included here. Unless otherwise noted, they were printed in London.

Also reproduced, to indicate other sorts of ephemera concerning witchcraft, are a ballad and an extract from a pamphlet that, although mainly concerned with the trial of a well-known minister, appends two vivid sketches of witchcraft accusations. In 1650 came the only witchcraft pamphlet by a woman, Mary Moore. The final pamphlet included here, published in 1712, deals with the last successful prosecution of a woman for witchcraft under English law. The contrast with the 1566 pamphlet is instructive. The last pamphlet was among many polemics on a violently controversial case. Hastily produced and partly reprinting existing work, it is unembellished by poem or illustration and of interest mainly to those interested in the political debate over witchcraft prosecutions. The witch's cultural place had changed decisively. The witchcraft pamphlets began in a world where witchcraft was a matter of God's providence (Lake), a world in which print was still rare and could be employed to encourage the wider community to prosecute witches. They ended when witchcraft was being relocated in a superstitious and semi-literate past, after a battle in the late seventeenth century over the literature of witchcraft as well as over the crime itself. The battle was between those who sought to treat witchcraft as a matter for rational debate, one beyond the judgement of wisewomen, maidservants, wives and female authors like Mary Moore, and those who still thought the crime worth universal concern. It is debatable which side was the more misogynist. Society did not stop prosecuting witches from shame at the wrongs done to woman. Although the significance of witchcraft changed greatly, English society's misogyny and the restricted ways in which women viewed themselves were always key to this significance.

The texts collected here, then, offer a sample of the forms in which witchcraft and the women involved in its prosecution were presented to readers. They suggest the range of activities and characteristics attributed to female witches and the kinds of interventions made by female witnesses and accusers. Most of these women were relatively poor, as their stories suggest. Resources such as a dish or a pint of milk were valuable, and disputes over them were behind many witchcraft accusations. For accusers, the belief that such items might be stolen or spoilt magically by witches was intolerable. Equally, accused witches, who were often as poor as or poorer than their 'victims', often called their female accusers intolerably unneighbourly and perhaps deserving of magical punishment. Women thus fell out with each other over borrowing and lending, payment (often 'in kind'), hotly-contested job opportunities in, say, childcare and wet-nursing, and occasionally over such moral issues as reputation, bastardy and adultery. Some witches are specifically said to have 'base' children or to behave whorishly. Often, therefore, witchcraft accusations were made over matters traditionally assigned to the female, domestic realm, and were made both by and against ordinary, lower-class women.

Less frequently, but significantly, witches and accusers fell out over more conventionally masculine issues such as inheritance, disruption of trade or damage to property. Some witches represented here were accused by propertied gentlemen of causing damage to their stock and their businesses, whilst others were thought to have attacked the male heirs of such families, who had their own anxieties about resources. These latter cases are intelligible from a feminist perspective: rich, powerful men attack poor, disempowered women in an explosion of culturally-sanctioned violence (Hester). But women, too, had businesses and income to protect. They also played a part in cases where expert witnesses such as midwives or respectable 'matrons' were called to search the bodies of accused women for any marks or teats from which spirits might have sucked blood, making an implicit pact between the witch and Satan (Sharpe 1996; Holmes). Frequently, they believed they found them and reported back to the uniformly male magistrates the evidence that sealed the fate of the accused woman. This collection also includes a work by a female pamphleteer, Mary Moore, who thought her claims that her children were bewitched by her female neighbour were not being taken seriously, and who, exceptionally, turned to print in an effort to make her voice heard.

Mary Moore was atypical of witchcraft pamphleteers. Most were anonymous and, where they can be identified, often worked for London publishers to supplement other income. Rather like modern freelance journalists, they had a variety of roles. Frequently, they brought a personal view, that of the moderately educated hack, to the stories they were asked to edit and frame with commentary, often on the criminal and sinful nature of womanhood and on women as socially and sexually disruptive. Each writer takes a different approach – a godly denunciation, humble prayers, a discussion of the competing theories on how the witch gained her power from the devil, a plea for the law to be tightened. Most who worked up a witchcraft case for print did not, apparently, greatly disrupt their source material, for there seems to have been a strong interest in preserving and making available actual courtroom records in such difficult, sensational cases. Many pamphleteers thus maintain distinctions between preface and story, commentary and *verbatim* transcript. This practice offers us several ways of reading the stories: the accused women can be read as negative exemplars, as subjects of fantasy and wonder, and as topics of masculine scientific and theological debate. Most strikingly, all these women are agents or authors, participating with surprising vigour in the creation of stories about witches, including those about themselves.

The Examination and Confession of certaine Wytches… : Representing Women as Witches in 1566

The Examination and Confession of certaine Wytches discusses three 'witches', all women. Each is, in her own way, typical of women suspected of and indicted for witchcraft in the period of the assize witch-trials and then represented in print.

The pamphlet's first accused witch, Elizabeth Fraunces, admits, apparently freely, that she had indulged in pre-marital fornication, attacked both her lover and her husband by magical means, and killed two of her children, one an unborn baby whom she aborted using her knowledge of herbs. She is thus presented as an unwomanly woman who threatens men and their children. A verse preface by John Phillips highlights Elizabeth's unmatronly nature – as part of a general attack on sinful behaviour – and relates how Satan had 'infected' her. The second accused is Agnes Waterhouse, who, we will learn from the second pamphlet reproduced here (*A Detection of damnable driftes*, 1579), was Elizabeth's sister. Agnes was 64, poor and still relying for religious knowledge on the pre-Reformation Catholic teachings of her youth. Like Elizabeth, she confesses that she was a man-killer, and in this case guilty of petty treason in murdering her husband. She appears with the classic witch attributes of economic dependency, unattractive and unproductive old age, and faulty faith. The third accused is her eighteen-year-old daughter Jone, who had, she says, learned witchcraft from her mother. She does not describe any formal initiation or say that she has a familiar spirit, unlike her mother and aunt, but admits to being tempted to witchcraft when denied charity by a neighbour and to using her mother's familiar to bewitch her. Jone is the stereotypical young witch: brought up by her mother, she follows her example by experimenting with satanic magic as she contemplates a life of poverty and isolation in a small village. In the eyes of the pamphleteers, then, Elizabeth, Agnes and Jone are typically witch-like, and *The Examination* brings these stereotypes into popular print.

The English witch is usually portrayed as female, poor and uneducated. She often has religious beliefs unacceptable to post-Reformation English authorities and often violates early modern ideologies of morality and femininity, deliberately or not. Witches are often related to one another, witchcraft descending through the female line. Yet the three women in *The Examination* also differ – suggesting that to stereotype the witches found in legal records or in literature is less helpful than it seems. We all think we know the 'stereotypical' witch, but our stereotypes often display inner contradictions that should prevent us from applying them to any one woman. Witches could be young and sexy, old and ugly, or ordinary-looking women of middle age. They could be socially and economically marginal or possess some lucrative skill or asset. They could be uneducated, or recusant or have an intelligently articulated sectarian (or simply idiosyncratic) faith. They could be married, widowed, virgin or none of these. The pamphlet about Elizabeth, Agnes and Jone begins the stereotyping of English witches, but each is distinct, just as each pamphlet is distinct. Each is a real woman frozen at a moment of crisis in a few pages of opaque text that raise more questions than they answer about each woman's life and her representation in print.

Questions about the relation of representation to reality are particularly troubling in the case of witchcraft, which most people now think unreal. Like *The Examination*, most surviving texts are partly polemical, their already ambiguous stories skewed by the desire to make a point. Additionally, witchcraft was conventionally presented as an exceptional crime, hard to prove and requiring special attention, so that stories told at every stage of a witchcraft trial lean towards typicality. Rather like precedent, typicality – of offender and crime – was some guarantee that the court, the texts produced for and by it, and the society they represented followed tried and tested guidelines. Many accusations and their printed incarnations thus aimed to show a reasonable supposition of guilt by offering a carefully crafted story of motive and crime. This happens in *The Examination*, where texts are shaped by the witches' questioners and by the narrator of the courtroom section. Prefaces and the narrative passages that intersperse transcribed documents often attempt to teach readers to recognize witchcraft, basing their conclusions on elements of the texts they select (Gibson, 1999, 2001; Rushton). The tone is often anxious, responding to an unvoiced questioning of specific evidence or to doctrinal scruples about magical power. Each story is meant to show why a particular woman was a witch and to support belief in witchcraft. We must be cautious in reading these stories, sensitive to the difficulties of deducing the lives of real women from the unreal ones in popular witch literature. Each pamphlet is selling a particular set of beliefs, even when inconsistent.

A Detection of damnable driftes… (1579): Witchcraft and Economics

A Detection of damnable driftes, like *The Examination*, comprises documents produced for the witch trial, with a pious preface. The main text is almost entirely focused on the economic dependency of women, which it and the preface present in a most unsympathetic light. One accused witch, Elleine Smithe, is represented by her accusers as having fallen out with her stepfather over her right to inherit her mother Alice Chaundeler's money. Chaundeler had been executed for witchcraft, and when Smithe's stepfather died of an apparently unnatural disease after the quarrel, Smithe was executed too. Readers are expected to conclude that Smithe was properly disposed of for killing the rightful male inheritor of her mother's wealth. Other women appearing in the pamphlet, including Elizabeth Frauncis/Fraunces from *The Examination*, were also apparently poor. *The Examination* presents Elizabeth as part of a needy underclass, and it is hard not to see *A Detection* as a sequel charting her further depredations. Fraunces explains that she had been denied charity by Alice Poole and had accordingly and effectively cursed her. Meanwhile, Margery Staunton (known here simply as 'Mother') is represented by the informations of her neighbours, two of whom had abused her verbally or physically, and nine others with whom she had fallen out over resources. Most of these had denied her charity or help, and again the reader is expected to side with them – although her acquittal is recorded in surviving trial records (perhaps the judge offered her more sympathy than the pamphleteer). But the final witch, Alice ('Mother') Nokes, who had quarrelled with neighbours over her husband's apparent adultery and various slights, does not, as represented, fit any economic category. Economics cannot account entirely for the representation of female witches in popular literature.

W.W., *A true and iust Recorde of the Information…* (1582): Witchcraft and Female Agency

The argument advanced by Clive Holmes – that female accusers and witnesses were to some degree ventriloquizing patriarchal concerns through a system devised, run and eventually abolished by men – also has merit, forcing us to think about the degree to which female witnesses and witches were in control of their own stories. This is evident in *A true and iust Recorde*, a detailed account of a mass trial of witches by "W.W." based, again, on pre-trial documents. It seems likely that W.W. worked for or with Brian Darcy (d.1587), the justice of peace who plays a prominent role in questioning the accused. W.W. may have been a clerk preparing trial materials for Brian Darcy or a member of the household of Brian's relative Lord Darcy, in whose home the accusations begin and to whom the pamphlet is dedicated. Barbara Rosen suggests William Lowth as a possible W.W., for he dedicates his translation of Bartholomew Batty's treatise *The Christian Mans Closet* to Brian Darcy in 1581 (Rosen, 106). But Brian Darcy himself is clearly responsible for much of the pamphlet's content, determining the questions asked of the accused and recording his own 'clever' attempts to trick them into confessing. The text portrays Darcy as having some knowledge of recent developments in demonology and the politics of prosecution, and the preface echoes this interest with specific reference to *De la Demonomanie des Sorciers* (Paris, 1580) by the French jurist Jean Bodin. The preface argues for tightening English laws on witchcraft, which the author views as heresy, after the French model. W.W. may be Brian Darcy himself, and the accusers and witches in the rest of the account seem to express some of Darcy's concerns. The pamphlet is included here because it raises significant questions about how such texts promote their orchestrators and disempower female witches and accusers proportionately.

Ursley Kempe's accuser Grace Thorlowe, for example, a servant of Brian's cousin Lord Darcy, began the accusations in her community. Her story is pointed and coherent, at least as it appears in the words of the scribe. She seems a confident, self-possessed woman. But there may be evidence of coaching in her testimony (Rosen). Before Grace fell out with Ursley and accused her of witchcraft, she had used Ursley's demonic skills to heal her lameness. But Grace presents this problematic information carefully: Ursley had not been 'sent for' but had offered her skills of her own accord. Thus Grace avoids damaging her testimony by appearing irreligious – resorting to witches for medical aid was officially condemned as ungodly. Meanwhile, Darcy had promised Ursley Kempe favour if she would confess, pressuring her so that 'bursting out with weeping, [she] fel upon her knees'. The superficial impression left by Grace and Ursley is of women confident of their identity and worth who think they can handle the male of the better sort and who expect to be listened to attentively. But both have stories of direct use to Brian Darcy, their questioner, in his own climb up the ladder of local influence, and this seems to be the purpose of their deployment in print. There is also an indication that Darcy used child witnesses' fantastic evidence to manoeuvre their parents into confessing witchcraft and then altered the dates of the children's examinations to make it appear that the adults were confessing freely. (See, for example, the evidence of Febey Hunt and her mother Ales, where on 24 February Ales is clearly responding to Febey's story although the testimony is dated 25 February.) At others' expense, Darcy advances his own reputation as a pious witch-hunter and effective magistrate.

Darcy was the son of Thomas Darcy of Tolleshunt Darcy and his second wife, Elizabeth Bedingfield, daughter of John Haydon of Baconsthorpe, Norfolk. He lived at Tiptree Priory, and his family's home St. Osyth Priory, Essex, features in the pamphlet. He married Brigit, daughter of John Corbett of Sprowston, Norfolk, and they had eight children. Two daughters and three sons survived Darcy. Two sons were educated at Caius College, Cambridge, and one at Lincoln's Inn. Darcy made his first appearance as a justice of the peace at the March assizes of 1581, at Brentwood, and seems to have regarded the massive witch prosecution of 1582 as a showcase for his godliness, efficiency and views on reform of the law against witchcraft. His desires did not prevail completely, for many of the accused were acquitted and the condemned pardoned. But perhaps because of public attention, he became Sheriff of Essex in 1586. He may have been knighted in the year of his death, 1587 (*DNB*). Given his ambition, and the ways in which he manipulated witnesses, we should be wary of seeing women's testimony in *A true and iust Recorde* as a window into their world. That the female protagonists of *A true and iust Recorde* can be so neatly tabulated at the end of the pamphlet, mere numbered entries on a list, suggests the status of their words in Darcy's scheme.

The table must have made the production of the pamphlet more expensive and increased its final price. It is on a large (foldout) paper, and would have demanded careful typesetting and binding work. The publisher, to whom the work was entered in the Stationers' Register on 6 April, evidently thought producing the table worth the trouble, perhaps to show the account's mastery of its subject. That there is a mistake in the ordering of the entries suggests, however, the difficulty of completely capturing such a vast array of contested material. The pamphlet was produced very soon after the events it describes, moreover, with mistakes in reporting verdicts and sentences that suggest an unseemly rush. The difficulty in reading the pamphlet and understanding its contents, which are unchronological, inconsistent and sometimes in conflict with surviving trial records, similarly suggests the inherent ungraspability of a mass witch trial. Since the author lacked organizational tools, the account fails as literature in a way that less ambitious pamphlets do not.

G. B., *A MOST WICKED worke of a wretched Witch* (1592): Truth, Fiction and Polemic

For pamphlets are, after all, literary works. *A MOST WICKED worke of a wretched Witch* clearly depends on Robert Greene's play *Friar Bacon and Friar Bungay* (performed earlier in 1592 at the Rose Theatre) for the story of a servant carried into the air and then to Hell and back by a witch. The servant, Richard Burt, is working in the barn and stops to eat some apple pie, when suddenly he hears a voice calling him away. Going to the door, pie in hand, he is hoisted into the air. Compare his story with that of Greene's Hostess at the Bell Inn:

> Enter a woman with a shoulder of mutton...
> HOSTESSE. As I was in the kitchen mongst the maydes,
> Spitting the meat against supper for my guesse [guests],
> A motion mooved me to looke forth of dore.
> No sooner had I pried into the yard,
> But straight a whirlewind hoisted me from thence,
> And mounted me aloft unto the cloudes (scene 2, lines 116–31)

The characters share the same desire to look out the door, the same immediate and surprising result, and the same verb 'hoisted'. Both victims are of the 'lower sort', comic characters whose basic instinct is to bring their food with them at all costs. Later in his flight, Richard Burt is taken to a place full of fire and doleful cries, where it is very hot. True to form, Richard looks around for an alehouse, because he is thirsty. Compare the servant Miles in *Friar Bacon and Friar Bungay*:

> MILES. But I pray you sir do you come lately from hel?
> DEVIL. I marry how then.
> MILES. Faith tis a place I have desired long to see, have you not good tippling houses there, may not a man have a lustie fier there, a pot of good ale...
> DEVIL. All this you may have there.
> MILES. You are for me, friende, and I am for you, but I pray you, may I not have an office there?
> DEVIL. Yes, a thousand, what wouldst thou be?
> MILES. By my troth sir, in a place where I may profit my selfe, I know hel is a hot place, and men are mervailous drie, and much drinke is spent there, I would be a tapster.
> DEVIL. Thou shalt... (scene 15, lines 30–45)

Like Miles, Richard Burt is worried about how he will earn a living in Hell. The witch, Mother Atkins, seems little more than an abstraction in comparison to her colourful victim and his adventures. *A MOST WICKED worke*, by the unidentified writer G.B., Master of Arts, thus powerfully shows how Elizabethan stories about 'real' witches shaded into popular fiction. The play was performed on 19 February and 25 March and the pamphlet entered in the Stationers' Register on 7 April 1592. G.B. probably saw the play rather than read it, for it was not printed until 1594, but he made good use of his viewing to produce a work meant to entertain rather than to give real information about a witch. Consequently, since there is no extant judicial record, we know nothing about Mother Atkins.

A. Ri. [James Balmford?], 'A Report Contayning a brief Narration' in *The Triall of Maist. Dorrell* (1600): Men and the World of Spirits and Devils

The Triall of Maist. Dorrell demonstrates another way by which pamphleteers could appropriate witch stories for their own purposes. Two of its stories have a potent atmosphere and set of concerns springing from the world of female storytelling and symbolic conflict, but they are extracted here because the pamphlet's powerful male figures test and describe the world of spirits and devils; the pamphlet deploys the stories in a war of words between 'Puritan' and mainstream Church of England officials over the reality of demonic possession. One story is about a poltergeist-like phenomenon linked to an old woman accused by an apparently possessed or obsessed young girl (in 'obsession' cases, the devil remains outside his victim's body but can still control it). The other is a classic story of neighbourly quarrels, likewise between a wicked old witch and innocent girls, with elements of folktale reminiscent of 'Sleeping Beauty'.

This largely anonymous pamphlet, part of whose commentary is signed by the unidentified A. Ri., belongs to the controversy over exorcisms performed between 1586 and 1598 by John Darrell, a Puritan minister from the English Midlands. Darrell was brought before ecclesiastical commissioners in 1598 after his dispossessions by prayer and fasting of William Sommers in Nottingham had led to witchcraft accusations, including that against a cousin of one of the town's aldermen. Nottingham was in sectarian uproar over these accusations and the validity of Sommers' complaint and cure; the Bishop of London, Richard Bancroft, and his chaplain Samuel Harsnett (one day to be Archbishop of York) assembled and interrogated at length many witnesses willing to swear that Darrell was a fraud. Darrell, however, asserted his innocence vigorously, and between 15 and 20 pamphlets were published between 1598 and 1603 debating the Sommers case and those of Darrell's other 'patients' (Rickert; Gibson, 2006). This pamphlet takes Darrell's side, pleading for a fair trial for him. One defence is the assertion that witches can act as Satan's agents in bringing about demonic possession, so the writers of *The Triall* use the two witchcraft cases as evidence that spirits and witches seek constantly to attack Christians in this way. Whatever the motivation and intention of the female accusers and accused, this text shows how the witches Barthram and Kerke and their victims are mere pawns in the wider argument.

Witches Apprehended, Examined and Executed (1613): Women, Witchcraft and Class

On the whole, in the pamphlets discussed so far, the poor accuse the poor. But in Jacobean times a higher proportion of pamphlets and other literature details accusations against the poor by the rich. One example is *Witches Apprehended*. This text concerns a parish swineherd and her daughter, accused of witchcraft by a landowner, Master Richard Enger, who was convinced that their witchcraft had cost him two hundred pounds in losses. His stock mysteriously died, his servants were subjected to strange accidents and illnesses, and one was made incapable of labour. Finally his son and heir died. The sufferings of this rich gentleman are counterpointed by the pamphleteer's commentary on the penniless witches. The older woman, Mother Sutton, had appeared dutiful and hard-working in the job assigned to her to help relieve her poverty – but secretly, the pamphleteer explains, she was harming stock and betraying the community's trust in her. Her daughter, the other accused witch, Mary Sutton, is an unmarried mother with 'three bastards', who appears as a satanic temptress in her victim's visions. The two women thus present both the deserving and the undeserving poor and, significantly, conspire to attack the wealthy and respectable because of supposed slights and ill-usage that the pamphleteer is careful to represent as entirely acceptable behaviour on the part of society's 'better sort'. Mary Sutton's son is beaten for throwing dirt into Master Enger's millpond, the pair are gossiped about as witches and stones are thrown at Mother Sutton, Mary is attacked and forced to visit her supposed victim so that he can scratch her (a common countermagical remedy to cure bewitchment), and finally she is beaten ''till she was scarce able to stirre' and thrown into the millpond. Yet the pamphleteer continues to regard the witches' supposed attack on Master Enger and his servants as motiveless.

The pamphlet is included here as representative of a genre of story told about witches in popular literature that uses third-person narrative rather than legal documents and that adopts the supposed victim's point of view. *A MOST WICKED worke* (1592) is a comic example. But in the more ideologically weighty of these works, the victim is represented as wealthy and entirely innocent, even when the text must acknowledge some falling out between victim and witch. The poor are presented as ungrateful and dangerous, stirring up trouble even when treated well. Tensions over poverty, class and rebellion are evidently behind such representations; later Elizabethan and Jacobean concern grew over the aspirations of the poor and the insecurity of the rich. The pamphlet offers a way for victims to fight back, giving one of the first accounts of how to perform the swimming test (in which a witch's guilt is determined according to whether he or she floats when 'swum' in water). This supposedly showed if the witch had renounced her Christian baptism. Such tests came to be frowned upon by the authorities as superstitious, but they provided an unofficial, vigilante way for those who felt persecuted to confront and disempower their supposed attackers. Once swum, a witch who had floated could be taken before the magistrate with some confidence, and the swimming test became popular. This witch-swimmer's manual was reused in the second and third editions of another pamphlet, *The Wonderfull Discoverie of the Witchcrafts of Margaret and Phillip Flower* (1619; retitled *Witchcrafts Strange and Wonderfull* in 1635).

Damnable Practises Of three Lincoln-shire Witches (1619): Rebellion by the Poor

The anonymous two-part ballad *Damnable Practises Of three Lincoln-shire Witches* was printed as an accompaniment to *Wonderfull Discoverie*, the pamphlet recounting these witches' story. The ballad represents Phillip (Phillippa), Margaret and Joan Flower's supposed activities in musical form, to the apt tune of 'the ladies fall'. Both works refer to the case of apparent bewitchment in the Earl of Rutland's family, in which the women of the Flower family were accused of causing the death of his two sons, leaving him with only a female heir. The women, with several others, were convicted in 1619. Once again, in ballad and pamphlet, poor and ungrateful women are seen rebelling against rich and rightfully powerful men. Margaret Flower was a servant at Belvoir Castle, home of the Earl and Countess of Rutland, but was apparently dismissed for misconduct that *The Wonderfull Discoverie* tells us involved stealing from her employer. Yet, once again, the pamphlet asserts flatly and inconsistently that no injury was done to the women; treated munificently, they had no genuine motive for attacking the Earl's family. The ballad, however, straightforwardly reports that Margaret was 'discharg'd' and that her family plotted 'revengement'. In both ballad and pamphlet women and servants are analogous classes of persons likely to rebel and give the devil access to respectable homes. Both texts also dwell on the witches' other moral shortcomings. The younger witches, especially Phillippa, are sexually threatening ('well knowne a Strumpet lewd') whilst the older woman is verbally so, swearing and blaspheming. Together, they conspire against God, the aristocracy and patriarchy. The ballad ends with an appeal to God to strike down or convert the wicked.

Henry Goodcole, *The wonderfull discouerie of ELIZABETH SAWYER, a Witch* (1621): Preaching and the Politics of Rebellion

Pamphleteers were often keen to adapt witchcraft stories to encourage female submission. Henry Goodcole (1586–1641) was the chaplain of Newgate prison when he wrote his account of an interview with a condemned witch, *The wonderfull discouerie of ELIZABETH SAWYER, a Witch*. He does not seem to have attended a university, but nevertheless describes himself as a 'minister of God's word'. In 1606 he married Anne Tryme; they had a daughter within six months. Goodcole did not obtain the ecclesiastical preferment that he must have desired, but his work at Newgate gave him access to another source of income, of which he made good use. Between 1618 and 1637 he wrote six pamphlets based on his experience of London's judicial system. Attending Old Bailey trials, ministering to Newgate's condemned and accompanying them to execution, he had remarkable access to London's underworld. Like many in his society, Goodcole was interested in female criminality, devoting four of his six works to the subject. The first was the pamphlet reproduced here.

With a focus on Elizabeth Sawyer's 'cursing, swearing and blaspheming', Goodcole's narrative is based on the binary of Christian and anti-Christian. His question-and-answer format, unusual for witchcraft accounts, carefully shapes Sawyer's pre-execution confession into a morality tale about the proper regulation of the Christian voice, especially the female voice. (See Leuschner.) He warns that to speak inappropriately 'is a playne way to bring you to the Divell; nay, that it brings the Divell to you'. Sawyer admits praying to the devil, but Goodcole's careful record of his questions dispels any impression that she originated this notion herself: 'Did the Divell at any time find you praying when he came unto you, and did not the Divell forbid you to pray to Jesus Christ, but to him alone? and did not he bid you pray to him the Divell, as he taught you?', he asks. Sawyer garbles a piece of the Latin *paternoster* in response. Goodcole's text is another reminder of the pamphlets' potential for manipulative mediation of female voices. He co-opts Elizabeth Sawyer, relying on her status as 'a very ignorant woman' to bolster his authority so that he can offer a providential message to his readers, as if preaching to the 'flock' he was never able to serve as a parson. Goodcole's pamphlet was the major source for John Ford, Thomas Dekker and William Rowley's play *The Witch of Edmonton* (also 1621), and it is his description of the witch–devil relationship that is at the heart of their play. The play's exploration of the relative morality of male and female crime and of women's subservient position is deeply indebted to Goodcole.

A MOST Certain, Strange and true Discovery of a WITCH (1643): Women in Opposition to the Godly

The Witch of Newbury represented in *A MOST Certain, Strange and true Discovery* is another woman taking inappropriate command of her world, this time when political authority was being openly contested in the Civil War. She is evidently a political creation, the superhuman adversary of Parliamentary troops, validating by her very opposition their claim to righteousness. She seems both to symbolize and to epitomize the evils against which Parliamentary troops fought the Battle of Newbury. (See Purkiss, 1997.) Firstly, when she appears to a soldier who notices her walking on water, this blasphemous imitation of Christ smacks of the pseudo-miraculous, of the Catholic and of the Royalist, and it is contrasted by the author to the safely Protestant 'Providence of God' that assists drowning persons. Secondly, her body is invulnerable to shot and sword, suggesting that a terrifying immortality might be granted by Satan to such ungodly Royalist enemies as Prince Rupert, widely believed to have a demonic familiar. Thirdly, by her sex she represents the effeminization that many Parliamentarians resented in Cavalier culture, with its long hair and decorative clothing. Finally, the woman identifies herself as a Royalist, scorning her persecutors and foretelling balefully that her loss of power and life means victory for the Parliamentary army. The pamphlet is Parliamentary propaganda, showing witches as enemies of the Commonwealth; here they represent the privileged and decadent Royalists – a very different meaning from that accorded them in earlier accounts.

THE EXAMINATION, CONFESSION, TRIALL, AND EXECUTION Of Joane Williford… (1645): Demonic Women in the Commonwealth

This sense that the emergent Commonwealth was beset by demonic forces is most strongly suggested by the witchfinding activity sweeping across eastern England in the 1640s. In the absence of centralized power and legal processes, swept away by the war, individuals and factions within towns carried out their own judicial processes, which often lacked even the meagre safeguards built into the assize system. The activities of the 'Witchfinder General' Matthew Hopkins were part of this widespread activity, although there is no evidence that he was directly involved in the cases of Joane Williford, Joan Cariden, Elizabeth Harris, and other witches who made similar confessions in *THE EXAMINATION*. But many English men and women shared Hopkins' belief that the devil was conspiring to flood godly society with witches, who represented all that was unwanted in their New Jerusalem. The witches of *THE EXAMINATION* offer very specific testimony of devil worship, highly unusual in earlier English accounts. But the questioning of witches described in Goodcole's pamphlet suggests that Cariden, Harris and the others probably did not originate the idea that they had made a written covenant with the devil. Their accusers found exactly what they were looking for, and it seems likely that leading questions, together with the extra measures, such as sleep deprivation, which Hopkins' supporters introduced to the interrogation process, led the witches to make such confessions. Hopkins denies this in his *Discovery of Witches* (1647), but in doing so he confirms precisely the kind of pressure and pointed questioning to which suspects were subjected – which were then publicized by such pamphlets.

The suspects in Faversham were questioned by its mayor and jurats (the equivalent of magistrates and/or aldermen in the other works reproduced here), for Faversham is one of the Cinque Ports and had its own judicial system even before the Civil War. The mayor himself was thought to be the target of witchcraft, and a diabolical society was imagined with confessions including a sabbath-like meeting with the devil and covenants with Satan that mirrored those made by the godly mayor and jurats with Christ. Although we have no details of the questions asked of these particular women, Goodcole's search for anti-Christianity and his barely-concealed desire to construct a sexual relationship between the heretical witch and devil resurface in Joan Cariden's confession of finding something lying on her in bed (echoed by Jane Hott) and visits to her bed by a devil-dog. Each woman believes she has given herself to the devil in some physical and spiritual way, but Joan Cariden's statement that 'she thought God forsooke her' is typical of the way in which such a belief was often represented – as a loss or feeling of failure by a woman under intense scrutiny. These women seem less in control of their stories than do some of the earlier witches represented in this collection. The pamphlet exemplifies the concerns of this mass witch-hunt that demonized women alongside political and religious enemies. However, it was perfectly possible for men to be accused in the Hopkins-related hunts, and for women to demonize other women, as the next pamphlet shows.

Mary Moore, *Wonderfull News from the North* (1650): Women Writing against Women

Whilst the Civil War continued around her, a wealthy Northumbrian, Mary Moore, wrote *Wonderfull News from the North* to chronicle the affliction of two of her daughters and a son by the 'witchcraft' of a neighbour, Dorothy Swinow (or Swinhoe). These women were on different sides in the conflict and it is hard not to see this division motivating Moore's antagonism. Here again the witch is the Royalist. But Moore also seems to have feared Swinow as an unmotherly, anti-familial woman. Swinow had begun her life as Dorothy Clavering, later Guevara, daughter of Sir Robert Clavering and Mary Collingwood (who, once widowed, married Sir Henry Guevara). She married Gilbert Swinhoe, later a colonel in the Royalist army, who died in the Tower for his offences against Parliament. He had raised the county's forces against Parliamentary troops, and had been the subject of a resolution by the House of Commons on 3 October 1644, barring him from employment. In 1645 he had been captured and imprisoned and was probably dead by 1651. In his absence, Dorothy Swinow had been forced into a position of authority and an attitude of self-defence. She had two sons, Gilbert, later the author of a play about Mahomet the Great's love for a Greek woman (*The Tragedy of the Unhappy Fair Irene* [1658]), and James, killed in a duel in 1671. The family, in fact, lived like classic Royalists, with a love of theatre and high living that had apparently made them enemies locally. They lived at Chatton, County Durham, across the county boundary from Moore in Northumberland.

All these factors – Swinow's status, support and place of residence – made it difficult for Mary Moore to prosecute her successfully. Magistrates could operate only within their own counties and it seems likely that they were also sympathetic to Swinow, in part because of her history and connections. In Moore's account they are seen buck-passing successfully over the Northumberland–Durham county boundary to keep Swinow out of jail. Moore managed to get two arrest warrants, but Swinow was (illegally, and apparently without examination) bailed, and not committed for trial as she should have been as a suspected felon. Moore also alleged that magistrates favoured Swinow by letting her see Moore's information against her and another legal document denied to Moore herself. Some legal action was taken, however. Moore also blamed John Hutton, probably a cunning man or village 'wiseman', for bewitching her children; he was arrested and put in prison, where he died. The pamphlet also prints the examination of another woman, Margaret White, who accused her own sister, Jane Martin, and Dorothy Swinow of joining her in witchcraft practises, including the attack on Margaret Muschamp and Mary Moore. Martin was later hanged.

In this text, Mary Moore appears to have been a potential murder victim herself. During her questioning, White says that Dorothy Swinow had tried to bewitch Moore's unborn child (Sibella) and had then murdered it, after its birth (24–5). An indictment of Swinow for this murder was drawn up and is printed by Moore, who also reports that it was 'found', or endorsed *Billa vera*, presumably by the grand jury at the Quarter Sessions of 24 April 1650, for which it was drafted (25). Yet from Moore's account, it seems that Swinow was not present at this hearing, and a further warrant was issued for her apprehension. No further action had been taken by the time the pamphlet was approved for publication in November 1650. It seems likely, therefore, that Swinow escaped prosecution; no record of an assize trial has been found. If so, Mary Moore had failed in her attempt to prosecute a witch; in any case, she turned to print to publicize her plight and the injustice she felt had been done. Her book is partly a Puritan 'complaint' about the ungodly inattention of local magistrates and partly a personal cry for help, playing on her status as a mother and a woman.

The pamphlet is included here as the only account of a witchcraft event known to have been written by a woman. It thus challenges the belief that prosecuting witches was a masculine activity and that women did not use the language of demonology. Although Elaine Hobby thinks it likely to have been written by a man posing as a woman, Frances Dolan finds 'no internal evidence for this claim'. In fact, there is strong internal evidence that Moore was the mother of the afflicted children and did write the pamphlet whose preface she signed. Her identity and the narrative itself are fractured and confusing, however. Wallace Notestein concludes that Mary Moore was a friend of the children's mother Mary Muschamp, whilst Malcolm Gaskill (2003), confused by Moore's narrative of unsuccessful attempts to make her miscarry, believes they succeeded. Such difficulties are caused in part by Moore's dual marital identity as both a Moore and a Muschamp; inheritance is again a key anxiety in this witchcraft pamphlet. The widow of George Muschamp, by whom she had had five children, Mary was married to Edward Moore when she wrote her pamphlet. Edward already had six sons and at least one daughter, and during the course of the narrative Mary Moore bore him another child, the same Sibella who soon died. Mary Moore is referred to in one of the legal documents with which she concludes her account as 'Mrs. Mary Moore Widdow' (27), but there is no other evidence to suggest that Edward Moore himself died before the completion of the work. Instead, this addition may reflect Mary's strong identity as the widow of George Muschamp, whose children are the victims of the supposed witchcraft. In another legal document she is simply 'Mary' (25), whilst in the text she once calls herself 'Mrs. Muschamp' (10).

Moore also speaks of herself in both third and first persons, introducing further confusion. After her direct address in the preface, she re-introduces herself to the reader very obliquely in a description of her daughter's first signs of supernatural affliction. 'Mistris Margaret Muschamp suddainely fell into a great Trance', she says abruptly, and 'her Mother' (that is, Mary Moore herself) 'being frighted, called Company'. Moore appears as her child's mother rather than as a person in her own right, and as a lonely, frightened figure calling for assistance from others. This can be read both as a gesture of the authorial modesty encouraged in female writers and as an indication that Mary Moore defined herself primarily by her motherhood and her desire to defend her children. Her identity is secondary and relational, and she seems to have no wish to assert herself. But, as the very act of writing and publishing her work suggests, Moore had a strong sense of her own opinion and worth. This bursts occasionally from her text, in a way familiar to readers of early modern women. It is especially explosive when she speaks of the woman she blames for bewitching her children: 'I got her apprehended', Moore says on page 12, suddenly slipping into the first person. Hers is a shifting, elusive and uncomfortable identity, with multiple names and viewpoints, alternating between assertion and shrinking. The account's very complexity seems designed, how consciously we cannot know, to veil or mitigate Mary Moore's insistent need to speak despite her sex. Her text reveals powerfully the stresses involved in maintaining a sense of self in a society identifying women as 'wife of' and 'mother of'. Recourse to the law over a magical matter both freed Mary Moore to speak as an abused individual and placed her in a position of extreme exposure so keenly felt that she is absent from her work's title and title page.

Frances Dolan has given a sensitive account of Mary Moore's identity based on a reading of her family as 'blended' yet riven by 'conflict between spouses and between stepparents and stepchildren'. She notes the pamphlet's references to Edward Moore's increasing disapproval of his wife's activities, expressed through the mouth of his stepdaughter Margaret Muschamp: the witches, says Margaret, will afflict her mother by hardening the hearts of her husband and others against her. Clearly, Mary Moore wrote and published in defiance of her second husband, making her work the more remarkable. She seems to invoke the aid of her first husband as the father of the afflicted children, but his presence can be no more than ghostly. Dolan also notes that the accusations of witchcraft made by Moore both displace tensions (some economic, some political) from her own family onto outsiders, and paradoxically make them more visible. Moore accuses Swinow of killing her sister, thus losing the family her estate, which had been settled on her only for life, and she clearly fears for her own children and their future if Swinow is allowed to escape. Because Swinow was the widow of a Royalist officer, the pamphlet may also be seen as an attempt by Northern Parliamentarians to remove a disorderly Royalist network from their border society. How important is her sex, and her role as an unmotherly adversary of her female accuser's children? Is the pamphlet more interested in family harmony, economic well-being, or the political unity of the divided English nation? As we have seen, witchcraft had a role to play in all these debates.

Francis Bragge, *WITCHCRAFT Farther Display'd* (1712): The Decline of Witchcraft Belief

Francis Bragge, author of *WITCHCRAFT Farther Display'd*, was a Hertfordshire gentleman who, aged 22, became involved in a witchcraft prosecution when the maidservant of his neighbour, Godfrey Gardiner the rector of Walkerne, fell mysteriously sick. The work reproduced here is Bragge's second on the case, chosen because it includes comments on the affliction of the 'victim' Anne Thorn and the *maleficium* of the 'witch' Jane Wenham, and also because it relates these cases to two others that Bragge had researched and reprinted from other works. It shows how intertextual the debate about witchcraft had become, and how it broadened in its final stage beyond the discussion of one individual woman; no wonder that this case became a matter of international import. Bragge, pious and soon to be ordained deacon, was visiting Anne Thorn's employer when she fell ill, on 11 February 1712, and he leapt to join the great debate. He observed the victim and became convinced that she was bewitched. Thorn identified her attacker as Jane Wenham, an elderly villager, and gave evidence of this to Bragge's grandfather, the magistrate Sir Henry Chauncy.

This is a conventional story of a witch's revenge that would once have commanded widespread belief, but by 1712 such reports had become controversial along political, party lines. Walkerne was sharply divided between 'low church' Puritans and Dissenters on the one hand, and 'high church' Anglicans on the other (Guskin). By their actions, Gardiner and his supportive fellow ministers Strutt and Bragge identified themselves with the hotly-contested beliefs in spectral evidence and devilish conspiracy, with the high Anglican and Tory party. Sir Henry Chauncy and Francis Bragge were identifiable with such Tories as Joseph Glanvill, whose *Saducismus Triumphatus* (1681) attacked those who disbelieved in witchcraft as atheist deniers of the entire spiritual world. Sir Henry, 80 years old at the time of the Wenham case, had followed an entirely secular career as a lawyer and antiquarian. He simply did what most magistrates would do when faced with accusations made by two clergymen against a suspect – he committed Wenham for trial at the assizes, which does not make him a Glanvillite. Bragge was obviously of Glanvill's mind, however. The son of Sir Henry's daughter Jane Chauncy and her husband Francis Bragge senior, the Vicar of Hitchin, he intended to follow his father into the Church. The sermons of the senior Reverend Bragge survive and suggest high levels of anxiety over the growth of 'profaneness and infidelity', a concern that his son inherited. In *WITCHCRAFT* he amplifies them into outright accusations of saducism against those who did not believe Jane Wenham to be a witch; he even reproduces some of Glanvill's book. Controversialist writers who later commented on the case took great pains to protect the reputations of Gardiner and Strutt as men of the cloth, so little is known of their theological bent, and thus the brunt of their criticism was borne by Bragge, who was not yet eminent or in orders.

The case came to court and Wenham was found guilty – but not before a blast of judicial scepticism that shocked her accusers. Bragge was appalled by what he saw as the perverse attitude of the Judge, Sir John Powell, a prominent and jocular politician whom Bragge regarded as a supporter of Whiggish scepticism. That the jury ignored Powell's view was of little comfort, for the Judge used his power to reprieve Wenham. A later account suggests that she was freed and given protection on the estate of a Hertfordshire landowner, Colonel Plummer of Gilston. One of Bragge's most earnest complaints, marking him out as a Glanvillite, was that at Powell's instigation the idea that prayer might recover a victim of witchcraft was laughed out of court. To Bragge, this seemed atheist. Fuming, he published an anonymous account of the case, *A full and impartial account* (1712), provoking vigorous public debate. He published two more works, *WITCHCRAFT Farther Display'd* and *A defence of the proceedings against Jane Wenham* (1712). But Bragge was on the losing side. Despite his attempts to prove that Wenham was thievish, whorish, blasphemous, and reviled by her own family, she was not pursued further and was the last person prosecuted for witchcraft in England. In 1736 the Witchcraft Act of 1604, under which Wenham had been prosecuted, was repealed. The new Witchcraft Act made it an offence to pretend to have magical skill, removing the last official endorsement of belief in witchcraft.

Wenham's experience helped prompt the Suffolk curate Francis Hutchinson to publish his *Historical Essay* on witchcraft (1718), firmly consigning the subject to the past. Another factor was Hutchinson's interest in a case from his own parish, one also used as evidence by Bragge in *WITCHCRAFT Farther display'd*, that of Amy Duny and Rose Cullender of Bury St Edmunds. Hutchinson investigated both cases and went to Gilston to meet Jane Wenham, who was still alive. He says:

> I have very great Assurance that she is a pious sober Woman ... She would make me hear her say both Lord's Prayer and Creed and other very good Prayers beside; and she spake them with an undissembled Devotion, tho' with such little Errors of Expression, as those that cannot read are subject to. I verily believe, that there is no one that reads this, but may think in their own Minds, such a Storm as she met with, might have fallen upon them, if it had been their Misfortune to have been poor, and to have met with such Accidents as she did, in such a barbarous Parish as she liv'd in.

Hutchinson mentions in the same passage that Francis Bragge, 'the most vehement Writer, who press'd her most severely with his Pen', had died by 1718.

The case is as notable for the continuing importance of gender politics as it is for its relation to the world of party politics – although it has not traditionally been discussed in these terms. Whilst Bragge was being dismissed as a superstitious, backward fool by the Whiggishly-inclined, little had changed in the way that women were viewed by society. As so often in the past, the reputations of two women were pitted against one another. Bragge had dwelt in his first pamphlet on Wenham's 'Idleness and Thievery', her 'common Swearing and cursing', and her 'Character of a Whore' (*A full and impartial account* 33). This view was rejected by Hutchinson. Yet Wenham's gain was at the expense of her supposed victim, Anne Thorn. Writing later in 1712, the author of *The Case of the Hertfordshire Witchcraft Consider'd* (whom Francis Hutchinson would identify on page 171 of the second edition of his 1720 *Historical Essay* as the Reverend Henry Stebbing) casts doubt on Thorn's chastity and suspects a sexual motivation for her actions:

> Anne Thorne is not so silly and undesigning a Girl, as [Bragge] would make us believe. If she has got nothing else by playing these Pranks, she has got what she calls a good Husband; but it is possible it may hereafter appear, that she got something more.

Stebbing goes on to explain that, on the advice of a 'White Witch', Thorn had been performing a daily ritual of washing her hands with special water designed to procure a husband. While ill, she had then been attended by a 'brisk Fellow' who was often left alone with her for hours at a time. He had given evidence against Jane Wenham, and had now married Thorn and taken her away with him. Her fellow-accuser, Anne Street, had also married one of the trial witnesses. Stebbing lets us imagine the rest of the story, noting only that Thorn had now entirely lost the trust of Mrs. Gardiner. He concludes:

> the Policy of such Girls as these, is not always open to every one's View: They have sometimes Designs too deep to be presently discover'd; and are able to manage such dark Intrigues, as one would hardly suspect in them ... a firm Resolution, join'd with a moderate Share of Cunning, might be able to carry her thro' it: And if what she had was any ways deficient, we know there is one abroad in the World, who is forward enough to encorage People in ill Designs, and who could spare her some of his Policy, to make up those Defects in her own.

With that 'one', Satan, at her side, the accuser Anne Thorn is Stebbing's choice for the role of witch because of her unchastity, dishonesty and cunning. Hutchinson goes further: 'the Maid that was thought to be bewitch'd, was an idle Hussy, with Child at the Time, and was well as soon as her Sweetheart came and married her'. Witchcraft did not disappear in 1736 – it became a metaphor for wicked female charm.

Acknowledgements

Many thanks to the staffs of The British Library, Bodleian Library, Lambeth Palace Library, and Exeter University Library, and to Aude Fitzsimons at the Pepys Library, Magdalen College, Cambridge, for all their help.

References

STC 19869.5 [*Examination and confession*], STC 5115 [*A detection*], STC 24922 [W.W., *A true and iust*], STC 1030.5 [G.B., *A MOST WICKED worke*], STC 6287 [*The triall*], STC 25872 [*Witches apprehended*], STC 11106 [*Damnable practises*], STC

12014 [*The wonderfull discouerie*], Wing M2870 [*A most certain*], Wing E3712 [*The examination*], Wing M2581 [Moore], and ESTC T68954 [Bragge]

Ankarloo, Bengt and Gustav Henningsen (eds) (1993), *Early Modern European Witchcraft: Centres and Peripheries*, Oxford: Clarendon
Bostridge, Ian (1997), *Witchcraft and its Transformations c.1650–c.1750*, Oxford: Clarendon
Clark, Sandra (1983), *The Elizabethan Pamphleteers: Popular moralistic pamphlets 1580–1640*, London: Athlone Press
Clark, Stuart (1980), 'Inversion, Misrule and the Meaning of Witchcraft', *Past and Present* 87: 98–127
—— (1997), *Thinking with Demons: The Idea of Witchcraft in Early Modern Europe*, Oxford: Clarendon
—— (ed.) (2001), *Languages of Witchcraft: Narrative, Ideology and Meaning in Early Modern Culture*, Basingstoke: Macmillan
Cockburn, J.S. (1975–85), *Calendar of Assize Records. Home Circuit Indictments. Elizabeth I and James I*, 10 vols, London: HMSO
Dolan, Frances (1994), *Dangerous Familiars: Representations of Domestic Crime in England 1550–1700*, Ithaca and London: Cornell University Press
Ewen, Cecil L'Estrange, (1929), *Witch Hunting and Witch Trials*, London: Kegan Paul, Trench, Trubner
—— (1933), *Witchcraft and Demonianism*, London: Heath Cranton
Gaskill, Malcolm (1994), 'Witchcraft and Power in Early Modern England: The Case of Margaret Moore', in *Women, Crime and the Courts*, Jenny Kermode and Garthine Walker (eds), London: UCL; partly reprinted in *The Witchcraft Reader* (2002), Darren Oldridge (ed.), London and New York: Routledge, 343–52
—— (2003), *English Witchcraft 1560–1736: The Matthew Hopkins Trials*, Vol. 3, London: Pickering and Chatto
Gibson, Marion (1999), *Reading Witchcraft: Stories of Early English Witches*, London and New York: Routledge
—— (2000), *Early Modern Witches: Witchcraft Cases in Contemporary Writing*, London and New York: Routledge
—— (2001), 'Understanding Witchcraft: Accusers' Stories in Print in Early Modern England', in *Languages of Witchcraft: Narrative, Ideology and Meaning in Early Modern Culture*, Stuart Clark (ed.), Basingstoke: Macmillan, 41–54
—— (2006), *Possession, Puritanism and Print*, London: Pickering and Chatto
Ginzburg, Carlo (1986), *Myths, Emblems and Clues*, trans. J. and A. Tedeschi, London: Hutchinson Radius
Glanvill, Joseph (1681), *Saducismus Triumphatus*, London: for J. Collins and S. Lownds
Guskin, Phyllis J. (1981), 'The Context of Witchcraft: The Case of Jane Wenham 1712', *Eighteenth-Century Studies* 15 (1): 48–71
Harsnett, Samuel (1599), *A Discovery of the Fraudulent Practises of John Darrell*, London: by John Windet for John Wolfe
Hester, Marianne (1996), 'Patriarchal Reconstruction and Witch-hunting', in *Witchcraft in Early Modern Europe: Studies in Culture and Belief*, Jonathan Barry, Marianne Hester and Gareth Roberts (eds), Cambridge: Cambridge University Press
Hobby, Elaine (1989), *Virtue of Necessity: English Women's Writing 1649–88*, Ann Arbor: University of Michigan Press
Holmes, Clive (1993), 'Women, Witches and Witnesses', *Past and Present* 140: 145–79
Hutchinson, Francis (1718), *An Historical Essay Concerning Witchcraft*, London: for R. Knaplock and D. Midwinter
Jackson, Louise (1995), 'Witches, Wives and Mothers: Witchcraft Persecution and Women's Confessions in Seventeenth-Century England', *Women's History Review* 4:1; partly reprinted in *The Witchcraft Reader* (2002), Darren Oldridge (ed.), London and New York: Routledge, 353–66
Lake, Peter and Michael Questier (2002), *The Antichrist's Lewd Hat: Protestants, Papists and Players in Post Reformation England*, New Haven: Yale University Press
Larner, Christina (1981), *Enemies of God*, London: Chatto and Windus
—— (1984), *Witchcraft and Religion*, Alan Macfarlane (ed.), Oxford: Blackwell
Leuschner, Kristin Jeanne (1992), 'Creating the "Known True Story": Sixteenth and Seventeenth Century Murder and Witchcraft Pamphlets and Plays', Ph.D. dissertation, University of California
Macfarlane, Alan (1991), *Witchcraft in Tudor and Stuart England*, Prospect Heights, Illinois: Waveland Press
Notestein, Wallace (1911), *A History of Witchcraft in England from 1558–1718*, New York: Apollo
Oldridge, Darren (2002), *The Witchcraft Reader*, London and New York: Routledge
Pollard, A.W. and G.R. Redgrave (1986–91), *A Short-title Catalogue of Books Printed in England, Scotland and Ireland 1475–1640*, 2nd edn, 3 vols, London: Bibliographical Society
Purkiss Diane, (1996), *The Witch in History: Early Modern and Twentieth-Century Representations*, London and New York: Routledge
—— (1997), 'Desire and Its Deformities: Fantasies of Witchcraft in the English Civil War', *Journal of Medieval and Early Modern Studies* 27:1: 103–32
—— (1998), 'Invasions: Prophecy and Bewitchment in the Case of Margaret Muschamp', *Tulsa Studies in Women's Literature* 17:2: 235–53
Rickert, Corinne Holt (1962), *The Case of John Darrell, Minister and Exorcist*, Gainesville: University of Florida Press
Roper, Lyndal (1994), *Oedipus and the Devil: Witchcraft, Sexuality and Religion in Early Modern Europe*, London and New York: Routledge
Rosen, Barbara (1991), *Witchcraft in England 1558–1618*, 2nd edn, Amherst: University of Massachusetts Press

Rushton, Peter (2001), 'Texts of Authority: Witchcraft Accusations and the Demonstration of Truth in Early Modern England', in *Languages of Witchcraft: Narrative, Ideology and Meaning in Early Modern Culture*, Stuart Clark (ed.), Basingstoke: Macmillan, 21–39

Scot, Reginald, (1584), *The Discoverie of Witchcraft*, London: by Henry Denham for William Brome

Sharpe, James (1991), 'Witchcraft and Women in Seventeenth-Century England: Some Northern Evidence', *Continuity and Change* 6: 179–99

―――― (1994), 'Women, Witchcraft and the Legal Process', in *Women, Crime and the Courts*, Jenny Kermode and Garthine Walker (eds), London: UCL, 106–24

―――― (1996), *Instruments of Darkness: Witchcraft in England 1550–1750*, London: Hamish Hamilton

[Stebbing, Henry] (1712), *The Case of the Hertfordshire Witchcraft Consider'd*, London: for John Pemberton

Stephen, Leslie and Sidney Lee (1921–22), *The Dictionary of National Biography*, 22 vols, Oxford: Oxford University Press

Thomas, Keith (1971), *Religion and the Decline of Magic: Studies in Popular Beliefs in Sixteenth- and Seventeenth-Century England*, London: Peregrine

Watt, Tessa (1991), *Cheap Print and Popular Piety*, Cambridge: Cambridge University Press

Willis, Deborah (1995), *Malevolent Nurture: Witch-hunting and Maternal Power in Early Modern England*, Ithaca and London: Cornell University Press

MARION GIBSON

The Examination and Confession of certaine Wytches (*STC* 19869.5) is reproduced from the unique Lambeth Palace Library copy by permission of the Trustees of Lambeth Palace Library (shelfmark ZZ.1587.12 [03] and ZZ.1587.12 [04]). The pamphlet was entered in the Stationers' 'Register' printed in two parts, although it is in three textual sections. The second is entitled *The second examination and Confession of mother Agnes Waterhouse & Jone her Daughter*. The text blocks of the originals measure 115mm × 65mm and 115mm × 66mm.

Hard-to-read passages in *The seconde examination*:

A3v.30:	good Reader
A3v.31:	To God the Lorde
A3v.32:	woulde
A3v.33:	And thus I ende hopinge
A3v.34:	my traveil well
A3v.35:	And judge the truth when
A3v36:	of this the full effect.
²A3.9:	and
²A3.10:	Sathan she
²A4v.1:	was chirning of butter and
²A4v.16:	wolde have, and he saide he
²A4v.17:	would have butter, and I
²A4v.18:	said I had none for him and
²A4v.19:	then he saide he wolde have
²A4v.20:	some or he went, and then he
²A5.6:	he opened the dore and went
²A5.7:	uppon the shelfe, and there
²A5.11:	and locked the dore and said
²A5.12:	that he had made flap but-
²A5.13:	ter for mee, and so departed,
²A5.14:	and then she saide shee tolde
²A5.15:	her aunte of it, and then she
²A5.16:	sent for the priest, and when
²A5v.1:	to me with the keye of oure
²A5v.2:	milkehouse dore in his mou-
²A5v.3:	the, and then I saide in the
²A5v.4:	name of Jesus what haste

The Examina-
tion and Confession of certaine Wytches at Chensforde in the Countie of Essex, before the Quenes maiesties Judges, the xxvi. daye of July.
ANNO. 1566,
at the Assise holden there
as then, and one of them put to death for the same offence, as their examination declareth more at large.

The Epistle to the Reader.

GOD whych of hys singuler goodnesse (as the sage philosopher Hermes hath plainly discribed) to each of his creatures hath added a reasonable soule, which is the chiefe and most excellent treasure that any man can be indued withall: Let vs then consider gods inerplycable benefits alwayes of his owne free wyll (and not of our desertes) geuen and bestowed vpon vs, and sith that the soule of man is of great estimation in his fatherly presence, let vs endeuour our selues to walke, that by continuall exercise of vertuous and holesome documēts, I meane not onely by hearing of the sincere veritie: neither yet by much talkyng of the same to heare, and not to bear awaye is altogether friuolous: To babble and prate much of Christ and hys gospell (as though we would be counted ghostly gospellers) & to wante the chefest thing, I meane the frutes of well gouerned conuersacion, and to be cleane voyde of integritie, and cleanesse of lyfe, in my iudgement and as the sacred scripture verifieth, is nothynge but folly: (example) A tree that is altogether barren, and at

A ii. the

The Epistle to the reader.

the required time destytute of fruyte hauing a trim shewe of leaues, deserueth to be hewed downe and made meete for the fier: so we wantinge fruites required, but hauing plenty of leaues be of lyke effect, and for all the outwarde shewe that we haue, we shall in like case be cut downe & throwen into the fyer prepared for the deuill and his aungelles, from which (gentell reader) God defende vs all, and geue vs suche grace that we maye henceforthe walke in our vocation, that god in al our workes may be vnfeynedly glorified, and by thadmonitiō of this littel boke learne in such sorte to keepe our soules, by fixed and assured faith in Christ, from the stinking puddle of filthy pollution, then shal we escape that horrible place prepared for the vngodly and wycked liuers, & as profitable seruants be counted apt members to dwell wyth our Sauiour Christ aboue the cloudes in his heuenly kingdome, to the which god for hys mercies sake bring vs all. Amen.

The

The Preface.

My tremblinge hande for feare doth
    quake,
my dolour doth excede:
My ioyes decrese to tender teares
my sportes are turnd in dede.
The gredy gulfs of grysly griefe,
    so gripe my restles harte:
& my pore pen can scantly shewe,
    the passions of my smarte.
Drawe nere you patrones with your babes,
    come viewe this haples happe:
In flushing fluddes of cominge teares
    your tender bewtyes lappe.
Ye matrones milde drawe nere in haste,
    this yrksome acte beholde:
Then Nature shall her rufull playnts,
    by you her Nimphes vnfolde.
Eche wight in whom the skilfull skyll,
    of natures arte is shown:
Surrender may them selues to me,
    this cruell acte to mone.
The heapes of griefs so hugie are,
    that sobbes must nedes abounde:
Yea shrilly shrickes to passe the skies,
    your voyces shall redounde.
The dolour nowe so doutfull is,
    that skante my warbling penne:
Can forth expresse the sence thereof,
    vnto the sonnes of men.
Agayne the blubringe teares whych glide,
    from my poore pincked eyes:
Besmerde my face that scarce I can,
    my inwarde griefes supprise.
One while I blushe for shame to showe,
    these pageantes worthy blame:
Some other time my thoughtes me let,
    these bluddy factes to name.   Thus

The Preface

Thus as I stay in doubt alas,
  my dumpes are passinge great:
My clogged ioyntes benomd with feare,
  haue got Dame sorrowes seat
Her massy mace with direful stroke,
  hath stroke my members all:
But these Periphrases I leaue,
  and will discourse my thrall.
Which to conceaue each reader wyll,
  well way I do not doubt:
Of late in Chencefozde towne deare friendes,
  before the noble route.
Of Iudges iust plast in that seate,
  by our moste famous Queene:
Iudgement to giue as iustice leades,
  as daily well is seene.
The Sessions there by order kepte,
  offenders to correct:
Thre feminine dames attached were,
  whom Sathan had infect.
With Belials sprite whose sorcery did,
  the simple so molest:
That when they woulde with present death,
  they were full sore opprest.
Here after shall succede the actes,
  that they them selues haue wrought:
As they them selues confessed haue,
  to iudgement being brought.
Which thing when thou hast viewed well,
  good Reader do thou praye:
To God the Lorde that he from vs,
  woulde witches take away.
But thus I ende hapinge thou wilte,
  my trauell well accept:
And iuge the truth when thou hast hearde,
  of thys the full effect.

        Finis Prolog.

An exhortacion to all faithfull men wyllinge them to set Gods feare before their eyes and Sathans practises vtterly to despise annexed to the same, profitable for euery Christian man to reade and to imbrace.

Ehold these acts & scan thē well,
behold their peruers sway:
these left ẏ lord these did his truth
which shold haue ben their stay:
In them such power sathan had,
that Christ they did refuse:
his precious blud shed thē to saue
to much they did abuse.
Sin death and hell did spreade their flagge,
in them they bare the sway:
His worde was yrkesome to their hartes,
they walked farre astray.
What tender harte woulde god renounce,
who woulde his gospell leaue:
What godly one woulde hate his lorde,
and vnto Sathan cleaue.
What wight woulde gods good benefites,
so lightly nowe esteme:
Which sent his Christ into the worlde,
from hell vs to redeme.
Who by his might did vanquishe sinne,
and layed Sathan waste:
By whose dere death eternall lyfe,
his flocke shall surely taste.
His loue to vs his creatures did,
in ample wise excede:

A.iiii   When

An exhortation.

When by the paynes of paynefull death,
   to saue vs he decrede.
What durst harte or selly brest,
   coulde finde Christe to repaye:
With such contempte as did these nymphes,
   which here beholde ye may.
What matrones harte woulde hyde the skyll,
   of Nature that meke dame:
And toyle by such vngodly artes,
   to extinquishe cleane the same.
I meane if God shoulde sende encrease,
   and multiply her sede:
Woulde she frequent it to destroy,
   by wicked meanes in dede.
I thinke no tender harte coulde finde,
   an infantes bloude to spill:
Nor yet no spoused wife I thinke,
   her husbande dere woulde kyll
Sith that by witchcraft witches vse,
   all euilles to sequest:
Let such as feare the liuynge God,
   their practises detest.
Sith whoredome in the same I saye,
   her force doth plainly showe:
Let euery wight the same abhorre,
   and scape infernall wo.
Sith this arte doth such yll conteyne,
   as swearinges manifolde:
Let faithfull hartes forsake the same,
   and fixe on Christ their holde.
Sith by that practise vile dere frendes,
   man slaughter put in vre:
Let vs contemne those godles actes,
   and leade a life most pure.
Sith Christ the rocke of lastinge life,
   must cleane renounsed be:

                                       And

An exhortation

And Sathan as the gouernour,
  must haue the dignitie.
what cursed state shall they abyde,
  which Christ their guide refuse:
And study still the deuilles minde,
  by practise still to vse.
Did Christ in vayne bestowe his bloude,
  to saue our soules from hell:
Did Christ in vaine prepare the heauens,
  for his elect to dwell.
Not so I iudge, why shoulde we then,
  his lawe and worde contemne:
The scripture doth rebellious folke,
  euerlastingly condemne.
I meane such as his worde detest,
  his lawe condemneth playne:
To taste with him whom they do serue,
  in hell eternall payne.
Such as do in sinne delighte,
  frequenting mischiefe styll:
Be Sathans owne, for Jesus Christe,
  for his deny them wyll.
Sith Christ in heauen will them forsake,
  which him in earth denye:
Let vs henceforth learne so to walke,
  his name to magnifye.
Let vs that swearers be in dede,
  our swearinge cleane refrayne:
So shall we scape the gredy gulphes,
  of hell and burninge payne.
Let whoremongers which whoredome vse,
  cast cleane away the same:
And pardon craue, for Christ is prest,
  for to forgeue the blame.
Let such men as delight in sinne,
  forsake their sinfull waies:

And

An exhortation

And study nowe that all your actes,
  may tende the Lorde to prayse.
Let filthy swynishe dronkardes nowe,
  abhorred in Gods sight:
Leaue of their quaffing in excesse,
  in modesty delight.
Then shall Gods armes be opened wide,
  vs wretches to embrace:
And with his sainctes in his kingedome,
  he will vs surely place.
To whych kingedome for Christes sake,
  vouchsafe thy flocke to bringe:
That we as thy electes deare God,
  to thee may prayses singe.

    Finis. ❧ Iohn Phillips

The examination of them with their confession before Doctor Cole and master Foscue at the same Sise verbatum as nere as coulde be gathered, and firste of Elizabeth Frauncis who saide as here foloweth.

First she learned this arte of witchcraft at the age of .xii. yeres of hyr grandmother whose nam was mother Eue of Hatfyelde Peuerell disseased.

Item when shee taughte it her, she counseiled her to renounce GOD and his worde, and to geue of her bloudde to Sathan (as she termed it) whyche she delyuered her in the lykenesse of a whyte spotted Catte, and taughte her to feede the sayde

The examinacion

sayde Catte with breade and mylke and she dyd so, also she taughte her to cal it by the name of Sathan and to kepe it in a basket.

When this mother Eue had geuen her the Cat Sathan, then this Elizabeth desired firste of the sayde Cat (callinge it Sathan) that she might be ryche and to haue goodes, and he promised her she shoulde, askinge her what she would haue, and she sayde shepe (for this Cat spake to her as she confessed in a straunge holowe voice, (but suche as she vnderstode by vse) & this Cat forthwith brought shepe into her pasture to the nūber of .xviii. blacke

and Confession

blacke and whyte, whych continued wyth her for a tyme, but in the ende dyd all weare awaye she knewe not howe.

Item when she had gotten these shepe, she desired to haue on Andrew Byles to her husband, which was a man of some welth, and the cat dyd promyse she shold, but that he sayde she must fyrste consent that this Andrew shuld abuse her, and she so did.

And after when this Andrew had thus abused her he would not mary her, wherfore she willed Sathan to waste his goodes, which he forthwith did, and yet not beyng contentid with this, she wild him to touch his body, whych he forthewith dyd whereof he died.

Item that euery tyme that he did any thynge for her, she sayde that he required a drop of bloude, which she gaue him by prycking herselfe, sometime in one place & then in an other, and

The examination

and where she pricked her selfe there remayned a red spot, which was styl to be sene.

Item whē this Andrew was dead, she douting her selfe with childe willed sathan to destroye it, and he bad her take a certayne herbe and drinke it whych she did, and destroyed the childe forthwyth.

Item when she desyred an other husbande, he promysed her an other, naminge this Frauncis whom shee nowe hath, but said he is not so rich as the other, willynge her to consent vnto that Frauncis in fornycation which she did, and therof conceaued a daughter that was borne within a quarter of a yere after they were maried.

After they were maryed they liued not so quietly as she desyred, beinge stirred (as she said) to much vnquietnes and moued to swearing and cursinge, wherfore she willed sathan her

Cat

and Confession

Cat to kyll the childe, beinge aboute the age of half a yere olde and he did so, and when she yet founde not the quietnes that she desyred, she wylled it to lay a lamenes in the leg of thys Frauncis her husbande, and it did in this maner. It came in a morninge to this Frauncis shoe, lying in it lyke a tode, and when he perceiued it putinge on his shoe, and had touched it with his fote, he being sodenly amased asked of her what it was, and she bad him kil it, and he was forthwith taken with a lamenes wherof he can not healed.

After all this when shee had kept this Cat, by the space of .xv. or xvi. yeare, and as some saye (though vntruly) beinge wery of it, she came to one mother Waterhouse her neyghbour (a pore woman) when she was going to the oue, and desired her to geue her a cake, & she wold geue her a thing that she should be the better
for

The examination

for so lõg as she liued, & this mother waterhouse gaue her a cake, where vpon she brought her this cat in her apron and taught her as she was instructed before by her grandmother Eue, tellig her that she must cal him Sathan and geue him of her bloude and bread and milke as before, and at this examination woulde confesse no more.

¶ Mother waterhouse of Hatfylde peuerell of the age of. lxiiii. yeares being examined the same day confessed as folioweth, & the xxix. daye suffered.

Yrst she receyued this cat of this frances wife in y order as is before sayde, who wild her to cal him sathã, and told her that yf she made muche of him he would do for her what she wolde haue him to do.

Then when she had receyued him
she

and Confession

she (to trye him what he coulde do) wyld hym to kyll a hog of her owne which he dyd, and she gaue him for his labour a chicken, which he fyrste requyred of her & a drop of her blod. And thys she gaue him at all times when he dyd any thynge for her, by prickyng her hand or face & puttinge the bloud to hys mouth whyche he sucked, & forthwith wold lye downe in hys pot agayne, wherin she kepte him, the spots of all the which prkks are yet to be sene in her skin.

Also she saythe that another tyme being offended with one father Kersye she toke her catte Sathan in her lap and put hym in the wood before her dore, & willed him to kyll three of this father Kersyes hogges, whiche he dyd, and retourning agayne told her so, and she rewarded hym as before, wyth a chicken and a droppe of her bloud, which chicken he eate vp cleane as he didde al the rest, and she

B   colde

The examination

colde fynde remaining neyther bones
nor fethers.

Also she confessed that fallyng out
with one widdow Gooday she wylled Sathan to drowne her cow and
he dyd so, and she rewardid hym as
before.

Also she falling out wyth another
of her neyboures, she killed her three
geese in the same maner.

Item, shee confessed that because
she could haue no rest (which she required) she caused sathan to destroye
the brewing at that tyme.

Also beyng denyed butter of an o-
ther, she caused her to lose the curdes
ii. or. iii. dayes after.

Item fallinge out with an other of
her neybours and his wife, shee wylled sathan to kyll hym with a blud-
dye flixe, whereof he dyed, and she
rewarded him as before.

Likewyse shee confessed, that because she lyued somwhat vnquietly

and Confession

with her husbande she caused sathā
to kyll hym, and he did so about. ix.
yeres past, syth which tyme she hath
lyued a widdow.

Also she said that when she wolde
wyl him to do any thinge for her, she
wolde say her Pater noster in laten.

Item this mother Waterhouse
confessed that shee fyrst turned this
Cat into a tode by this meanes, she

kept the cat a great while in woll in
a pot, and at length being moued by
pouertie to occupie the wol, she prai-
B.ii   ed in

The examinacion

ed in the name of the father, and of
the sonne, and of the holy ghost that
it wold turne into a tode, and forthwith it was turned into a tode, and
so kept it in the pot without woll.
¶ Also she said, that going to Black
stede a lyttle before her apprehen-
tyon, this Sathan wylled
her to hye her home,
for she shulde haue
great trouble,
and that
shee shoulde be eyther hanged
or burned shortly, more at
this tyme she wolde
not confesse.

and Confession

⁋Ione Waterhouse, daughter to the
mother Waterhouse, beinge of the
age of. xviii. yeres, and examined, cōfesseth as foloweth.

Fyrst, that
her mo-
ther this
laste wyn
ter would haue lear
ned her this arte,
but she lerned it not,
nether yet the name
of the thinge. She
saith she neuer saw
it but once in her
mothers hand, and
that was in the like
nes of a tode, and at
that time comming
in at a sodeyn when
her mother called it oute to worke
some thynge withall, she herde her
to call it Sathan, for shee was not
B iii   at

The examination.

at any tyme truely taught it, nor did never exercise it before this time as foloweth.

Item she confessed that when her mother was gone to Breakstede, in her absence lacking breade, she went to a gyrle, a neighbours childe, and desired her to geue her a pece of bred and cheese, whiche when she denied and gaue her not, or at the least not so muche as wolde satisfye her, shee goinge home dydde as she had seene her mother doe, callynge Sathan, whiche came to her (as she sayd) she thoughte out of her mothers shewe frome vnder the bedde, in the lykenes of a great dogge, demaundynge

w h

and Confession.

what she wolde haue, wherewithall she beyng afearde, sayd she wold
haue him to make such a gyrle aferd
naminge this gyrle, then asked hee
her what she wolde geue hym, and
she saide a red kocke, then sayde hee
no, but thou shalt geue me thy body
and sowle, whereby she beinge soore
feared, and despzous to be rydde of
hym, sayd she wold: And herewith
he went to this gyrle in the lykenes
of an euyll sauoured dogge with hoz
nes on his head, and made her very
muche afearde, and dothe yet haunt
her, nowe can not these witches (as
they saye) cal hym in agayn, because
they dyd not let hym out. And more
(sayth shee) she neuer dydde, but
this her doinge was the re-
uealyng of all the rest.

FINIS.

Imprynted at London by
Wyllyam Powell for Wyllyam
Pickeringe dwelling at Sainte
Magnus corner and are there
for to be soulde.

Anno 1566. the 13. August.

The second exa=
mination and Confession of
mother Agnes Waterhouse & Jone
her daughter, vpon her arainement
with the questions & answeres of Agnes
Browne the childe, on whom the spirite
haunteth at this present, deliberately declared before Justice Southcote and
master Gerard the quenes atturney, the. xxvii. day of July
Anno. 1 5 6 6. no lesse
wonderfull then
most true.

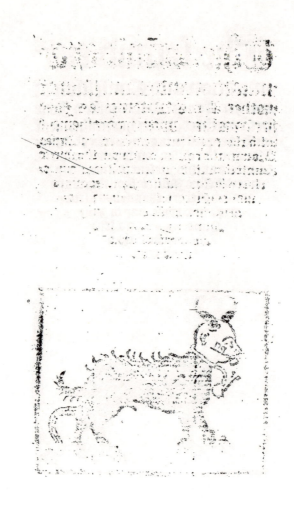

¶ The Confession of Agnes Waterhowse the . xxvii . daye of July in Anno. 1566. at Chelmsforde before Justice Southcote and M. Gerard the quenes Atturney.

Fyrst being demaunded whether that shee were gyltye or not gilty vpon her araynement of the murtheringe of a man, she confessed that she was gilty, and then vppon the euidence geuen a gaynst her daughter Jone Waterhouse, she sayde that she hadde a white Cat, and wylled her cat that he shuld destroy many of her neyghbours cattell, and also that

A ii   he

The examination

he shoulde kyll a man, and
so he dyd, and then after she
must go. ii. or. iii. mile from
her house, and then she toke
thoughte howe to kepe her
catte, then she and her catte
concluded that he the sayde
catte wolde become a tode,
and then she shuld kepe hym
in a close house & geue hym
mylke, and so he wolde con=
tinue tyll she came home a=
gaine, and then being gone
forth, her daughter hauing
ben at a neyghbours house
there by, required of one A=
gnes Browne, of the age of
xii. yeres or more, a peece of
breade and cheese, and the
sayde Agnes saide that shee
had

and Confession

had none, and that she had not the key of the milkhouse dore, and then the said Ione went home and was angry with the said Agnes broun and she said that she remembred that her mother was wonte to go vp and downe in her house and to call Sathan Sathan, she sayde she wolde proue the like, & then she went vp and downe the house and called Sathan, and then there came a black dogge to her and asked her what she woulde haue, and then she saide she was aferd and sayd I wold haue thee to make one Agnes browne afrayde, and then he asked

A iii   her

The examinacion

her what she wold giue him
and she saide she wolde geue
hym a red kock, and he said
he wolde haue none of that,
and shee asked him what he
wolde haue then, & he sayde
he wold haue her body and
soule, and so vpon requeste
and feare together she gaue
him her body and soule, and
then sayde the quenes attur
neye, Howe wylt thou do before
god. O my lord, I trust god
wyll haue mercy vpon mee,
and then he saide, thou saiste
well, and then he departed
from her, and then she saide
that she herde that he made
the sayde Agnes Browne a
fearde.

The

and Confession

The said Agnes Brown was then demaunded and called for, and then she came in, and beinge asked what age she was of she sayde she thoughte she was, xii. yeres old, and then the quenes atturney asked her what shee could say, and then she saide that at suche a day naming the daye certayne that shee

A iiii   was

The examinacion

was chirning of butter and there came to her a thynge lyke a blacke dogge with a face like an ape, a short taile, a cheine and a sylver whystle (to her thinking) about his neck, and a peyre of hornes on his heade, & brought in his mouth the keye of the milkehouse doore, and then my lorde she saide, I was fearde, for he skypped and leaped to and fro, and satte on the toppe of a nettle, and then I asked hym what he wolde haue, who he saide he woulde haue butter, and I said I had none for him and then he saide he wolde haue some or he went, and then he dyd

and Confession

dyd run to put the keye into the locke of the mylkehouse dore, and I sayde he should haue none, and he sayde he wolde haue some, and then he opened the dore and went vppon the shelfe, and there vpō a new chese laid downe the key, and being a whyle within he came out againe, and locked the dore and said that he had made slay but ter for mee, and so departed, and then she saide shee tolde her aunte of it, and then she sent for the priest, and when he came he bad her to praye to god, and cal on the name of Jesus, and loo the nexte day my lord he came again

to

The examination.

to me with the keye of oure milkehouse dore in his mouthe, and then I saide in the name of Jesus what haste thou there, and then he layed downe the key and sayde that I spake euyll woordes in speakynge of that name, and then hee departed, and so my aunte toke vp the key for he had kept it from vs. it dayes and a nyghte, & then we went into the milkhouse and there we did se the print of butter vpon the chese, and then within a few daies after hee came againe with a beane pod in his mouth and then the queenes attourney asked what that was, and

so

and Confession

so the other Justices declared, and then shee sayde my lorde I saide in the name of Jesus what hast thou there and so then he laid it downe and saide I spake euil wordes and departed and came agayne by & by with a pece of breade in his mouth, and I asked hym what he wold haue and he sayde butter it was that he wolde haue, & so he departed, and my lord I dyd not se hym noo more tyll wenseday laste, whiche was the. xxiiii. day of July why said the quenes atturney was he with the on wēseday last, ye she said, what did he then to thee sayde he, my

The examination.

my lorde saide shee he came with a knyfe in his mouthe and asked me if I were not dead and I said no I thanked god, and then hee sayde if I wolde not dye that hee wold thrust his knife to my harte, but he wold make me to dye, and then I sayde in the name of iesus lay down thy knyfe, and hee sayde he wolde not departe from his sweete dames knyfe as yet, & then I asked of hym who was his dame, and then he nodded & wagged his head to your house mother Water house, then the queenes attourneye asked of the sayde Agnes Waterhouse what she

and Confession.

she saide to it, then she demāded what maner knife that it was, and Agnes Browne said it was a daggar knife, there thou liest saide Agnes Waterhouse, why quod the quenes atturney, mary my lord (quod she) she saith it is a daggar knif, and I haue none suche in my house, but a greate knyfe, and therein she lieth, yea yea, my lorde, quoth Ione Waterhouse she lieth in that she saith that it hadde a face like an ape, for this that came to mee was like a dogge, well sayde the quenes attourney well, can you make it come before vs nowe, if ye can we will dyspatche

The examination

patche you out of pryson by and by, no faith said Agnes Waterhouse I can not, for in faith if I had let hym go as my daughter did I could make hym come by and by, but now I haue no more power ouer him, then said the queenes atturneye, Agnes waterhouse when dyd thye Cat suck of thy bloud neuer saide she, no saide hee, let me se, and then the iayler lifted vp her kercher on her heade and there was diuerse spottes in her face & one on her nose, then sayde the quenes atturney, in good faith Agnes when dydde he sucke of thy bloud laste, by my fayth my

and Confession.

my lorde sayde she, not this fortnyght, and so the iurye went together for that matter.

Imprynted at London by Wyllyam Powell for Wyllyam Pickeringe dwelling at Sainte Magnus corner and are there for to be soulde.

Anno 1566. the. 13. August.

To Bishop,
**uprighte typers, not the
Latinysh, and to the
intercession tonge
ther for the
himselfe.**

Imprinted at London by
Henry Denham for Andrew
Maunsell in the Bucklers
bery at the

Anno Domini 1579.

¶ The ende and last confes-
sion of mother Waterhouse at her
death, whiche was the
xxix. daye of July.
Anno. 1566.

Mother wa-
terhouse.

Fyrste (beinge redi prepared to receiue her death) she confessed earnestly that shee had bene a wytche and vsed suche execrable sorserye the space of. xv. yeres, and had don many abhominable dede, the which she repented earnestely & vnfaynedly, and desyred almyghty God forgeuenes in that she had abused hys most holy name by

A   her

The last ende

her deuyllishe practyses, and trusted to be saued by his most vnspekeable mercy. And being demaunded of the by standers, shee confessed that shee sent her sathan to one Wardol, a neibour of hers, beinge a tayler (with whō she was offended) to hurte and destroy him & his goodes. And this

her Sathan went therabout for to haue done her wyll, but in the ende he returned to her agayne, and was not able to do this myschiefe, she asked the cause, and he aunswered because the said Wardol was so strong in fayth that he hadde no power to hurt hym, yet she sent hym dyuerse and sundry time (but all in vayne)to haue

of mother VVaterhouse.

haue mischeufd hym. And being demaunded whether she was accustomed to go to church to the common prayer or deuine seruice, she saide yea & being required what she dyd there she saide she did as other women do, and prayed right hartely there, and when she was demanded what praier she saide, she aunswered the Lordes prayer, the Aue Maria, and the belefe, & then they demaunded whether in laten or in englyshe, and shee sayde in laten, and they demaunded why she saide it not in englyshe but in laten, seing that it was set out by publike aucthoritie and according to goddes worde that all men shoulde pray in the englyshe & mother toung that they best vnderstande, and shee sayde that sathan wolde at no tyme suffer her to say it in englyshe, but at all tymes in laten: for these and many other offences whiche shee hathe commytted, done and confessed, shee
bewayled

The last ende
bewayled, repented, and asked mercy of God, and all the worlde for-
gyuenes, and thus she yelded vp her sowle, tru-
sting to be in ioye
with Christe
her sauiour, whiche dearely had
bought her with his most
precious bloudde.
Amen.

Imprynted at London by
William Powell for Wyllyam
Pickeringe dwelling at Sainte
Magnus corner and are there
for to be soulde.

Anno 1566. the. 23. August.

A Detection of damnable driftes (*STC* 5115) is reproduced by permission from the unique copy at The British Library (shelfmark C.27.a8). The Library mark is illegible. The text block of the original measures 112mm × 63mm.

Hard-to-read passages in the original:
A3v.12:   meri‹te›s
A4v.22:   widowe dwellyng in the same parishe of Hat-
A4v.25:   she brought drinke in a crewse, and gave it to
A4v.26:   one Jhon Fraunces servaunte to goodman

A Detection
of damnable driftes, practized by three VVitches arraigned at
Chelmifforde in Essex, at the
laste Assises there holden, whiche
were executed in Aprill.
1579.

Set forthe to discouer the Ambushementes of
Sathan, whereby he would surprise vs
lulled in securitie, and hardened
with contempte of Gods
vengeance threatened
for our offences.

Imprinted at London for Edward White,
at the little North-dore of Paules.

To the Reader.

Ccept this pamphlet (Christian Reader) view, and peruse it with discretion, and hedefulnesse. No trifles are therin conteined worthy to be contēned, nor pernicious fantazies deseruyng to bee condemned. But contrariwise in this pretie plot may holsome hearbes of admonitions for the vnwarie, and carelesse, and soote flowers to recreate the wearied senses, be gathered. For on thone side the cleare sight maie espie the ambushmentes, whiche Sathan the secrete woorkemaister of wicked

TO THE READER.

wicked driftes, hath placed in moste partes of this realme, either by craftie conueighaunces, to creepe into the conceiptes of the simple, or by apparaunt treacherie to vndermine and spoile the states of suche as God permitteth him to haue power ouer. And on the other side the eye that is wimpled, may hereby be aduertised of the darkenesse, wherewith his vnderstandyng is ouercast, and puttyng of the veile of vanitie, maie reclaime his concept, and esteeme of the impietie of the offendours and vilanie of their actes, accordyng to the woorde of God, and waightinesse of the case. And if in tyme past he hath escaped their Sorceries, let hym not the lesse

feare

TO THE READER.

feare the harmes that maie hereafter ensue. For the Deuill by the sufferaunce of almightie God, is as well able to plague the persone, that moste presumeth of safetie, as any haue bin who in this treatise are mentioned. Some with muche ados cã be awaked out of their drousie dreames, though thei bee tolde that their neighbours house is on fire. But when their owne walles are inuaded with like flames, thei shall finde that it had bin better to haue come an hower too soone, to quenche those forrein fires, then to haue risen one minute too late to extinguishe the same, creepyng into their owne chambers. If therefore thou be assured that thy neighbour,

A.ij. *either*

TO THE READER.

either in bodie, familie, or gooddes is impaired by damnable witchcrafte, or perceiuest by information, or otherwise ought of suche deuises, inteded to be practized, or likely presumption of suche Deuilishe deedes contriued, for Charitie to thy Christian brother, and tender regard of thine owne state, preuente or stop the mischief by all possible meanes. And for thyne owne parte with praier, and assured faithe in the merittes of Christ Jesus shield thy self, so shal neither the Deuill nor his Angelles haue power, ouer thee, or thine.

Farewell.

¶ *The Confession of Elizabeth Fraun-*
ces, late of Hatfeelde in Essex.

Mprimis, the saied Elizabeth
Frauncs cōfessed that about
Lent last (as she now remembreth) she came to one Pooles
wife her neighbour, and requi-
red some olde yest of her, but beyng denied the
same, she departed towardes one good wife
Osbornes house a neighbour dwelling thereby
of whome she had yest, and in her waie going
towardes the saied goodwife Osbornes house,
shee cursed Pooles wife, and badde a mischief
to light vppon her, for that she would giue her
no yest, Whereuppon sodenly in the waie she
hard a greate noise, and presently there appe-
red vnto her a Spirite of a white colour in see-
myng like to a little rugged Dogge, standyng

A.iiij. neere

neere her vppon the grounde, who asked her whether she went? shee aunswered for suche thinges as she wanted, and she tolde him therewith that she could gette no yeest of Pooles wife and therefore willed the same Spirite to goe to her and plague her, whiche the Spirite promised to doe, but first he bad her giue him somewhat, then she hauing in her hand a crust of white bread, did bite a peece thereof and threwe it vp on the grounde, whiche she thinketh he tooke vp and so went his waie, but before he departed from her she willed hym too plague Pooles wife in the head, and since then she neuer sawe him, but she hath harde by her neighbours that the same Pooles wife was greuously payned in her head not longe after, and remayneth very sore payned still, for on saterdaie last past this Examinate talked with her.

2 Item this Elizabeth Fraunces saieth further, that she knoweth one Elizabeth Lorde a widowe, dwellyng in the same parishe of Hatfielde and so hath doen of longe tyme, of whom she hard, that about seuen or eight yeres paste she brougbt mylke in a crewse, and gaue it to one Thon Fraunces seruaunte to goodman
Some

Some of thesame parishe, shortly after the taking of whiche drinke he sickened, and died.

3. Item she further confesseth that she likewise knoweth that the same Widowe Lorde,
was saied to haue bewitched one Ione Rober-
tes, seruaunte to old Higham, in a peece of an
Apple cake whiche she gaue her, vpon the ea-
tyng whereof she presently sickened, and not
long after died.

4. Item she also confesseth, that she knowes
one Mother Osborne, a Widowe in the same
toune to be a witche, and that she hath a marke
in the ende of one of her fingers like a pitt, and
another marke vppon the outside of her right
legge, whiche she thinketh to bee pluckt out by
her Spirit: and that one Mother Waterhouse
her owne sister (long since executed for Witch
crafte) had the self same markes, whiche she
termeth (nippes) and she saieth that this Mother Osborne lying lame, and complainyng of
her sore legge, she the saied Elizabeth Fraunces came vnto her, and required to see her leg,
whiche beeyng shewed vnto her, she the saied
Elizabeth badde to put it into the bedde again,
saiyng: that she her self knewe that the same

A.v.   came

came, by wante of well seruyng of God. And thus muche for Elizabeth Fraunces.

¶ *The Euidence giuen against Elleine Smithe of Maldon.*

There was one Jhon Chaundeler dwellyng in Maldon, whose wife vaimed Alice Chaundeler, was mother vnto this Elleine Smithe, and for Witchcrafte was executed long before, after whose execution he went vnto his daughter in lawe Ellein Smithe, and demaunded certaine money of her, whiche she had receiued of her mother his wife, by meanes of whiche money thei fell out, and in fallyng out the saied Elleine in greate rage saied vnto hym, that it had been better for hym, he had neuer fallen out with her, and so it came to passe, for the same Jhon Chaundeler confessed before his death, that after the same hower that she had saied so vnto hym, he neuer eate any meate that digested in hym, but euer it came vp againe as soone as it was doue, by whiche meanes he consumed, and wasted awaie to his death.

2 The sonne of the foresaid Ellen Smithe,

of

of the age of thirteene yeres, or there aboutes, came to the house of one Jhon Estwood of Malden, for to begge an almose, who chid the boye awaie from his doore, whereuppon he wente home and tolde his mother, and within a while after the said Estwood was taken with very greate paine in his bodie, and the same night followyng, as he satte by the fire with one of his neighbours, to their thinkyng thei did see a Ratte runne vp the Chimney, and presently it did fall doune again in the likenesse of a Tode, and takyng it vp with the tongges, thei thruste it into the fire, and so helde it in forcesibly, it made the fire burne as blewe as Azure, and the fire was almoste out, and at the burnyng thereof the saied Ellen Smithe was in greate paine and out of quiete, whereuppon dissemblyngly she came to the house of the foresaied Jhon Estwood, and asked how all that were there did, and he saied well I thanke God, and she said, I thought you had not been well, and therefore I came to see how you did, and so went her waie.

3 Also it was auouched, and by this prisoner confessed, that where as her daughter, and the daughter of one Widowe Webbe of Maldon afore saied, did fall out and fight, the same Ellein

lein Smithe offended thereat, meetyng good wife Webbes daughter the nexte daie, gaue her a blowe on the face, wherevpon so soone as the childe came home she sickened, and languishyng twoo daies, cried continually, awaie with the Witche, awaie with the Witch, and so died. And in the mornyng immediatly after the death of the same childe, the saied good wife Webbe espied (as she thought) a thyng like to a blacke Dogge goe out at her doore, and presently at the sight thereof, she fell distraught of her wittes.

4 Besides the sonne of this Mother Smith, confessed that his mother did keepe three Spirites, whereof the one called by her greate Dicke, was enclosed in a wicker Bottle: The seconde named Little Dicke, was putte into a Leather Bottle: And the third termed Willet, she kepte in a Wolle Packe. And thereuppon the house was commaunded to bee searched. The Bottles and packe were found, but the Spirites were vanished awaie.

The effecte of the Euidence againste Mother Staunton, late of Wimbishe in Essex, who was arraigned, but not executed, for that no manslaughter, or murder was obiected against her.

Impri-

Mprimis, this Mother Staunton, late of the parishe of Wimbishe in Essex, came to the house of one Thomas Prat of Broke Walden, Thou Farrour of Libleburie beeyng presente, and one Thomas Swallowe, and the saied Mother Staunton, beyng demaunded by one of them how she did, she aunswered, that a knaue had beaten her: saiyng she was a Witche, then saied he again, in good faithe Mother Staunton, I thinke you bee no Witche, no Maister ꝙ she, I am none in deede, although I can tell what belongeth to that practise, of whiche woordes, the goodman of the house tooke witnesse of the aforenamed parties, and deliuered a bill subscribed with their handes thereof, to Maister George Nicolles.

2 Item, the saied Mother Staunton came to his house an other tyme, and after certaine woordes of anger betweene hym and her, he raced her face with a Nedle, what quoth she, haue you a Flea there: and the nexte night after, the saied Pratte was so greeuously taken with tormente of his Limmes, that he neuer thought to haue liued one hower longer, which also was subscribed and sent.

                                              Item

3   Item, she came the third tyme by his dore with Graines, and he demaundyng a fewe of her, she asked what he would doe with them, I will giue them, saied he, to my Chickens, and snatchyng a handfull from her, did so. But after thei had tasted of them, three or fower dousen of them died, and onely one Chicken escaped of them all.

4   Item, she came on a tyme to the house of one Richard Saunder of Brokewalden, and beeyng denied Yeest, whiche she required of his wife, she went her waie murmuryng, as offended with her aunswere, and after her departure, her yonge child in the Cradle was taken vehemently sicke, in a merueilous strange maner, whereuppon the mother of the childe tooke it vp in her armes to comforte it, whiche beyng doen, the Cradle rocked of it self, fire or seuen tymes, in presence of one of the Earle of Surreis gentilmen, who seyng it stabbed his dagger three or fower tymes into the Cradle or it staied: Merily iestyng and saiyng, that he would kill the Deuill, if he would bee rocked there.

5   Item, the saied Mother Staunton, came on a tyme to the house of one Robart Petie of
                                   Broke-

Brookewalden, and beyng denied by his wife diuerse thynges, whiche she demaunded at once, and also charged with the stealyng of a Knife from thence, she wente her waie in greate anger, and presently after her departure; the little childe of the saied Petie fell so straungely sickeas for the space of a Weeke, as no bodie thought it would liue.

6 Item, the saied Stauntons wife, came also to one Willyam Torners house of Brokewalden vpon a Fridaie, as she had doen often in tymes paste, and beeyng denied of certaine thynges whiche she craued, as a peece of Leather &c. She asked the good wife how many children she had, who aunswered one, whiche childe beeyng then in perfite healthe, was presently taken with suche a sweate and coldnesse of bodie, and fell into suche shrickyng and staryng, wringyng and writhyng of the bodie to and fro, that all that sawe it, were doubtfull of the life of it.

7 Item, she came on a tyme to the house of Robart Cornell of Suersem, and craued a Bottle of Milke of his wife, but beyng denied it, she departed for a little while, leauyng her owne Bottle behinde her, and tooke an other with her, that belonged to the afore saied Cornel,

nell, after three daies she came againe, and requested her owne Bottle, and restored the other, crauyng Milke as before, the wife of the house alwaies suspectyng her to bee a Witche denied her requeste, and barred the doores against her, whereuppon she satte doune vppon her heeles before the doore, and made a Circle vppon the grounde with a knife. After that she digged it full of holes with in the compasse, in the sight of the saied wife, her man, and her maide, who demaundyng why she did so: She made aunswere, that she made a shityng house for her self after that sorte, and so departed, the nexte daie the wife commyng out at the same doore, was taken sicke, and began to swell frō tyme to tyme, as if she had been with child, by whiche swellyng she came so greate in bodie, as she feared she should burste: and to this daie is not restored to healthe.

8. Item, she came often to the house of one Jhon Hopwood of Walden, and had continually her requestes, at the laste beyng denied of a Leathern thong, she went her waie offended and the same night his Geldyng in the stable, beyng the daie before in very good case, died sodainly, and afterward beyng burdeined withall, she neuer denied it.

Item,

Item, she commyng to the house of Thou Cornell the yonger of Wimbishe, and beeyng denied her demaunde, she tooke offence, and immediatly after his cattell in steede of sweete Milke, yelded gore stinkyng blood, and one of his Kine fell into suche miserable plight, that for a certaine space, he could by no meanes recouer her.

Item, she came on a tyme to the Vicars house at Wimbishe, and beyng denied her errande by his wife (he beeyng as then from home) his little soune in the Nurses lapp was taken with suche vehemet sicknes, that the beholders supposed no lesse, but it would straight haue died, the saied Mother Staunton sittyng by, and hauyng touched the child before it grew sicke: but within one hower after the Vicar came home the childe recouered perfectly, and plaied as before.

Item, also she came on a tyme to the house of oue Robart Lathburie, of the same Toune, who dissikyng her dealyng, sent her home emptie, but presently after her departure, his Hogges fell sicke and died, to the number of twentie, and in the ende he burned one, wherby as he thinketh, he saued the reste: He also had a Cowe straungely caste into a narrowe

B.j.   grip,

gripe, and beyng holpen out in the presence of maister Henry Morraunt, notwithstandyng the diligent care that was takn of her, she was in fewe daies three tymes like to be loste in the mire. And thus muche for Mother Staunton.

¶ The effecte of the Euidence geuen in against Mother Nokes late of Lamberd Parishe in Essex.

Certaine Seruant to Thomas Spycer of Lamberd Ende in Essex yoman, sporting, and passing away the time in play with a great nymber of youth, chaunced to snatche a paire of Gloues out of the pockette of this Mother Nokes Daughter being a yong woman of the age of xxviij yeres, which he protesteth to haue done in iest. Her Mother perceiuyng it, demaunded the Gloues of him, but he geuing no greate eare to her wordes departed towardes the feeldes to fetch home certeine Cattell. Immediately vpon his departure quoth the same Mother Nokes to her Daughter, lette him alone, I will bounce him well enough, at what time he being sodainely taken, and refte of his limmes fell doune. There
was

was a boye then in his companie by whome he sent the Gloues to Mother Nokes, Notwithstanding his Maister was faine to cause him to be set home in a Wheele Barrowe, and to bee laide into a bedde, where with his legges a crosse he lay bedded eight daies, and as yet hath not atrayned to the right vse of his lymmes.

Further it was auouched that mother Nokes had saied that her housbande laie with one Tailers wife of Lamberd Ende, and with reprochfull wordes reuiled her saiyng at last; thou hast a Nurse childe but thou shalte not keepe it long, and presently thereupon the Childe diet.

An other affirmed, that when he had reproued the said Tailers wife, and Mother Nokes as thei were at Churche, and willed them to agree better, the same Mother Nokes in a fume aunswereth that she cared for none of them all, as longe as Tom helde on her side, meanyng her Feende.

The same man hauing a seruaunt of his at Plough, this Mother Nokes going vp, asked the felowe a question but getting no aunswere at him she went her way. Forthwith one of his horses fell downe. At his coming home to dynner, he tolde his Maister howe the same horse was swolne about the head. His Maister at first supposing that it came by a stripe, was greately offended at the ploughman, but afterwardes vnderstandyng of Mother Nokes goyng by, and the circumstance afore mentioned, went to the said Mother Nokes and chid and threatned to haue her to her aunswere, howbeeit the horse died.

FINIS.

W.W., *A true and iust Recorde* (*STC* 24922) is reproduced by permission from the fine copy at The British Library with the table from another copy of the same (shelfmarks G.2359 and C.27.a.2). The text block of the original measures 116mm × 67mm.

Hard-to-read passages in the original:

A3v: [marginalia] Bodinus in confutatione
A4: [marginalia] futilis opinionis Wieri; Lamias, lamiarumq; Venefica astruentis. [Bodin {i.e., Jean Bodin, De la Demonomanie des Sorciers (1580)} in confutation of the futile opinion of Wier {Johann Wier, De Praestigiis Daemonum (1563)} supporting witches and the poisonings of witches.]
A4.18: to be notable: undertooke briefly to knit up in a
²A4.18: dwelleth in yᵉ next house unto yᵉ saide Joan
²A4.22: she ye saide Joan received beefe & bread, the which
B8v.24: Lyard in ye likenes of a Lion to goe & to plague
B8v.25: the saide Byets beastes unto death, and the spi-
B8v.27: plagued two of his beastes, the one a red Cow,
B8v.28: the other a blacke. And saith that the spirits
E4v.18: very extreame
E4v.19: and most straunge sorte, and so continued about
E4v.20: three quarters of a yeere, and then died: and hee
E4v.21: sayeth, that his saide wife did tell him severall
E4v.22: times that Ursley kempe his sister, had forspoke
E4v.23: her, and that shee was the onely cause of that her
E4v.24: sicknesse.

Foldout following G8v:

.41: [T]he sayd Ursley Kemp had foure spyrites viz. their names Tettey a hee like a gray Cat, Jack a hee like a [bl]ack Catt Pygin a she, like a
.42: black Toad, & Tyffyn a she, like a white Lambe. The hees were to plague to death, & the shees to punish with bodily harme, & to destroy cattell.
.43: Tyffyn, Ursleys white spirit did tell her alwayes (when she asked) what the other witches had done: And by her the most part were appel-
.44: led, which spirit telled her alwayes true. As is well approved by the other Witches confession.
.45: The sayd Ales Newman had the said Ursley Kemps spirits to use at her pleasure.
.46: Elizabeth Bennet had two spirits, viz. their names Suckyn, a hee like a blacke Dog: and Lyard red [lyke a Lyon a shee].
.47: Ales Hunt had two spirits lyke Coltes, the one blacke, the other white.
.48: 11 Margery Sammon had two spirits like Toads, their names Tom and Robyn.
.49: Cysly Celles had two spirits by severall names viz. Sotheons Herculus, Jack or Mercury.
.50: Ales Manfield and Margaret Grevell had in common by agreement iiii spirits, viz. their names Robin, Jack, Will, Puppet, alias Ma-
.51: met, whereof two were hees, and two shees, lyke unto black Cats.
.52: Elizabeth Ewstace had iii. Impes or spirits, of coulour white, grey and black.
.53: Annis Herd had vi. Impes or spirites like avises and black byrdes. And vi. other like Kine, of the [bignes of Rats, with short hornes, the]
.54: Avises shee fed with wheat, barly, Otes and bread, the Kine with strew and hey.

2359

¶ A true and iuſt Recorde, of the Information, Examination and Confeſſion of all the Witches, taken at S. Oſes in the countie of Eſſex: whereof ſome were executed, and other ſome entreated according to the determination of lawe.

Wherein all men may ſee what a peſtilent people Witches are, and how vnworthy to lyue in a Chriſtian Commonwealth.

Written orderly, as the caſes were tryed by euidence, By W. W.

¶ Imprinted in London at the three Cranes in the Vinetree by Thomas Dawſon. 1582.

¶ A true and iuſt Record, of the Information, Examination and Confeſsion of all the Witches, taken at S. Oſes in the countie of Eſſex: whereof some were executed, and other some entreated according to the determination of lawe.

Wherein all men may ſee what a peſtilent people Witches are, and how vnworthy to lyue in a Chriſtian Commonwealth.

Written orderly, as the cases were tryed by euidence, by W. W.

¶ Imprinted in London at the three Cranes in the Vintree, by Thomas Dawſon. 1582.

¶ To the right honourable and his singular good Lorde, the Lord Darcey, W. W. wisheth a prosperous continuaunce in this lyfe to the glory of God, and a dayly preservation in Gods feare to his endlesse ioye.

F THERE HATH BIN at any time (Right Honorable) any meanes vsed, to appease the wrath of God, to obtaine his blessing, to terrifie secreete offenders by open transgressors punishments, to withdraw honest natures from the corruption of euil company, to diminish the great multitude of wicked people, to increase the small number of virtuous persons, and to reforme all the detestable abuses, which the peruerse witte and will of man doth dayly deuise, this doubtlesse is no lesse necessarye then the best, that Sorcerers, Wizzardes, or rather Dizzardes, Witches, Wisewomen (for so they will be named) are rygorously punished. Rygorously sayd I? Why it is too milde and gentle a tearme for such a mercilesse generation: I should rather haue sayd most cruelly executed: for that no punishment can bee thought vpõ, be it in neuer so high a degree of tormẽt, which may be deemed sufficient for such a diuelishe

A 3

The Epistle

uelish & dánable practise, And why? Because al the imaginatiõs, al the cõsultatiõs, al the conferences, al the experimentes, finally all the attemptes, proceedinges and conclusions of Sorcerers, Witches, and the rest of that hellishe liuerie, are meere blasphemers against the person of the most high God, and draw so neere to the nature of idolatrie (for they worshippe Sathan, vnto whome they haue sworne allegiaunce) that they are by no meanes to be exempted from the suspition of that most accursed defection, nay rather they are guiltie of apparaunte apostasie, which is more heynous (considering the circumstances of their ordinarie actions, then any trespasse against the seconde table, which ouglye sinnes of blasphemie, and grosse, or rather diuelish idolatrie cõcurring in no malefactor so roũdly, as in sorcerers, witches, Inchaũters &c. in whõ the meete with a millian of enormities more, as it were in a centre; the magistrates of forren landes, noted so precisely, that weighing the qualitie of the cryme, they kept a due analogie and proportion of punishment, burning them with fire, whome the common lawe of Englande (with more measure of mercie then is to be wished) strangleth with a rope. An ordinary fellon, and a murtherer offending against the morrall lawe of iustice, is throtled: a Sorcerer, a Witch, (whome a learned Phisitian is not ashamed to auoche innocent, and the Iudges that denounce

odinus confutationa

Dedicatory.

denounce sentence of death against them no better than hangmen) defying the Lorde God to his face, and trampling the pretious blood of that immaculate lambe Iesus Christ most despitfully vnder feete, is stiffled: the one dyeth on the gallowes, and so doth the other: wherein doubtlesse there is a great inequalitie of iustice, considering the inequalitie of the trespasse, which deserueth a death so much the more horrible, by how much the honour of God is eclipsed, and the glorye due to his inuiolable name most abhominably defaced, euen to the vttermost villanie that they can put in practise.

futilis opinionis Wieri; Lamias, lamiarumq; Veneficia astruentis.

This I speake (Right Honorable) vpon a late viewe of tryall, taken against certaine Witches in the countie of Essex; the orderly processe in whose examinations, together with other accidents, I dilygently obseruing and considering their trecheries to be notable: vndertooke briefly to knit vp in a fewe leaues of paper, their manifolde abuses: and obtaining the meanes to haue them published in print, for that a number of memorable matters are here touched, to present the same vnto your Lordship, of whose gentle acceptation though I dooe not doubt, yet will I not be ouer bolde thereupon to presume: but rather refer the same to your honours iudgement and patronage, by way of humilyation, that going abrode vnder couerte of your honourable name, the discourse maye seeme the

more

The Epistle

more credible, your lordship knowing the grounds of this whole booke to be true and iustifiable, and therefore the further off from feare of impugning. But supposing I haue beene too tedious, and sparing to trouble your Lordship with multitude of words, I buyld vpō hope, & so put forth my booke, praying the Lord here to blesse your Honour, and all about you with the increase of
his grace in this life, and with
the presence of his diui-
nitie in the lyfe to
come. Amen.
(`.`.)

*Your Honours to com-
maund* W. W.

¶ The xix. day of February
the xxiiii. yeere of the raigne of
our Soueraigne Ladie Queene
Elizabeth.

*The information of Grace Thurlowe, the wife of
Iohn Thurlowe, taken before mee Brian Darcey,
the day and yeere aboue saide, against
Vrsley Kempe alias Grey,
as followeth.*

THe saide grace sayeth, that about xii. monethes past, or neere there abouts, her sonne Dauye Thurlowe, beeing strangely taken and greatly tormented, Ursley Kempe alias Grey came vnto the said Grace to see how the childe did: At which time the childe lying vpon a bed in the chimney corner, shee the said Ursley tooke it by the hande, saying, A good childe howe art thou loden: and so went thrise out of the doores, and euery time when shee came in shee tooke the childe by the hande, and saide, A good childe howe art thou loden: And so at her departure, the saide Grace prayed the saide Ursley to come againe vnto

A　　　　　　　　　　her

The Apprehension

her at night to helpe her. And thereupon the the saide Ursley replied, and saide, I warrant thee I, thy Childe shall doe well enough: and that night it fell to rest, the which it did not of a long time before. And the next day the said Grace going to mille warde meeting the said Ursley, shee asked her howe her childe did, and shee said it tooke good rest this night God be thanked, I saide the said Ursley, I warrant thee it shall doe well. Note, that the palmes of the childes handes were turned where the backes shoulde bee, and the backe in the place of the palmes.

The said Grace saith also, that about three quarters of a yeere agoe she was deliuered of a woman childe, and saith, that shortly after the birth thereof, the said Ursley fell out with her, for that shee woulde not suffer her to haue the nursing of that childe, at suche times as she the said Grace continued in woorke at the Lorde Darcies place: And saith, that shee the saide Grace nursing the said childe, within som short time after that falling out, the childe lying in the Cradle, and not aboue a quarter olde, fell out of the saide Cradle, and brake her necke, and dyed. The which the saide Ursley hearing to haue happened, made answere it maketh no matter. For shee might haue suffered

of certaine whitches.

red thee to haue the keeping and nursing of &c.

And the saide Grace saith, that when shee lay in, the saide Vrsley came vnto her, and seemed to bee very angrie for that shee had not the keeping in of the saide Grace, & for that she answered vnto her that shee was prouided: And thereupon they entred further into talke, the saide Grace saying, that if shee should continue lame as shee had doone before, shee woulde finde the meanes to knowe howe it came, and ẏ shee woulde creepe vpon her knees to complaine of them to haue iustice done vpon them. And to that shee the saide Vrsley saide, it were a good turne. Take heed (said Grace) Vrsley, thou hast a naughtie name. And to that Vrsley made answere, though shee coulde vnwitche shee coulde not witche, and so promised the saide Grace, that if shee did sende for her priuily, and send her keeper away, that then shee woulde shew the said Grace, how shee shoulde vnwitch herselfe or any other at any time.

And the said Grace further saith, that about halfe a yeere past she began to haue a lamenesse in her bones, & specially in her legges, at which time ẏ said Vrsley came vnto her vnsent for and wtout request: And said, she would helpe her of her lamenes, if she the said Grace woulde giue

her

The Apprehension

her iii. pence, ý which the said Grace speaking her fayre, promised her so to doe, and thereupon for the space of v. weekes after, she was wel & in good case as shee was before. And then the said Vrsley came vnto the saide Grace, and asked her ý money she promised to her. Wherupon the saide Grace made answere, that shee was a poore and a needie woman, and had no money : & then the said Vrsley requested of her cheese for it : but she said she had none. And shee the said Vrsley, seeing nothing to be had of the saide Grace, fell out with her, and saide, that she woulde bee euen with her : and thereupon shee was taken lame, and from that day to this day hath so continued.

And she saith, that when she is any thing well or beginneth to amend, then her childe is tormented, and so continueth for a time in a very strange case, and when he beginneth to amend: Then shee the saide Grace becommeth so lame, as without helpe shee is not able to arise, or to turne her in her bed.

The information of Annis Letherdall, wife of Richard Letherdall, taken by mee Brian Darcey Esquire, against Vrsley Kempe, alias Grey the xix, day of February.

The

of certaine witches.

The said Annis saith, that before Michaelmas last, she the said Ursley sent her sonne to the said Letherdals house, to haue scouring sand, and sent word by the said boy, ý his mother would giue her the dying of a payre of womens hose for the sand: But the said Annis knowing her to be a naughtie beast sent her none. And after she the said Ursley, seeing her gyrle to carry some to one of her neighbours houses, murmured as the said childe said, & presently after her childe was taken as it lay very bigge, with a great swelling in the bottome of the belly, and other priuie partes. And the saide Annis saith, ý about the tenth day of Februarie last shee went vnto the said Ursley, and tolde her that shee had been foorth with a cunning body, which saide, ý she the said Ursley had bewitched her childe: To ý the said Ursley answered, that shee knewe shee had not so been, and so talking further she said, that she would lay her life that she the said Annis had not been with any: whereupon shee requested a woman being in the house a spinning with the said Ursley, to beare witnesse what shee had said. And the next day the childe was in most piteous case to beholde, whereby shee thought it good to carry the same vnto mother Ratcliffe, for that shee had some experience of her skill, The which when the said mother

A 3   Ratcliffe

The apprehension

Ratcliffe did see, shee saide to the saide Annis that shee doubted shee shoulde doe it any good, yet shee ministred vnto it, &c.

The enformation of Thomas Rabbet, of the age of viii. yeres or there abouts, base sonne to the said Vrsley Kempe *alias* Grey, taken before me Brian Darcey esquire, one of her Maiesties Iustices, the xxv. day of February, against his said mother.

The saide Thomas Rabbet saith, that his said mother Vrsley Kempe alias Grey hath foure seuerall spirites, the one called *Tyffin*, the other *Tittey*, the third *Pigine*, & the fourth *Iacke* & being asked of what colours they were, saith, that *Tyttey* is like a little grey Cat, *Tyffin* is like a white lambe, *Pygine* is black like a Toad, and *Iacke* is black like a Cat. And hee saith, hee hath seen his mother at times to giue them beere to drinke, and of a white Lofe or Cake to eate, and saith that in the night time the said spirites will come to his mother, and sucke blood of her vpon her armes and other places of her body.

This Examinat being asked, whether hee had seene Newmans wife to come vnto his mother, saith, that one morning he being in ye chamber

of certaine witches.

her with his mother, his Godmother Newman came vnto her, and saith, that then hee heard her and his mother to chide, and to fall out: But saith before they parted they were friends: and that then his mother deliuered an earthen pot vnto her, in the which he thinketh her spirites were, the which she carried away with her vnder her aperne.

And this examinat saith, that within a fewe daies after the said Newmans wife came vnto his mother, and y he heard her to tel his mother that she had sent a spirit to plague Johnson to y death, and another to plague his wife.

The enformation of Ales Hunt, taken before mee Brian Darcey Esquire, the xxiiii. day of February, against Ioan Pechey widdow.

THis examinat Ales Hunt saith, that shee dwelleth in y next house vnto y saide Ioan Pechey, & y she the said Ioan two or three daies before Christmas last, went to y house of Iohnson y Collector appointed for y poore, whereas she y said Ioan receiued beefe & bread, the which this Examinat saith, shee hearde to bee of the gift of y said Bria Darcey) And this examinat saith that y said Ioan going homewardes, murmured & found great fault at Johnson, saying, he might haue giuen that to a gyrle or another,

A 4   and

The apprehension

and not to her, saying, the bread was to hard baked for her, and that shee then seemed to bee in a great anger therewithall. This examinat saith, shee was at that present in the house of the wydow Hunt, and that there was but a wall betweene them, The saide Ioan comming to her house did vnlocke her dore, the which this examinat did see her doe: And after shee was entred into her house, this examinat saith, she hard the said Ioan to say, yea are you so sawsie: are yee so bolde: you were not best to bee so bolde with mee: For if you will not bee ruled, you shall haue Symonds sause, yea saide the saide Ioan, I perceiue if I doe giue you an inch, you you will take an ell: and saith she is assured that there was no christian creature with her at that time, but that she vsed those speeches vnto her Imps.

And this examinat saith, that she hath heard her mother say, that she the said Ioan was skilfull and cunning in witcherie, and could do as much as the said mother Barnes, this examinats mother, or any other in this towne of S. Osees. And further saith, she hath hard her mother to say, y the said Ioan did know what was saide or done in any mans house in this towne.

The

of certaine Witches.

The information of Margerie Sammon, sister to the saide Ales Hunt, taken before mee Brian Darcey Esquire, the xxv. day of Februarie against the said Ioan Pechey as foloweth.

The said Margerie sayth, that she hath hard the widowe Hunt to say, that the sayde Ioan Pechey shoulde say that shee coulde tell what any man saide or did at any time in their houses, when & as often as shee listed: and sayth, that the saide widowe Hunt did tell her that shee hath harde the saide Ioan Pechey, being in her house, verie often to chide and vehemently speaking as though there had been some bodye present with her: And sayth, that shee went in to see to whome the saide Ioan should speake, but shee founde no bodie but her selfe all alone: And sayeth, that shee the sayd Ioan Pechey was with this examinates mother, mother Barnes, the day before shee departed, where this examinate left them together while shee went home to her mistris house to doe her businesse and worke.

The enformation of Iohn Tendering of Saint Osees, také before me Brian Darcey esquire, the xxvi. of Februarie 1582.

A 5   The

The Apprehension

The said John sayth, that William Byette hauing occasion to come to this examinate, sayeth, that after they had conferred and talked, hee the saide William Byet did declare to this examinate, That, that morning he did tell him that he had a Cow ŵ had lien two dayes or longer in a strange case, and had eaten nothing, and was not likly to liue, & that he and his seruants seuerall times had lifted at the said cowe to raise her vpon her feet, but they could not make her to arise or stand: wherevpon he told this examinat, that he had caused his said seruāts to fetch straw, and to lay the same round about her: And that he hunselfe tooke an Axe, minding to knocke her vpon the head, and so to burne her: And said that the fire being kindled, the said Cowe of her selfe start vp, and rā her way vntil it came to a wood stack, and there stood still, and fell a byting of stickes, bigger then any mans finger, and after liued and did well.

The enformation of Febey Hunt, daughter in lawe to Ales Hunt, of the age viii. yeeres or there abouts, taken before mee Brian Darcey esquire, the xxv. day of Februarie agaynst Ales Hunt her mother.

The sayd Febey hunt sayth, ŷ shee hath seen her mother to haue two litle thinges like horses,

of certaine Witches.

horses, the one white, the other blacke, the which shee kept in a litle lowe earthen pot with woll, colour white and blacke: and that they stoode in her chamber by her bed side, and saith, that shee hath seene her mother to feede them with milke out of a blacke trening dishe, and this examinat being caried after this confessiō by the Counstables to her fathers house, shee shewed them the place were they stood and the boxe that couered them: And this examinate chose out the dishe, out of which they were fedde, from amongst many other dishes. Shee this examinat did also confesse that her mother had charged her not to tell any thing what shee had seene: And if shee did those thinges woulde take her, and this examinate saith, that her mother did send them to Hayward of Frowicke, but to what end shee can not tell, & shee being asked howe she knew the same, saieth, that shee hard her mother bid them to go.

The enformation of William Hooke Painter, taken before me Brian Darcey esquire, the xxiii of Februarie, against Ales Newman.

This examinate William Hooke sayth, ÿ he dwelleth in the next house vnto Ales Newmā, & saith, that he hath hard William Newemā her husband to say vnto ÿ said Ales his wife, ÿ she was

The Apprehension

was the cause of her husbands great miserie and wretched state, and sayeth, that when the saide Ales doeth giue her husbande any meate to eate, then presently he the saide William saith to his wife, doest thou not see? doest thou see? wherevnto this examinate sayth, that he hath hearde the saide Ales to say, if thou seest any thing, giue it some of thy meat. And saith further, that he hath hearde the saide William Newman bid the said Ales his wife to beate it away.

The enformation of Elizabeth Bennet, taken by me Brian Darsey esquire, the xxiiii. day of Febrnarie 1582. against Ales Newman.

The sayde Elizabeth saith, that shee neuer sent any spirite to plague Johnson or his wife, neither knew shee mother Newmā to haue sent any of her spirits to plague him or his wife, shee this examinate for her part sayth, shee was greatly beholding to the sayde Johnson and his wife. But denieth that euer shee sent any spirit to hurt him and his wife: or that shee knewe mother Newman to haue hurt them. But this examinat saith, that shee being at Johnsons to haue wool to spinne, hē bēing a clothmaker, of whom shee had many times worke, At that present mother Newman being come thither, shee this examinate
minate

of certaine Witches.

minate saith she hard the sayd mother Nowman to desire Iohnson to giue her xii.d. saying: her husbande lay sicke, whervnto shee heard him answere that hee woulde gladly helpe her husbande: but that hee had laide out a greate deale more then he had receiued, saying, he was a pore man, and hee, his wife and familie, might not want for the helping of her husband, saying that hee coulde not helpe her with any, vntill he had collected more money, wherupon shee departed, and vsed some harde speeches vnto him, and seemed to be much angrie.

The examination & confessiō of Vrsley Kemp alias Gray, taken at S. Osees, and brought before me Brian Darsey esquire, one of her Maiesties Iustices of the peace, the xx. day of Februarie 1582.

Condemned.

The saide Vrsley Kempe sayeth, that about tenne or eleuen yeeres paste, shee this examinate was troubled with a lamenes in her bones, and for ease thereof, went to one Cockes wife of Weley, nowe deceased, who telled this examinate that shee was bewitched, and at her entretie taught her to vnwitche her selfe: And bad her take hogges dunge and charuell,

and

The Apprehension

and put them together and holde them in her left hand, and to take in the other hande a knife, and to pricke the medicine three times, & then to cast the same into the fire, and to take the said knife & to make three pricks vnder a table, and to let the knife sticke there: & after that to take three leues of sage, and as much of herbe John (alias herbe grace) and put them into ale, and drinke it last at night and first in the morning, & that shee taking the same, had ease of her lamnesse.

The sayde examinate sayth, that one Pages wife, and one Grayes wife, beeing eyther of them lame and bewitched: shee beeing requested and sent for to come vnto them, went vnto them: And saieth, that shee knewe them to bee bewitched, and at their desires did minister vnto them the foresaid medicine, whereupon they had speedie amendement.

The saide Brian Darcey then promising to the saide Vrsley, that if shee would deale plainely and confesse the trueth, that shee should haue fauour: & so by giuing her faire speeches shee confessed as follloweth.

The saide Vrsley bursting out with weeping, fel vpon her knees, and confessed that shee

of certaine Witches.

shee had foure spirits, wherof two of them were hees, and the other two were shees: the two hee spirites were to punishe and kill vnto death, and the other two shees were to punishe with lamenes, and other diseases of bodyly harme, and also to destroy cattell.

And she this examinate, being asked by what name or names shee called the sayde spirits, and what maner of thinges, or colour they were of: confesseth and saith, that the one is called *Tittey*, being a hee, and is like a gray Cat, the seconde called *Iacke*, also a hee, and is like a blacke Cat, the thirde is called *Pigin*, being a she, and is like a blacke *Toad*, the fourth is called *Tyffin*, being a shee, and is like a white lambe.

This examinate being further asked, whiche of the saide spirites shee sent to punishe Thorlowes wife and Letherdalls childe, confessed and sayed, that shee sent *Tyttey* to punishe Thorlows wife, and *Pigen* Letherdalls Childe.

And this examinate, without any asking of her owne free will at that present, confessed and saide, ẏ shee was the death of her brother Kemps wife, and that she sent the spirite *Iacke* to plague her, for that her sister had called her whore and witche.

And this examinate further confessed,
that

The Apprehension

that vpon the falling out betweene Thorlowes wife and her, shee sent *Tyffin*, the spirite vnto her childe, which lay in the Cradle, and willed the same to rocke the Cradle ouer, so as the childe might fall out thereof, and breake the necke of it.

These foresaide 5. last recited matters, being confessed by the saide Ursley priuately to me the sayde Brian Darcey, were afterwardes (supper being ended, and shee called agayne before mee, the saide Brian) recited and particularlie named vnto her all which shee confessed, as before in the presence of vs, whose names bee hereunder subscribed.

Also after this examinates aforesaide confession, the saide Thorlows wife, and Letherdalles wife being then in my house, and shee the saide Letherdalls wife hauing her chylde there also, were brought in my presence before this examinate: who, immediatly after some speeches had past betweene them, shee this examinate burst out in teares and fell vpon her knees, and asked forgiuenesse of the sayde Letherdalls wife, and likewise of Thorlows wife, and confessed that shee caused Newmans wife to sende a spirite to plague the childe, asking the saide Letherdalls wife, if shee were not afraide that night that the spirite came vnto the childe, and telled her a-
bout

of certaine whitches.

about the same houre, and said that shee her selfe by reason thereof was in a great swett. And this examinate confesseth, that shee caused the saide Newmans wife, to send a spirite to Thorlowes wife, to plague her where that thought good, &c.

The said Letherdals childe (being a woman childe)) at the time of this examination, appeared to bee in most pitious sort consumed, and the priuie and hinder partes thereof, to be in a most strange and wonderfull case, as it seemed to verye honest women of good iudgement, and not likely to liue and continue any long time.

Note also that it is specially to be considered, that the saide childe beeing an infante and not a yeere olde, the mother thereof carrying it in her armes, to one mother Ratcliffes a neighbour of hers, to haue her to minister vnto it, was to passe by Ursley this examinates house, and passing bye the wyndowe, the Infante cryed to the mother, wo, wo, and poynted with the finger to the wyndowe wardes: And likewise the chyld vsed the like, as shee passed homewards by the said window, as which she confessed her conscience moued her, so as shee went shortly after and talked with the said Ursley, whereupon

The Apprehension

vpon shee vsed suche speeches as mooued her to complaine.

The seconde confession and examination of Vrsley Kemp, takē the xxi. day of Februarie.

The said Vrsley, being committed to the ward & keeping of the Constable that night, vpon some speeches that shee had passed, said, that shee had forgotten to tell M. Darcey one thing, wherevpon the next day she was brought before Brian Darcey, & the second time examined, who confessed and said.

That about a quarter of a yeere last past, one Ales Neweman, her neere neighbour came vnto this examinates house and fel out with her, and said shee was a witche, and that shee woulde take away her witcherie, and carrie the same vnto M. Darcey: But this examinate saieth, shee thought shee did not meane it, but after they had chidden they became friendes, and so shee departed carying away with her, her spirites in a pot, as this examinate sayth.

And shee further sayth, that about Christmas last, shee went to the said Ales Newman, and declared to her that Thorlows wife and shee were fallen out, and prayed the saide Newmans wife,

to

of certaine witches.

to sende the spirite called *Tittey*, vnto her to plague the sayde Thorlowes wife, where that thought good: The which this examinate saith, shee did, and at the returne of the saide spirite it tolde this examinate, that it had punished Thorlowes wife vpon her knee, And then it had a reward by sucking blood of this examinate, and so returned as shee saith to the said Ales Newman.

This examinate saith, that about three monethes past, shee and one Iohn Stratton fel out, and the saide Iohn called her whore & gaue her other euill speeches, wherevpon this examinate sayth, that shortly after shee sent her Boy for spires vnto the wife of the said Iohn: But shee sayeth, shee sent her none, whervpon this examinate sayeth, shee went vnto the said Newmans wife, and tolde her of the falling out between Stratton and her, and requested the saide Newmans wife, to sende *Iacke* the spirite vnto Strattons wife to plague her, ẏ which the said Ales Newman promised this examinate to doe the nexte night, as this examinate saith shee did: And the spirite tolde this examinate when it returned, that it had plagued her in the backe euen vnto death: and the spirite did sucke of this examinate vpon the left thigh, the which when she rubbeth (shee saith) it will at all times bleede.

B 2   An

The Apprehension

And shee sayeth that then the spirite did returne to the sayde Newmans wife agayne, and had the like rewarde of her as shee thynketh.

This examinate sayeth, that about Friday was seuennight beeing about the nienth of Februarie, shee went vnto the said Ales Newman, and did shewe her that one Letherdalls wife and shee were fallen out, and sayth, that shee prayed her to sende one of the spirites vnto her younge chylde: wherevnto shee the sayd Ales answered well, she would: and this examinate saith, that at that time shee coulde haue no longer talke with her, for that her husband was then present in the house: and this examinat saith, that the said Ales sent the spirit *Pigin*, to plague the said child where that thought good, and after that it had sucked of this examinate, shee saith it returned to the saide Newmans wife, and more at that time the saide examinate confessed not.

The third examination & confession of Vrsley Kempe alias Gray, taken before me Brian Darsey esquire, one of her Maiesties Iustices of the peace, the xxiiii. day of Februarie.

This examinate, being asked how she knew the said Elizabeth Bennet to haue two spirites,

of certaine witches.

rits, saith, that about a quarter of a yere past, she went vnto mother Bennets house for a messe of milke, the which shee had promised her: But at her comming this examinate saith shee knocked at her dore, and no bodie made her any answere, whereupon shee went to her chamber windowe and looked in therat, saying, ho, ho, mother Bennet are you at home? And casting her eyes aside, shee saw a spirit lift vp a clothe lying ouer a pot, looking much lik a Ferret. And it beeing asked of this examinate why the spirite did looke vpon her, shee said it was hungrie.

This examinate, beeing asked howe shee knewe the names of mother Bennets spirites, sayth, that *Tyffin* her spirite did tell this examinate that shee had two spirites, the one of them like a blacke Dogge, and the other redde like a Lyon, and that their names were *Suckin* and *Lyerd*, and sayeth that *Suckin* did plague Byettes wife vnto death, and the other plagued three of his Beastes whereof two of them dyed, and the third leyer sire or drooping, & not likly to liue: Byette caused his folkes to make a fire about her: The Cowe feeling the heate of the fire, starte vp and ranne her way, and by that occasion was saued.

This

The apprehenſion

This examinate ſaieth, that about the fourteene or fifteene day of Januarie laſt, ſhee went to the houſe of William Hunt to ſee howe his wife did, and ſhee beeing from home, ſhee called at her chamber window and looked in, and then eſpied a ſpirite to looke out of a potcharde from vnder a clothe, the noſe thereof beeing browne like vnto a Ferret. And ſayeth, that the ſame night ſhee aſked *Tyffin* her white ſpirite, what Hunts wiues ſpirite had done: And then it tolde this examinate, that it had killed Heywarde of Frowicke ſixe beaſtes which were lately dreſſed of the gargette. And ſayeth, that her ſayde ſpirite tolde her, that Huntes wiues ſpirite had a droppe of her blood for a rewarde: but ſhee ſayeth, that ſhee aſked not her ſpirite vpon what place of her body it was.

This examinate ſayeth, that one Michell a ſhoomaker of Saint Oſees did tell her, that he thought that Glaſcockes wife had bewitched his Chylde, whereof it dyed: Wherevpon ſhee this examinate ſayeth, that ſhee went home, and aſked *Tyffin* her white ſpirite, whether the ſame were ſo: whiche tolde this examinate, that ſhee had bewitched the ſayde chylde, and ſent one of her ſpirites to plague it to the death.

And

of certaine witches.

And sayeth also, that the sayde Glascockes wife did bewitche the Base childe that Page and his wife haue in keeping, and that her sayde spirite telled her so. And being demaunded, howe many spirits Glascockes wife had, and by what names shee called them, this examinate sayeth, that shee asked not her spirite *Tyffin* any such questions.

This examinat sayeth, that the sayde Elizabeth Bennette did sende her spirite *Suckyn* to plague one Willingall, whereof hee languished and died: beeyng sicke of an impostume.

This examinate sayeth also, that the sayde Elizabeth sente the sayde spirite to William Willes his wife to plague her, whereof shee languished many yeeres and dyed.

This examinate sayeth, that the sayde Elizabeth (not aboue three weekes sithence) sent her spirite *Lyerd* to plague Fortunes wife and his chylde.

This examinate sayeth, that the sayde Elizabeth did sende her spirite *Lyerd* to Bonners wife to plague her, the whiche her sayde spirite, tolde this examinate to bee done vpon the knee.

This examinate saith further, that Ales Newman went vnto Johnson beeing Collectour

B4

The apprehension

for the pome, and did require him to giue her xii. d. for her husbande whiche was sicke. But hee aunswering her that he had disbursed more money then hee had collected, saying, therefore hee coulde not then helpe her with any: The sayde Newmans wife fell out with him very angerly, and the next day after sent one of the spirites that shee had from this examinate to plague the saide Johnson and his wife vnto the death: And that her spirite called *Tyffin* did tell the same vnto her, and shee beeing asked what woordes the sayde Newmans wife vsed to Johnson vpon the falling out, sayth, that shee asked not her said spirite.

This examinate sayeth, that Newmans wife beeing at Butlers, and asking a peece of meate, was denyed thereof: whereat shee went a way mourmuring, And then shortely after sent one of her spirites to punishe him vpon the backe: The whiche *Tyffin* her sayde spirite telleth this examinate was done, whereof hee languisheth and is greatly payned.

This examinate being asked, whether her white spirit called *Tyffin* did euer at any time tell her any vntruths, or whether she had foūd it at any time

time to tell any thing contrary to truth, saith, that the saide spirite did euer tell her true, in any matter shee required of it, and saith, that shee neuer knewe it to tell her otherwise then truth.

This Exam. being asked, whether she sent any of her spirits to plague or punishe John Strattons childe, confesseth and saith, that the spirite which plagued Strattons wife to the death, did also punishe the saide Strattons childe, saying, that the saide childe shoulde not complaine thereof vntill the mother were departed.

Note, it is to bee considered, that the saide Vrsley Kempe in this her confession hath vttered many thinges well approued and confessed to bee most true: And that shee was brought thereunto by hope of fauour.

The Examination and confession of Ales Newman, taken before mee Brian Darcie Esquire, the xxi. of February.

Condemned.

This examinat saith, that shee went vnto the house where the saide Vrsley Kempe alias Grey dwelt, and entred into communication with her, and that they fell out greatly: and confesseth that shee saide vnto the saide Vrsley

The Apprehension

that she knew her to be a witche, but denieth the residue of y⟨e⟩ speeches alleadged by the said Vrley against this Examinat.

The said Brian Darcey finding this examinat to bee obstinate, and that shee coulde bee brought to confesse nothing, said to this Examinat, that hee woulde seuer and part her and her spirites a sunder, nay sayth shee this examinat, that shal ye not, for I wil carry thē with me, and hold being taken of her wordes, after some distance she added (if she haue any.)

The enformation of William Bonner, taken before me Brian Darcey Esquire, the xxiiii. day of February.

The said William Bonner saith, that y⟨e⟩ said Elizabeth Bennet and his wife were louers and familiar friendes, and did accompanie much together: and saith that since Candlemas last his wife hath complained of a lamenesse in her knee, and that sithence also shee hath been much troubled. And saith also that not ten daies past the saide Elizabeth Bennet being with his wife, shee beeing sickely and sore troubled, the saide Elizabeth vsed speeches vnto her, saying, a good woman how thou art loden, & then clasped her in her armes, and kissed her: Wherupon

of certaine Witches.

on presently after her vpper Lippe swelled & was very bigge, and her eyes much sunked into her head, and shee hath lien sithence in a very strange case.

Vpon the saide enformation made by Vrsley Kempe *alias* Grey, against Elizabeth Bennet, I Brian Dercey directed my warrāt for her apprehēsiō, wherupō she was brought before me the said Brian, whose confession being taken the 22. day of February.

Condemned.

THe said Elizabeth Bennet being charged with the foresaid information, denieth the same in generall, & after many and sundrie demāds being asked, whether she had not a pot or pitcher of earth stāding vnder a paire of staires in her house & wool in the same, in the which vsually the said two spirits did lie, denied ye same with many othes, saying, yt she was wel assured yt she had none such, wherupō it was said to her, if it be proued to your face, what will you say to al the other matters you haue bin charged with, are they true? To that she made answere & said yea: Then was the pot brought before her, the which she then confessed to be her pot, but denied yt the wool therin was any of hers, thē I calling her vnto mee, saide, Elizabeth as thou wilt

The Apprehenſion

wilt haue fauour confeſſe the truth. For ſo it is, there is a man of great cunning and knoweledge come ouer lately vnto our Queenes Maieſtie, which hath aduertiſed her what a companie and number of Witches be within Englande: whereupon I and other of her Iuſtices haue receiued Commiſſion for the apprehēding of as many as are within theſe limites, and they which doe confeſſe the truth of their doeings, they ſhall haue much fauour: but the other they ſhall bee burnt and hanged. At which ſpeeches ſhee the ſaide Elizabeth falling vpon her knees diſtilling teares confeſſed as heereafter followeth.

Saying, that one William Byet dwelt in the next houſe vnto her three yeres, ſaying, ÿ the firſt yeere they did agree reaſonably well, but ere the ſeconde yeere paſſed they fell out ſunny and oftentimes, both with this examinat & her huſbande, Byet calling her oftentimes olde trot and olde witche, and did banne and curſe this examinat and her Cattell, to the which this examinat ſaith, that ſhee called him knaue ſaying, winde it vp Byet, for it wil light vpon your ſelfe: and after this falling out this examinat ſaith, that Byet had three beaſtes dyed, whereof hee ſeeing one of them ſomewhat to mowe, hee did beat the ſaide Cowe in ſuch ſorte, (as this

Examinat

of certaine Witches.

Examinat saith, that shee thought the said Cow did die thereof.

This examinat saith further, that Byets wife did beate her swine seuerall times with greate Gybets, and did at an other time thrust a pitch-forke though the side of one of this examinats swine, the which Durrant a Butcher did buie, and for that when hee had messed it, it prooued A messell, this Examinat saith, shee had nothing for it but receiued it againe, &c.

This examinat saith also, that aboue two yeeres past there came vnto her two spirits, one called *Suckin*, being blacke like a Dogge, the other called *Lierd*, beeing red like a Lion, *Suckin* this examinat saith is a hee, and the other a shee. And saith, on a time as this examinat was comming from mill, the spirite called *Suckin* came vnto her and did take her by the coate, and helde her that shee coulde not goe forwarde nor remooue by the space of two houres, at the which (this examinat saith) she was much amased, and shee saith, that the spirite did aske her if she this examinat woulde goe with it : Whereat shee this examinat saide, In the name of God, what art thou ? Thou wilt not hurt mee, at the which speeche it said no, & this Examinat saith, that shee then prayed deuoutly to Almightie God to deliuer her from it : at which time the

spirite

The Apprehension

did depart from her vntill shee had gone a good way, and being come within xxx. or xl. rodes of her house, this examinat saith, that the said spirite came againe vnto her and tooke her by the coates behind, & held her fast, whereat this examinat saith, that she desired God to deliuer her frõ that euill spirite, and then that did depart to the Wel. And this examinat saith, y within one houre after, the same same spirite came againe vnto her she being a sifting of her meale, & saith, the same remained with her vntill she had laied her leauen, and then departed.

The saide examinat saith, that the next day shee being a kneading of her bread, the said spirite came againe vnto her, and brought the other spirite with it called Lierd, and that one of them did aske her why she was so snappish yesterday, to that this examinat saith, that shee made answere, I trust I am in the faith of God, and you shall haue no power ouer mee, at which wordes this Examinat saith, the saide spirites departed.

Then shee this examinat saith, that shee beeing a making of a fire in her Ouen, the said spirits came againe vnto her, and tooke her by the legge, this examinat feeling it to take her by the leg saith she said, God and the holy Ghost deliuer me from the euill spirites, at which words
this

of certaine Witches

this examinat saith, that the said spirites did depart to her thinking.

But this examinat saith, that within halfe an houre after she hauing a fier forke in her hãd, and beeing a stirring of the fire in the Ouen, the spirit (called Suckin) came vnto her & tooke this examinat by the hippes, and saide, seeing thou wilt not be ruled, thou shalt haue a cause, & would haue thrust this examinat into ye burning Ouen, & so had (as this examinat saith) but for the foresaide forke, but this examinat striuing and dooing what shee coulde to her vttermost, the saide spirite burnt her arme, the which burning is apparaunt and euidently too bee seene, and when it had thus doone it did depart.

And this Examinat saith, that about a moneth after or more, shee beeing a walking in a croft neere vnto a Barne called Heywoods Barne, the spirite called Suckin came and followed this examinat, she spying the same as she looked backe, at the sight thereof this examinat saith, ye her eies wer like to start out of her head: then she saith ye she did beseech God to gouerne and guide her from the euill spirites, whereupon shee saith they did depart.

But the same euening she this examinat being set a milking of a red Cowe with a white face,

saith

The Apprehension

saith that *Suckin* and *Lired* came againe vnto her, and saith that *Suckin* appeared at that time in the likenesse of a blacke dogge, and *Lired* in the likenesse of a Hare, the one sitting on the one side of her, the other on the other side of her within lesse then two yardes: And saith, that the Cowe shee was then a milking of, snorted and ranne away, and brake her paile and spilt al her milke, neither coulde she get the said Cow any more that night to stand still, and saith, that for the losse thereof her husband did much chide her, but shee woulde not tell him what was the cause: and she praying to the father, the sonne, & the holy ghoste, saith that they did depart, and that shee sawe them not a quarter of a yeere after, nor aboue three times since Midsommer last.

The said exam. saith, that about that time they appeared againe vnto her, and saith that a little before there was a falling out betweene her and the saide Byet, whereupon and for that Byet had oftentimes misused her this examinat and her Cattell, shee saith, that shee caused *Lyard* in þ likenes of a Lion to goe & to plague the saide Byets beastes vnto death, and the spirite returning tolde this examinat that it had plagued two of his beastes, the one a red Cow, the other a blacke. And saith that the spirit

told

of certaine Witches

tolde her, that hee plagued the blacke Cowe in the backe, and the read Cowe in the head.

This Examinate saieth further, that aboute Whitsontyde last past, the spirit called *Suckin*, did come againe at that tyme vnto her, sayeing to this Examinate, that hee had mette Byettes wife two seuerall tymes, tellyng this Examynate, that it mette her once in this Examinates yarde, and the next day after it sayde, that it met her at the style, going into her grounde: And saieth it tolde this Examinate, it had plagued y̨ said Byets wife to the death. She this Examinate saying it was done by the spirite, but not by the sending of this Examinate. The sayde spirite sayeing, I knowe that Byet and his wife haue wronged thee greatly, and doone thée seuerall hurtes, and beaten thy swyne, and thrust a pytchforke in one of them, the which the spirite sayde to haue doone, to winne credit with this Examinate.

And this Examinate saieth further, that aboute Lammas last past: For that the sayde William Byet had abused her, in calling her olde trot, old whore, and other lewde speaches, shee this Examinate, caused the spirite, called *Suckin*, to goe and plague the sayde Willyam Byrtte where that woulde: The which the sayd spyrite did, and at the retourne of it, it

C.　　　　　　　　　colde

The Apprehension

tolde this Examinate, that it met Byet in the barne yarde, and that it had plagued him in the hippes, euen vnto death: And saith she gaue it a rewarde of mylke; and saith, that many tymes they drinke of her milke bowle. And being asked how shee came by the sayde spirites, she confessed and sayde, that one Mother Turner did sende them vnto her to her house (as shee thinketh) for that she had denyed the sayde Mother Turner of mylke: And when, and as often as they did drinke of the mylke: This Examynate saith they went into the sayd earthen pot, and lay in the wooll.

The Examynation and Confession of Annis Glascocke, wife of Iohn Glascocke, sawyer, taken before me Bryan Darcey Esquyre, the xxiiii. of February.

This Examinate beeing charged by Mychel the shoomaker, that a womā, sotimes fellowe with her in the house, shoulde reporte her to bee a naughtie woman, and a dealer in witchcrafte, denyeth that she knewe anye such woman, or that any such speaches were vsed vnto her.

This Examinat being charged that one sparrowe being lodged in her house, shoulde heare a strainge noise or rumbling since Christmas last,

of certaine Witches.

laſt, ſaith, that ſhe made a noyſe by remouing of boards one night for that ſhe woulde haue him to lye in an other chamber.

This Examinate ſaith alſo, that long ſithence ſhe dwelt by the ſpace of one quarter or more with her brother Edward Wood, and that at ſeueral tymes in that time certain ledde weights and great ſtones were caſt into the houſe, and diuers ſtraunge noyſes of rumblinges hearde: the which weights & ſtones came alwayes neereſt one Arnoldes head, being then a boorder in that houſe, and ſaith that Arnoldes wife was accompted a witch: And was ſuſpected to cauſe the ſame ſtones to be caſt, to the intent to dryue her huſband from boording there being in Ieloſie of this Examinate: She being at that tyme not aboue the age of xx. yeares.

This Examinate ſaith, that by many yeares paſt ſhe was much troubled with ſtraung aches in her bones, and otherwiſe: wherof ſhe conſumed by the ſpace of two or three yeares: And ſaith, ẏ ſhe was told, that about Sudbery there dwelt one Herring (named to bee a Cawker) to whome ſhe went, who declared to this Examinate, ẏ ſhe was hauted with a witch (naming Arnolds wife) And that ſhe ſhould not eſcape death wout ſhe had ſome remedy, wherupon this examinat ſaith, ẏ ſhe praied ẏ ſaid Herring to helpe

C 2   her, And

The Apprehension

And that hee then deliuered vnto her a little lynnen bagge of the breadth of a groate, full of small thinges like seedes, and willed her to put the same where her payne was most, the which shee proued by sewing it vppon her garmente, neare the place where her greefe was: And after a while this Examinate saieth, she recouered, and was well.

This Examinate denyeth that euer she hurt the base Childe, which Pages his wife kept, or that there was anye falling out betweene this Examinate and her: And sayeth, that shee knoweth not, whether the sayde Childe bee a base Childe or not.

This Examinate beeing charged, that shee sent a spirite to plague Michell, the shoomakers Childe, or that shee had bewitched the said Childe, denyed that shee had doone eyther of both. And she being asked, whether she euer fell out with one Fortune or his wife, or whether shee hurt any of their children, saieth, that there was no falling out betweene them, or that shee hurt any of his Children.

Annys Letherdall and Margaret Sympson women appoynted, to see and view the body of this Examinate: sayde, and affyrme vppon their credites, that vpon the left side of the thighe of this Examinate, there be some spots,

an

of certaine Witches.

and vpon the left shoulder likewise one or two: Which spottes bee like the sucked spots, that Ursley Kempe hath vppon her bodie.

This Examinate and the sayde Ursley Kempe, alias Greye being brought before mee face to face, the sayde Ursley then charged this Examinate to haue plagued and punyshed Mythelles Childe, whereof it dyed: And also Fortunes wiues Childe, whereof it languyshed. At which speaches this Examinate vsed outragious wordes, calling the sayde Ursley whore, saying, shee would scratch her: for shee was a Witch, and that shee was sure shee had bewitched her: For that shee coulde not nowe weepe.

The Confession and Examynation of Ales Hunt, the Wife of Willyam Hunt, taken before me Bryan Darcey Esquyre, the xxiiii. of February.

The sayd Ales Hunt beeing asked, whether there was anye falling out beetwene this Examinate, and Haywarde of Frowycke, or his Wyfe: saieth, there was none: But rather shee had cause to be beeholding vnto them: saying, that Haywardes wife did christen her a Childe. And she being charged to haue a spirit

C 3   in

The Apprehenſion

in a potſharde, which Urſleye Kempe had ſeene, denyed that ſhee had anye ſuch, or that ſhee had plagued Haywardes Cattell with that or with any other ſpirite.

This Examinate being aſked, if ſhe neuer did feede her ſpirits with mylke out of a lyttle trenyng diſhe, ſayde no: the which dyſhe was brought by the Conſtable from her houſe, and then ſhewed to this Exampnate, the which ſhee denyed to bee her dyſhe, or that ſhe had any ſuch in her houſe.

This Examinates warrant beeing made, and to her read, and ſhee committed to the Counſtable to be carryed to the Gaile, deſired to ſpeake alone with mee the ſaide Bryan Darcey: wherevpon I wente into my Garden, and this Examinate followed mee, ſhee then falling vppon her knees with weeping teares, confeſſed and ſayde, that ſhee had within vi. dayes before this examination, two ſpirits, like vnto little Coltes, the one blacke, and the other white: And ſaith ſhe called them by the names of *Iacke* and *Robbin*: And that they tolde her, that the ſayde Urſleye Kempe woulde bewray her this Examinate, and willed her therefore to ſhift for her ſelfe. And ſo they went from her, and ſithence this Examinate ſaith ſhee ſawe them not.

This

of certaine Witches.

This Examinate saith, that her sister (named Margerie Sammon) hath also two spirites like Toades, the one called *Tom*, and the other *Robbyn*: And saith further, her sayde Syster and shee had the sayd spyrites of their Mother, Mother Barnes: who departed out of this world within xii. dayes before the taking of this examination.

The Examination and confession of Margery Sammon, taken before mee Brian Darcie Esquire, the xxv. of February.

The sayde Margerie Sammon, sister to the sayde Ales Hunt, daughter to one mother Barnes lately deceased, (which mother Barns was accompted to bee a notorious Witche) saith, that shee remayned at home with her mother by the space of halfe a yeare, and saith shee was with her mother seuerall times, when shee laye sicke, and also at the houre of her death: But denyeth the hauing of any spirites of her sayd Mother, or that her mother had any to her knowledge.

The said Margery ye night being cōmitted to ye ward & keeping of ye counstable, and the nexte daye brought before mee the sayde Bryan in the presence of her sister Ales Hunte, And beeing charged by her sayde Syster to haue

The Apprehesion

two spirites like toades, giuen her by her mother at her death, vtterlye denyed the same saying, I defie thee, though thou art my sister, saying she neuer sawe anye such: At which speaches her sister taking her aside by the arme, whyspred her in the eare: And then presentlye after this Examinate with great submission and many teares, confessed that she had two spirites delyuered her by her mother, the same day shee departed. And that shee this Examinate caryed them awaye with her in the euening, they beeing in a wicker basket, more then halfe full of white and blacke wooll: And that she asking her mother what shee should doe with them, she bad her keepe them and feede them: This Examinate asking wherewithall; her mother answered, if thou doest not giue them mylke, they will sucke of thy blood: And sayeth, she called them by the names of *Tom* and *Robbin*. And this Examinate beeing asked how often she had giuen them meate sithence shee had them, saieth and confesseth, that she fed them twise out of a dyshe with mylke: And beeing asked when shee fed them last, this Examinate sayde, vppon Twesday last past before this examination, and that with mylke.

This Examinate sayeth also, that when shee tooke them of her mother, shee sayde vnto her,

if

of certaine Witches.

if thou wilte not keepe the said spirits, then send them to mother Pechey, for I know she is a Witch, and will bee glad of them. And saith further, that shee hearing, that Ursley Kempe was apprehended, and fearing that shee shoulde bee called in question, saieth thereupon shee tooke the saide spirites beeing in a basket, and in the euening wente into the grounde of her Master, and so into Reads grounde, and bad them goe to the sayde mother Pechey: At which wordes they skypped out of the said basket, and wente before this Examinate, shee this Examinate sayeing, all euill goe with you, and the Lorde in heauen blesse mee from yee: And sayeth, shee myghte see the sayde spyrites goeing towarde a barred style, goeing ouer into Howe lane: And when they came at the style, shee saieth, they skypped ouer the same style and wente the readye waye to mother Pecheyes house: And saieth shee verilye thinketh the sayde mother Pechey hath them.

The Examination and confession of Ioane Pechey widdowe, taken before mee Brian Darcie Esquire, the xxv. of February.

The

The Apprehension

This Examinate Ioan Pechey beeing asked how olde shee was, saith, shee is threescore yeares and vpwardes: And saith that sheehath dwelt in the Towne of S. Oseys about xl. yeares: And saith she knew Mother Barnes, and she knewe her to bee no witch, or that she euer heard her to bee accompted, or to haue skill in any witchery. And she being asked whether shee was with her when she lay vpon her death bed, saith that she was not.

This Examinate also denyeth, that she hath or euer had any Puppettes, Spyrites or Maumettes: Or that shee had any Spirites, which she bought, or were conueyed vnto her by Margerie Barnes, or sent by any other sithence the death of Mother Barnes.

This Examinate also denyeth, that euer shee sayde to any of her neighbours, or to any other person in secrete sorte or meerely, that she knew or could tell what any man in the Towne at any time dyd or sayed, when she her selfe listed, or would know.

This Examinate saith, that she neuer vsed any of those speaches, which Ales Huntt hath enformed against her, As yea art thou so sawsie? art thou so boulde? thou were not best to bee so bould, for if thou beist, thou shalt haue Simonds sauce.

This

of certaine Witches.

This examinate being asked, what she thought of the sodaine death of Johnson the Collector, saith, he was a very honest man, and dyed very sodainly: And saith she heard, that one Lurkin shoulde saye, that hee heard Johnson to saye, that Mother Newman had beewitched him. And beeing asked of whome shee heard it, shee aunswered shee coulde not tell: And sayth that shee her selfe neuer vsed anye harde speaches against the sayde Johnson.

This Examinate beeing charged to haue willed her Sonne Phillip Barrenger, beeing of the age of xxiii. yeares to lye in bedde with her, denyeth that shee had so doone, other then shee had willed him at some tymes to lye vppon the bedde at her backe.

But the saide Phyllyppe beeing examined, confesseth and saith, that manye tymes and of late hee hath layne in naked bed with his owne mother, being willed and commaunded so to doe of her.

This Examinate beeing asked, whether she had any Cat in her house, sayth that shee hath a Kyttyn, and a little Dogge, And beeing asked, what coulour the Kyttyn was of, shee this Examinate sayed she could not tell, saying yee maye goe and see.

The

The Apprehension

The Information of Iohn Sayer one of the Constables of Thorpe, taken before mee Bryan Darcey Esquyre, one of her maiesties Iustices against Als Manfielde, the xiii. daye of March.

The sayde Iohn saieth, that aboue one yeare sithence hee had a Thetcher, which was a thetching of a barne of his, neere Mother Manfieldes house, and that then shee the sayde Ales came vnto the Thetcher, and would haue had him to thetche ouer an ouen of hers, wherunto this Thetcher made aunswer and saydz, hee woulde doe it, if his mayster woulde let him, but els hee woulde not doe it, whereunto shee saydz, hee had beene as good as to haue willed you to doe it. For I will bee euen with him. And hee saieth, that within a while after, hee had occasion to come by the house of the sayde Ales Manfielde with his carte, well neere three quarters loaden, and beeing before her doore vppon the harde grounde: saieth, his carte stoode, that hee coulde not make it goe forwarde nor backwarde, by the space of one howre and more: The which he saieth, hee thought to bee doone by some witcherie, which the sayde Ales Manfielde then vsed.

The

of certaine Witches.

The Information of Robert Sanneuet, taken before me Brian Darcey Esquire, one of her M. Iustices the xiiii. of March.

The sayde Robert saieth, that aboute xv. yeeres past, ther dwelt with him the daughter of Elizabeth Ewstace, and that for some lewde dealynges, and behauiour by her doone, hee saieth, hee vsed some threatning speeches vnto her, beeing his seruaunt: And that shortlye after shee wente home to her sayde mother, and telled her of her maysters vsing of her: And the nexte daye hee saieth, as hee was a sitting by his fire side, his mouth was drawne awrye, well neere vppe to the vpper parte of his cheeke: whereuppon hee sayeth, hee sent presentlye to one of skill to come vnto him, who came vnto him, And that hee seeing him in that case, tooke a lynnen cloath, and couered his eyes, and stroake him on the same side with a stronge blowe, and then his mouth came into the right course: and hee sayeth that hee willed this Examinate to put awaye his seruaunt, and that out of hand: the which he saieth he did.

This Examinat saith, that iii. yeres sithence his brother Crosse was taken verye sickly, and at tymes was without any remembrance, & that he sent for this Examinat, & when he came vnto him

The Apprehension

him, hee tolde him that Margaret Ewstace had bewitched him, and brought him into that weak state hee then was at: Wherto this Examinate saith, that if that bee so, hee then wished a spyt red hotte and in her buttocks, which speaches of his, hee sayth was carryed by one then in the house vnto the saide Mother Ewstace, and this Examinate saith, that shee seeing a neighbour of his going towardes this Examinates house, asked her whether shee was going, and she answered vnto this Examinates house: Whereunto she the sayd Mother Ewstace should say, naye goe not thyther, for he saith I am a witch: And sayed, his wife is with Childe and lustie, but it will bee otherwise, with her then hee looketh for: Whereuppon this Examinate saith, that his wife had a most straunge sicknes, and was deliuered of childe, which within short time after dyed.

This Examinate saith, that the Sommer after he milked vii. milche beasts, and that al that sommer many and very often tymes, his sayde beasts did giue downe blood in steede of milke and that hee had little, or no profit by them: And hee saith that about iiii. monethes after many of his hogges did skippe and leape aboute the yarde in a straunge sorte: And some of them dyed.

The

of certaine Witches.

The Information of Vrsley Kemp alias Grey, taken at Colchester by Thomas Tey and Brian Darcey Esquires, two of her M. Iustices the ix. of March.

This Examinate beeing charged that shee shoulde reporte to seuerall persons that haue comen vnto her, sithence her imprysonment, that Ales Newman shoulde send a spirit to plague the late Lorde Darcey, whereof hee dyed: And shee being asked, whether shee saied so, saith shee sayed, that *Tyffyn* her white spirit tolde her that Ales Newman had sent a spyrite to plague a noble man, of whome we (meaning the poore) had all reliefe: The which she saith she tooke to be the said Lord Darcey, And otherwise she sayed not.

The Information of Rychard Rosse of little Clapton, taken before mee Bryan Darcey Esquyre, agaynst Henry Cilles and Cysley his wife, the i. day of March.

The sayd Richard saith, that about vi. yeares past, the sayd Henry Cilles wrought with this Examinate in husbandry many and seuerall times, & saith y^t at one time he the said Henry beeing at plough in ye said Richardes ground with his plowgh of horses, they being as well and as likely to any mans iudgement, as any mens

horse

The Apprehension

horse myght be when they beganne to worke: yet before they had gone twise or thrise aboute the lande, two of his lykest horses fell downe in moste straunge wise, and dyed.

This Examinate sayeth, that a little before he had denyed the sayde Cillys of two bushels of maulte, which she would haue had for three shillings, but he helde it at tenne groates. And sayeth further, that within a whyle after the sayde Cysleye Cyllis did come vnto this examinates wife, brynging with her a poke, and desired to buye a bushell, or a bushell and a halfe of maulte of her, or as much as her bag would hould: But for that shee the sayd Cysley would not giue her her price, shee departed without hauing anye, vsing many harde speaches at that time: whereupon they fell out.

This Examinate saieth also, that his wife finding Cylles his cattell in his grounde, did hunt thē out therof, which Cylles his wife seeing, was thereat in a great anger, and gaue her lewd speeches, & saith that presently after, many of his beaste were in a most straung taking: the which he doth say, to be wroughte by some witchcraft, or sortery by þ said Hēry or Cisly his wife.

This Examinate saieth, that about xii. months & more past, a barn of his stāding in his groū, a good way of frō his dwelling house to

much

of certaine whitches.

much corne therein, was in a most sodeine sorte fired and burnt: But (hee saieth) hee cannot charge the said Henry or Cysley his wife, to bee the doers thereof, other then the youngest sonne of the saide Henrie and Cisley, should say heere is a goodly deale of corne, and a man vnknowen shoulde answere there was the diuels store.

The enformation of Henrie Sellys, sonne of the saide Henrie, taken before mee Brian Darcey Esquire, the saide day and yeere.

The saide Henrie saith, that hee is of the age of ix. yeeres, and that sithence Candlemas last, one night about midnight, there came to his brother John a spirite, and tooke him by the left legge, and also by the litle Toe, which was like his sister, but that it was al blacke: at which time his brother cryed out and said, Father, Father, come helpe mee, there is a blacke thing þ hath me by y legge, as big as my sister: whereat his father said to his mother, why thou whore cannot you keepe your impes from my childrē: whereat shee presently called it away frō her sonne, saying, come away, come away, At which speech it did depart.

This examinat saith, that the next day hee tolde

D

The Apprehension

tolde his mother hee was so afraid of the thing that had his brother by the legge that he swett for feare, and that he coulde scarse get his shirt from his backe: his mother answering thou lyest, thou lyest whoresonne. This Examinat being asked, wherewith hee had seene his mother to feede her Imps and wherein, hee saith, y⁹ she fed them out of a blacke dish, ech other day with milke: and saith, that he hath seene her to carry it vnto a heape of wood and brome standing vnder a crab tree by the house, and being asked what their names were, he saith, that one of them is called by two names which is Herculus, sothe hons, or Iacke, & that is a blacke one, & is a hee, and the other is called Mercurie, and is white, and is a shee: and that their eyes bee like vnto goose eyes, and saith, that he hath seen his mother to remooue foure Brome fagots, and so to creepe into the crabtree roote, whereas they stand and lye vpõ a fleese of wooll. And this Examinant saith further, y⁹ the same night Rosse his maide was taken: when his father came home, his mother told him her husbande, that she had sent Herculus to Rosse his maide: and he answered, yee are a trim foole. This examinat saith, that as hee and his mother were comming (they being in Rosse his Bromefield) she said vnto him, take heed ye say nothing.

The

of certaine whitches.

The information of Iohn Selles the youngest sonne of Henry and Cysley, taken before mee Brian Darcey Esquire, the third day of March.

The said Iohn Selles saith, that he is about the age of vi. yeeres iii. quarters, & saith, y^t one night there was a blacke thing like his sister, that tooke him by the legge and that hee cried out, saying, father, father, come helpe me and defende mee, for there is a blacke thing that hath me by the legge: at which he saith, his father said to his mother, ye stinking whore what meane yee? can yee not keepe your imps from my children? & beeing asked what colour they were of, & what they were called, he saith, that one is black, & another is white, & y^t he hath hard his mother to call them Imps, & that they haue eyes as big as himselfe: and he saith, y^t his father bad his mother put them away or els kill them. And saith, y^t a while sithence his mother deliuered the^m to one of Colchester (he thinketh his name is Wedon or Glascocke) and saith y^t Wedoⁿs wife had a cap to dresse of his mothers, and saith, that they were carried away in a basket at that time. And beeing asked, whether his father or mother bade him that hee shoulde saye nothinge, hee saieth, that his

D 2   mother

The Apprehension

mother said vnto him that hee should goe before a gentleman, and willed him to take heed he telled no tales nor lyes.

He saith, that his father called one of them, which is the blacke one, Iohn, which he said his father mocked him because his name was so: And his mother called ye white one an Impe. He saith he hath seene his father to feede them out of a blacke dish with a woodden spone, and y^t he knoweth the same dishe, & the last time he fed them it was behinde the Bromestacke at ye crabtree. And hee saith, that the man which carried them away gaue his mother a pennie, and that when she should goe to him she should haue another pennie, hee saith at that time his brother was from home at one Gardeners house.

And being asked, whether euer hee sawe his mother to feede them, he saith, that he hath seene his mother to feed them twise, and that out of a dish with a spone with thinne milke.

Note also, it is to be considered, that there is a scarre to bee seene of this examinats legge where it was taken, and also the naile of his little Toe is yet vnperfect.

The information of Ioan Smith wife of Robert Smith, take before mee Brian **Darcey** Esquire, the said day and yeere.

of certaine witches.

The said Ioan saith, that one holy day in the after noone sithence Michaelmas last, shee had made her selfe readie to goe to Church, and tooke in her armes her young childe & opening her dore, her mother (grandmother to the child) one redworths wife, and Selles his wife were at the said dore readie to draw the latch, shee this examinat telling her mother she was comming out of dores to Churchward: whereat the grand mother to the child, tooke it by the hand & shoke it, saying, a mother pugs art thou comming to Church: And Redworthes wife lokimg on it, said, here is a iolie & likely childe God blesse it: after which speeches, Selles his wife saide, shee hath neuer the more children for that, but a little babe to play wall for a time. And she saith within short time after her said childe sickned and died: But she saith y̶ her cõscience wil not serue her, to charge the said Cysley or her husband to be the causers of any suche matter, but prayeth God to forgiue them if they haue dealt in any such sort. &c.

The examination and confession of Henrie Selles and Cysley his wife, taken before mee Brian Darcey Esquire, the first day of Marche.

The said Henry saith, that he hath wrought in husbandry by some long time past with

D 3   Richard

The apprehension

Richard Rosse of litle Clapton, and þ one time he being at plough, two of his horses vpon a sodaine fell downe and were in most strange taking, but what the occasion should be thereof (he saith) he knew not. And saith, þ he doth not remember þ he would haue had any mault of the saide Rosse at his price, or þ there was any falling out betweene thē: and denieth þ his childe cried out vnto him, saying, father come helpe me, or that he called his wife stinking whore: and denieth all the residue of the matters in general enformed against him, &c.

Condemned.

The said Cysley his wife saith, that she doth not remēber þ Rosse his wife did at any tyme hunt her catell being in her ground, or þ shee vsed any hard speeches to his wife thereupon, or þ shee fel out for þ she could not haue any mault at her price: but she saith at one time she met Rosse his wife, & that there was some talke betweene them, the which shee doeth not remember more then that the saide Rosses wife saide, I shall see at your ende what you are. And being asked if shee knewe not mother Tredsall, shee saith shee knew her, but she denieth, þ she saide if she were a witche, she learned the same of the saide mother Tredsall: and denieth that her childe cryed out

of certaine witches.

ed out in the night to his father, and all the residue of ye matters ingeneral enformed against her.

Ales Gilney, Joan Smith, and Margaret Simson women of credite, appointed by mee Brian Darcey, to view and see the body of the saide Cysley, say, that shee hath vpon her body many spots very suspitious, and the said Margaret saith, that they bee much like the sucked spots, that shee hath seene vpon the body of Ursley Kempe and seuerall other.

The enformation of Ales Baxster seruãt with Richarde Rosse, taken by mee Brian Darcey Esquire, one of her Maiesties Iustices of the peace, the xix. day of Marche.

THE saide Ales saith, that about Hallamas last past about foure of the clocke in the after noone, shee went a milking into her masters grounde two closes of from the house, and that she had eight or niene beastes to milke, and saith y^t after she had milked all but one, and as shee was a milking of that one, before shee had halfe done, the Cow start and stroke downe her paile, and that shee saw all the rest to make a ſcaring and a looking about : And shee

D 4 saith,

The apprehension

saith as shee was a making an ende of milking of that Cowe, shee felt a thing to pricke her vnder the right side, as if she had been striken with ones hande, and she saith that after, as shee was going homewardes with her milke neere the style in the same closse, there came a thinge all white like a Cat, and stroke her at the hart, in such sort as shee could not stand, goe, nor speake, and so she remained vntill her said master & two of his workmen did carry her home in a chaire: she saith, she saw the said thing to go into a bush by the style, & that she knew not her master when he came vnto her.

Robert Smith saith, that about Hallamas last past he wrought wt Richard Rosse, and that about v. a clocke was called by the said Rosse to helpe him to fetch home his maid, & going then with him they found the said Ales his maide sitting leaning against the stile, & in yt case as she could not stand, go, nor speake, and yt he and one other with their masters helpe tooke her vp and brought her home in a chaire.

The information of Henrie Durrant, taken by mee Brian Darcey Esquire, one of her Maiesties Iustices of peace, the 26. day of March, against Ales Hunt.

The said Hery Durrāt saith, yt about the second day of this present month, he went to Colchester

of certaine Witches.

chester to appeare before the Iustices there to bee bounde from killing of fleshe, and after that hee had so done he saith, that he went with seueral of his neighbours vnto the Castle, to see the witches that were committed thyther, at which time he saith, he talked with Ursley Kemp alias Gray, who then tolde him after some demaunds which hee vsed vnto her, that Ales Hunt and her mother (the widow Barnes) had bewitched his daughter, whereof she dyed, saying, that because they were denied of a peece of Porke at suche time as they came for it, therefore they were offended with you: and saieth further, that hee doth remember that they came vnto him and woulde haue had a peece of Porke, the which for that it was newly dressed, and somewhat whot, he made them answere that he woulde not cut it out.

The enformatiō of Richard Rosse and others together, with the confession of Henrie Selles and Cisley his wife.

The examination and confession of Ales Mansfield, taken at Thorpe, and brought before me Brian Darcey esquire, one of her Maiesties Iustices, the xiii. day of Marche.

Con-

The Apprehension

Condemned.

THe saide Ales Manfielde saieth, that shee is of the age of three score and three yeeres or there aboutes, and that about xii. yeeres sithence one margaret Greuell came vnto this examinat and saide, that shee shoulde goe out of her house ỹ shee dwelt in vnto another house in the towne: And then telled her that she had foure Impes or spirites the whiche shee woulde not carrie with her to that house, for feare they shoulde be espied or seene, and prayed her this examinate that shee woulde keepe them, and also telled her what they woulde doe for her (saying shee should haue them vpon condition that shee the sayde Margaret might haue them at her pleasure, otherwise shee should not haue them) and with what, and howe shee shoulde feede them, and at her desire and request shee sayth that shee was contented to keepe them: And thereupon shee sayeth it was concluded and agreed betweene her and this examinate, that shee the sayde Margaret shoulde haue them as often and as many times as shee would at her pleasure, and that then shee receiued them.

This examinate being asked, what names they were called by, and of what likenes, saieth that one of thē was called *Robin*, an other *Iack*, the thirde *William*, the fourth *Puppet* alias *Mawset*

of certaine Witches.

met, & that two of them were hees and the other two were shees, & were like vnto blacke Cats, and sayth that she kept them in a boxe with woll therein: And ẏ they did stand vpõ a shelfe by her bed where she lay. This examinate saith also, ẏ ẏ said Margaret Grauel hath commen vnto her many & oftẽ times sithence ẏ saide agreemẽt betweene thẽ made, & according to ẏ said condition hath receiued of this examinat ẏ said imps or spirits: shee this examinat being telled of her some times wherfore she would haue thẽ, & that some times she knew by asking ẏ said imps or spirits where they had bin, & what they had done when they returned againe vnto her. And being asked how oftẽ & whẽ to her remẽbrãce, she this examinat saith, about 7. yeres since ẏ said mother Grauel came vnto this examinate & told her ẏ Chestons wife & she were fallẽ out, & had chiddẽ very much, & that she gaue her euill speeches, wherevpon shee requested to haue ẏ spirit *Robin* to go to plague his beasts: & thẽ sẽt it, which said when it returned, ẏ Cheston being at plow & leauing worke, ẏ it had plagued a bullocke of his ẏ was well liking & lustie, wherof it should pine & die.

This examinate saith, that the saide Margaret Greuell, well neere two yeres after, sent her spirite *Iacke* to goe to plague Cheston, vpon the great Toe vnto the death.

This

The Apprehension

This Examinate saieth, that when it returned it tolde her that it had plagued the saide Chesson vpon the Toe euen vnto death, and that it had sucked blood of the saide Margrettes bodie, and that besides it had of her Beere and Breade for the labour: and saith, that shee this examinate gaue it Beare and Breed then also for telling of her.

This examinate saith also, that fiue yeeres past or there aboutes, her spirit *Robin* tolde her that Margarette Greuell had sent the saide spirite vnto her husband to plague him, where of he pined aboue halfe a yeere and more, hauing by that meanes many and seuerall straunge sores, and thereof died. And this Examinate saith that, that hee woulde eate as much or more then two men woulde doe, and that it sucked blood vpon the bodye of the saide Margaret for the labour: she this examinate being asked vpō what place, saith the saide spirite did not tell her.

This examinat saith, that on a time she went vnto the house of Joan Chesson widow, and desired of her to giue her some Curdes: but shee sayeth shee gaue her none, wherevpon she saith, that shee sent her Impe *Puppet* alias *Mamet* to plague her Beastes, where that woulde, and so it did: And that when the saide Impe returned, it tolde this examinate that it had plagued

foure

of certaine Witches.

foure of her Beastes with lamenesse, and that it did sucke blood vpon this Examinates body for a rewarde.

This examinate sayth, that about two yeres past, one John Sayer did fetch doung out of an Orchard, from a pittes banke, neere this examinates house, and did by reason thereof, gulle a greene place before her doore, wherevpon shee saieth, shee sent her Impe called *Puppet* alias *Mamet* to stay the Carte being before the dore, the which it dyd, and shee saieth that shee sawe him and others to lift at the wheeles, and to set his hauser rope, the which did litle good, and that the same hauser rope and other of his horse harnesse burst a sunder, and shee saieth, shee gaue her said Impe Beere for the labour.

This examinate saieth, that litle before Michaelmas last, her saide foure Impes saide vnto her, saying, I pray you Dame giue vs leaue to goe vnto little Clapton to Celles, saying, they woulde burne Barnes, and also kill Cattell, and shee saith, that after their returne they tolde her that they had burnt a barne of Rosses with corne, and also tolde her that Celles his wife knewe of it, and that all they foure were fedde at Cels house by her al y̓ time they were away frō this examinate, w̓ shee sayeth was about a seuen night: And that *Puppet* sucked vpon this examinates

The Apprehension

aminates left shoulder at their returne vnto her:
And the rest had beere.

   This examinate saith, that *William*, one of
her Impes not aboue a seuēnight befoꝛe her ap-
pꝛehension, tolde her that shee shoulde be called
in question, and bad her shift foꝛ her self: saying,
they woulde nowe depart from her and goe vnto saint Osees vnto mother Gray, mother Toꝛ-
ner, oꝛ mother Barnes two daughters, but to
which of them it was that they would goe shee
doth not nowe remēber: but they told her ꝑ they
to whō they wēt had hurt mē & womē to death, &
seueral mēs cattel and other thinges.

This examinat saith, ꝑ about a quarter of a yere
since, she wēt vnto ꝑ house of mother Ewstace to
speake w̄ her, at w̄ time she saith, shee saw three
imps w̄ she had stāding in a yearthē pot in ꝑ one
side of her house next ꝑ heath, & saith that one of
thē was white, ꝑ other gray, & the third blacke,
& saith they were like cats. This examinat saith
also, that her white spirit told her, ꝑ mother Ewstace their dame, sent her impes to hurt a childe,
whereof it shoulde pine and become lame, but
whose childe shee remembꝛeth not.

   Also this examinate saith, ꝑ vpon some conference between mother Ewstace & her, shee this
examinate told mother Ewstace, ꝑ mother Gre-
uel did plague her husbād, wherof he died, which
was

of certaine Witches.

was done by her spirit *Robin*: & she saith that she also told mother Ewstace, y̶ mother Grauel set her spirite *Iacke* to plague Chettō to the death: but what answere she the said mother Ewstace then made, shee nowe remembreth not.

This examinate saith, that about a yere since the said mother Grauel told her, that she had caused her impes to destroy seuerall brewinges of beere, & batches of bread, being asked where, she saith a brewē at Reades, a brewē at Carters, and a brewē of three or foure bushelles of malte at Brewses.

The said confession being made by the saide Ales in maner and forme aforesaid, I the saide Brian in the presence of they cunstables & other the Townesmen of Thorpe, sayde as I had seuerall tymes before vnto the sayde Ales, what a danger it was, and howe highly shee should offende God if shee shoulde charge any person with any thing vntrue, and also telled her that her saide confession should bee read agayne vnto her, willing her that if shee hearde any thinge read that she knew was not true, that she should speake, and it shoulde be amended, the which being done, shee sayde her confession was true, and the sayde Margaret and Elizabeth beeing then also called before mee, shee affirmed her confession to their faces.

The

The Apprehenſion

The enformation of Thomas Death & Marie his daughter, taken by me Brian Darcey eſquire, one of her Maieſties Iuſtices, the xv. day of March.

THe ſayde Thomas Death ſaith, that about two yeeres ſithence, there was a great falling out betweene this examinates wife and the ſayde Ciſly Celles, for that one George Battell hauing put a child of his to the nurſing and keeping of the ſaide Ciſley, and after he taking the ſaide childe away from her, and put the ſame to this examinates wife to be nurſed & kept, whereupon at the next meeting of the ſayde wiues, the ſaide Celles his wife chid and rayled at her, and ſaide, thou ſhalt looſe more by the hauing of it, then thou ſhalt haue for the keeping of it, & within one moneth after (as he now remembreth) he ſaith that a child of his, of the age of foure yeres, being in good liking and well, went but out of the doores into the yarde, who preſently fell downe dead, and after by helpe being brought to life, the ſaide childe was in a pitious caſe, and ſo died preſently.

This examinate ſaith, that hee had preſently after ſeuerall Swine the which did ſkippe and leape about the yarde, in a moſt ſtraunge ſorte, and then died, And he ſaith that ouer night he had

a

of certaine witches.

a Calfe which was very fatt, and the next morning he found the same dead.

This examinate saith, that hee hauing bin at sea and newely arriued at Ipeswitch, a messenger which was newely come from his wife, by chaunce mette him, who told this examinate that his daughter Marie was taken very strangly, and lay in a most pitious case, saying he had brought her water to carry vnto a Phisition to haue his opinion thereof: Whereupon this examinate saieth, that hee and the messenger went therewith vnto one Berte dwelling in that Towne, and shewed him the same, hee sayeth, he asked him if that his daughter were not bewitched: But hee saide that hee woulde not deale so farre to tell him, whereupon hee not satisfied to his minde, met after with an acquaintaunce of his, and asked him where hee might goe to a cunning man, telling him in what case his daughter lay in: who then sent him to a man whome he knewe not, nor his name hee nowe remembreth not, with whome after hee had conferred and shewed his daughters saide water: This examinate sayeth, hee tolde hym if hee had not commen with some great haste to seeke helpe, hee had come too late: And this examinate

The apprehension

minate sayeth, that hee toulde him that within two nyghtes after the parties that had hurte his daughter shoulde appeare vnto her, and remedie her: And hee sayeth, that hee him selfe did not then come home, but went to sea: But hee sayeth hee sent his messenger home with thinges that were to bee ministred vnto his said daughter.

This examinate sayeth, that when he came home, his wife tolde him that the next nyght after his daughter had recevued the chinges ministred vnto her, that shee heard a noyse like a groning, and that shee did arise and went vnto her daughter, and asked her howe shee did: whereunto her daughter made answere and sayed, ah mother that you had commen a little sooner, you shoulde haue seene Celles wife and Barkers wife here standing before mee.

Marie Death, daughter of the sayd Thomas Death, sayeth, that about two yeeres sithence vpon a Sunday, shee was taken with an ache or numnes from her necke down her backe all ouer: And shee sayeth, that after her mother had ministred thinges vnto her sente from a Phisition: The nexte nyght after shee sayeth

eth shee hearde a voyce, saying vnto her, looke vp, at which shee saieth shee lifted vp her eyes, and then did see Celles wife and Barkers wife standing before her in the same apparell that they did vsually weare. And shee this examinat sayeth, shee thought they saide vnto her bee not afraide, and that they vanished away, as shee thinketh it was about midnight, And the nexte day after, this examinate saieth, shee amended, and was in case to arise without help, where afore two or three coulde scarce turne her in her bed as shee lay.

The enformation of Ioan Cheston widowe, Iohn Carter and other the inhabitantes of the Towne of Thorpe, taken before mee Brian Darcey Esquire, one of her Maiesties Iustices of the peace, the xiii. day of March, against Ales Manfielde.

The sayde Ioan saieth, that in sommer last, mother Manfielde came vnto her house and requested her to giue her Curdes, shee saith that answere was made that there was none, and so shee departed. And within a while after some of her cattell were taken lame & could not trauell to gather their meat, so that her seruants were constrained to mow down grasse for the by

The apprehension

the space of eyght dayes, shee sayeth, that afterwardes the saide mother Mansfielde came agayne vnto her, and demaunded Curdes, and shee sayeth, that shee then telled the saide mother Mansfielde, that shee had bewitched her Cattell, and that shee then sayde vnto her, that if her cattell did not amend and become well, shee would burne her: wherevpon shee sayeth, that her cattell did amende, and within a very shorte while after were as well as before.

Lyndes wife sayeth, that the sayde Mother Mansfielde came vnto her, and asked her a mease of Mylke, who answered that shee had but a little, not so muche as woulde suckle her calfe, whereat shee departed: and shee sayeth, that that nyght her Calfe dyed, being verye lustie, and xx. dayes olde.

The enformation of Iohn Carter & others of Thorpe, taken by mee Brian Darcey esquire, one of her Maiesties Iustices, the xx. day of March, agaynst Margarette Greuell.

Continued in prison.

The saide Iohn sayeth, that on a tyme Margaret Greuell came vnto this examinates house,

of certaine whitches.

house, desiring her to haue Godesgood, whiche was denied her, and sayeth that within a fewe dayes after his folkes went in hande with brewing: But of two brewinges after they coulde make no beere, but was fayne to put the same to the swill Tobbe, whiche was halfe a Seame at a brewing, & sayth, ỹ the third tyme they went to Brewing with the like quantitie, and that his sonne beeing a tall and lustie man, of the age of xxxvi. yeeres, was wished to take his Bowe and an arrowe, and to shoote to make his shaft or arrowe to sticke in the Brewing Fatte, and that he shotte twise and coulde not make the same to sticke, but at the thirde time that hee shotte, hee made the same to sticke in the brewinge Fatte, and after hee sayth they coulde brewe as well as before.

Nicholas Strickland Butcher, sayeth, that Margaret Greuell sent her sonne vnto him for a Racke of Mutton, hee hauing newely killed a Mutton, saying, the same was whot and that he coulde not cutte it out, and sayeth, that hee bad him come agayne in the after noone, and the Munday after his wife seething Mylke for the breakefaste of his woorkfolkes, the same Mylke and was bytter: And sayeth within fewe dayes

E 3 after

The Apprehension

after his wife went to chearne her Creame that shee had gathered, and that shee was from the morning vntill tenne of the clocke in the night a Chearning, and coulde haue no butter: the whiche this examinate seeing, hee sayeth hee caused his wife to powre the saide Creame into a Kettle, and to set it vpon the fire, the whiche was done: And making a great fire vnder it, this examinate sayeth, they coulde not make it to seeth ouer: Then this Examinate sayeth, that hee seeeing it woulde not doe, hee sayeth hee tooke the kettell off the fire, and powred the one halfe thereof into the fire, and the other halfe hee let stande in the Kettle, the whiche hee sayeth stancke in suche exceeding sorte, as they coulde not abyde in the house. And this examinate sayeth, that the seconde time that his wife went to to chearne her Creame, shee continued a chearning and coulde haue no butter, but that it was as the other, the which hee sayeth, his wife was constrayned to put it into ye swil Tub. And after y^t this Examinate saith, that the head and master Cowe of fiue beastes did also cast her Calfe, and presentlye after fell a haultynge, the whiche hee fearyng that it woulde haue dyed, sayung, that he fed it and killed it.

The

of certaine whitches.

The enformation of Felice Okey widowe, taken by mee Brian Darcey esquire, one of her Maiesties Iustices of the peace, the xx. day of March, against Elizabeth Ewstace.

The sayde Felice sayeth, that shee was the late wife of Thomas Crosse, and that shee on a time finding the geese of Elizabeth Ewstace in her grounde, did driue them out, and that by mischaunce one of her geese was hurt: whereat the sayde Elizabeth fell out exceedinglye with this Examinate, and gaue her harde speeches, saying, that thy husbande shall not haue his health, nor that whiche hee hath shall not prosper so well as it hath done, and that shee also sayde, thou haste not had so good lucke with thy gooslings, but thou shalt haue as badde: And shee sayeth that neuer after that, shee coulde haue any of them geese whiche shee her selfe kept: and also the same night shee sayeth, that one of her Kine gaue downe blood in steede of mylke, and after for the space of vii. dayes.

This examinate saith, that her late husbande T. Crosse, was takē in a strāge sort, & therof pined

E 4

The Apprehension

pyned, and sayeth, that on a time as her said husbande was a walking in his grounde, hee was cast amongest Bushes, and was in that case that hee coulde neyther see, heare, nor speake, and his face all to bee scratched: and shee sayeth, that hee beeing in that strange case, when hee came to his memorie, hee woulde alwayes crye out vpon the sayde Elizabeth euen vnto his dying day, and woulde say that sithence shee the sayd Elizabeth had threatned him he was consumed, and that shee had bewitched him.

The examination of Lawrance kempe taken before me Brian Darcey esquire, one of her Maiesties Iustices, the xx. day of Marche, against Ursley kempe.

The sayd Lawrence sayeth, that his late wife was taken in her backe, and in the priuie partes of her boodye, in a very extreame and most straunge sorte, and so continued about three quarters of a yeere, and then died: and hee sayeth, that his said e wife did tell him seuerall times that Ursley kempe his sister, had forspoke her, and that shee was the onely cause of that her sicknesse.

This

of certaine Witches.

This examinat saith, that his saide wife did tell him that two yeeres before shee mette the said Ursley his sister vpon Eliots heath, & that she fell vppon her, & then tooke vp her clothes and did beat her vpon the hippes, and otherwise in wordes did misuse her greatly.

This examinat saith, that when his wife lay a drawing home, and continued so a day and a night, all the partes of her body were colde like a dead creatures, and yet at her mouth did appeare her breath to goe and come: and that she so cōtinued in that case, vntil the said Ursley came vnto her without sending for, and then lifted vp the clothes and tooke her by the arme, the which shee had not so soone doone, but presently after she gasped, and neuer after drew her breath and so dyed.

The examination and confession of Margaret Greuell, taken before mee Brian Darcey Esquire, one of her Maiesties iustices of the peace, the 14 day of March.

Continued in prison.

This examinat saith, that she is of the age of lv. yeeres or there abouts, & being charged with the foresaide enformation and confession

E5 made

The Apprehension

made by the said Ales Manfield against her, denieth the same in generall, and saith, that shee her selfe hath lost seuerall bruings, and bakings of bread, and also swine, but shee neuer did complaine thereof: saying, that shee wished her gere were at a stay, and then shee cared not whether shee were hanged or burne, or what did become of her.

This examinat beeing asked, what falling out was or hath beene between Cheston & her, saith, on a time shee went to the saide Joan Ceston to buie a pennimorth of Rie meale, but shee woulde let her haue none, and saith, she said that it was pitie to doe her any good, saying, that she this examinat had told master Barnish þ thrises dogge did kil a Doe of his by the parke pale, and saith, that there was none other falling out as shee remembreth.

This examinat beeing viewed and seene by women, say, that they cannot iudge her to haue any sucked spots vpon her body.

This examinat and the saide Ales Manfield beeing brought before Brian Darcey, the saide Ales did affirme her confession made by her to her face to be true.

of certaine Witches.

The Examination and cōfession of Elizabeth Eustace, taken before mee Brian Darcey Esquire, the xiiii. day of marche.
Continued in prison.

THe said Elizabeth Eustace saith, shee is of the age of liii. yeeres or thereabouts, and denyeth the enformation and confession made by the sayd Ales Manfield in generall: Or that euer shee had any Impes or Mamettes saying, out vpon her hath shee tolde anye thing of mee: and shee beeing asked what conference had been betweene her the & sayd Ales Mansfielde saith, that there was none to her remembrance, other then once she went vnto her, and carried her ointment to annoynt her lamenesse that shee was troubled with, and that then there was no conference which she remembreth.

The saide Ales Mansfielde in my presence did affirme her confession made against the said Elizabeth to and before her face to face.

The enformation of Iohn Wadde, Thomas Cartwrite, Richard Harrison with seuerall others the parishioners of little Okeley, taken by mee Brian Darcey Esquire one of her Maiesties Iustices the 16. day of march.
Iohn

The Apprehension

John Wade saith, that about two moneth sithence Annis Heard saide vnto him, that shee was presented into the spirituall Courte for a witch, and prayed him to be a meanes to helpe her, that she might answere the same when the dayes were longer: whereunto he said, that hee told her that the Regester dwelt at Colchester, saying, it must be hee that therein may pleasure thee: whereto she saide, that shee woulde goe to John Aldust of Ramsey to speake vnto him, for that he goeth to Colchester that he might speak to the officers for her, and so she departed: this examinat saith, that since that time hee droue fortie sheepe and thirtie lambes to a pasture he had at Tendring, beeing thereof well neere fourescore Acres, the which hee had spared by somelong time, and knew the same to be a good sheepes pasture, and saith, that after they had bin there viii. or ix. dayes, hee went to see them (hauing neuertheleffe appointed one to looke to them): And at his comming, he found one to bee dead, another to bee lame, another to sit drowping, and a lambe in the same case by it, whiche all died, and he founde one other with the necke awry, which is in that case to this day, and one other whiche was so weake that it coulde not arise, & this examinat saith, that sithence he with others that presented her, and sithence shee the

saide

of certaine Witches.

saide Annis, talked with him, he hath had not so fewe as twentie sheepe and lambes that haue died, and be lame and like to die: & hee saith, that hee hath lost of his beasts & other cattell, which haue dyed in a strange sort.

Thomas Cartwrite saith, that after a great winde & snowe wel neere three yeeres sithence, there was an arme or boughe of a tree of his that was blowen downe, whereof Annis Herd had remoued a peece and laid the same ouer a wet or durtie place to goe ouer, which being to this examinat vnknowen, hee tooke the same & the rest and carried it home: the which the saide Annis knowing, that hee had carried the same away, she said, that the churle (meaning this examinat) to a neighbour of hers had carried away the peece of the bough that she had laied to go ouer, saying, that shee woulde bee euen with him for it. After which this Examinat saith, within three nights after, there then beeing a snowe two of his beasts went from all the rest, where as they lay as he might well perceiue by the snowe, and the head Cowe fell ouer a great bancke into a ditch on the other side, and there lay with the necke double vnder her, and the head vnder the shoulder, but a liue, and he saith, he gate it home by good helpe and laied it in his barne, and saith, that it lay fourteene dayes in a groning

The Apprehension

groning and piteous sort, but of all that time woulde eate nothing: whereupon hee saith hee tooke an axe & knocked it on the head. And also the other Cowe that was with the said Cow being a caluing in a most strange sorte died, the which this examinat saith, ẏ hee verily thinketh to be done by some witchery by the saide Annis Herd.

Bennet Lane wife of William Lane, saith, ẏ when she was a widdow, Annis Herd beeing at her house she gaue her a pint of milke & also lent her a dish to beare it home, the which dishe she kept a fortnight or 3. weekes, & then ẏ girle of the said Annis Herds came to her house on a message: & she asked the girle for the dish, & said though I gaue thy mother milk to make her a posset I gaue her not my dish, she this examinat being then a spinning: & so ẏ girle went home, & as it seemed told her mother, who by her sent her dish home to her, ẏ which girle hauing done her arrand, & being but a while gone: shee this examinat saith, she could no longer spin nor make a thread to hold, whereat she was so greeued ẏ she could not spin, she saith, she tooke her spindle and went to the grindstone therewith once or twise, & grownd it as smoth as she coulde, thinking it might be by some ruggednesse of ẏ spindle that did cause her thread to breake, and so

when

of certaine Witches.

when she had grownd it as wel as she could, she went againe to worke therewith, thinking that then it would haue done, but it would not do no better then it did before: then she saith, ỹ shee remembred her self and tooke her spindle and put it into ỹ fire, & made it red hot, & then cooled it gaine and went to worke, and then it wroughte as well as euer it did at any time before.

This examinat saith, that an other time the saide Annis Herd owed her two pence, and the time came that shee shoulde pay the Lordes rent, and she beeing a poore woman was constrained to aske her the two pence, and to borow besides (as shee said): whereto she the saide Annis answered, that shee had paied eight or nine shillings that weeke, and shee had it not nowe: saying she should haue it the next weeke, whereto shee this Examinat saide, you must needes helpe me with it now, for this day I must paye the Lordes rent, then shee saide shee must goe borrowe it, and so went and fetched it, saying, there is your money, whereunto shee this examinat answered, and said, now I owe you a pynt of milke, come for it when you will & you shall haue it: the which she came for ỹ next day, & had it with ỹ better, this examinat saith, ỹ ỹ next day she would haue fleet hir milk bowle, but it wold not abide ỹ fleeting, but would rop & role as it
were the

The Apprehension

the white of an egge, also the milk being on the
fier it did not so soone seath but it would quaile,
burne vp and stincke, the which shee saide shee
thought might be lõg of ye feeding of her beasts,
or els that her vessels were not sweete, wherevpon she saith, she scalded her vessels, and scou-
red them with salt, thinking that might helpe,
but it was neuer the better but as before: then
she saith, shee was full of care, that shee shoulde
loose both milke and creame, then shee saith it
came into her minde to approoue another way,
which was, shee tooke a horse shue and made it
redde hote, and put it into the milke in the ves-
sals, and so into her creame: and then she saith,
shee coulde seath her milke, fleete her creame,
and make her butter in good sort as she had before.

  Andrewe West and Anne saith, that on a
time the said Annis Herd came vnto his house,
saying, she had been at mill, and that she coulde
get neither meale nor bread, at which her speeches hee knowing her neede, saith, hee caused
his wife to giue her a peece of a lofe: and that
thẽ he said vnto her, Annis, thou art ill thought
of for witchcraft, the which she then vtterly denyed yt she coulde or did any such thing: wherevnto he saith, his wife saide wee haue a sort of
Pigges I wote not what we shall doe with thẽ,

say

of certaine witches.

saying, I woulde some body had one or two of them, to that the said Annis said, that if a poore body should haue of them and bestow cost, & that then if they should die it would halfe vndoe the, and said if her Landlord would giue her leaue to keepe one, she the wished that she would giue her one of them, whereunto this examinat said, shee should haue one: But for that she came not for it, this examinat saith, that he did thinke that she cared not for it, and after a while one of her neighbours bought two of them, and within ii. or iii. dayes after the said Annis came for one: to whom this examint said, for y they had not hard no more of her, that he thought she would haue none, and told her that he had sold two of them, and so the said Annis departed and went home.

This examinat saith, y his wife the next day sent vnto the said Annis a pound of wooll to be spun: and that she said to the boy that brought it, saying, can she not haue her weeders to spin the same: and that she then said to y boy, your Aunt might as well giue me one of her pigges, as to Penly. and this examinat saith, that within two houres after, one of the best pigs that he had fel vpon a crying as they stood all together before the dore in the yard, and the rest of the pigs wēt away from y: at the length the pig that cried folowed stackering as though it were lame in the hinder partes, and y then he called his weeders

The Apprehension

to see in what strange case the pig was in, and asked them what was best to doe therewith, to which some of them said, burne it, other said, cut of the eares & burn them, and so they did, & then the pig amended by & by, and within two daies after this examinats wife met with the said Annis Herd, and shee then burdened her with that she had said to her boy: To the which ye said Annis made answere, y^t she did say so: and then this examinats wife told the said Annis in what case her pig was, saying, thou saidest the other day thou hadst no skill in witcherie, his saide wife then said, I will say thou hast an vnhappie tongue. After which, this examinats wife could not brewe to haue any drinke y^t was good, so as she was full of care, saying, y^t somtimes she put one thing into her brewing fat, sometimes another thing to see if it could doe it any good, but shee saith, it did none: then she saith one gaue her counsell to put a hot yron into her mesh fat, the which she did, and then shee could brewe as well as she did before.

Edmond Osborne and Godlife his wife, said that a litle before Christmas last past, he bought at Manitree mault, and brought it home, and said to his wife, good wife, let vs haue good drinke made of it. And the next day shee went in hand to brew the same, and when she had meshed her first worte and did let it goe, that did verye

well

of certaine whitches.

well: Then his said wife hauing occasion to send her lad to their ground, she bade the lad call at Annis Herds for iii. d. the which shee owed her for a pecke of Aples, and that the lad so did: And she answered him very short, and saide, shee had it not now, saying, she shold haue it as soone as ye Wooll mã came: and the lad came home, & tolde his dame what she had said. And at ye time, she this examinat was readie to meshe ye seconde time, & whẽ she had done, her mesh fat wrought vp as the fat doth when it was set a worke with good beere, and bare vp a hand breadth aboue ye fat, and as they thrust in a sticke or any other thing, it would blow vp and then sinked againe, then she saith, ye she did heat an yron redde hot, and put ye same into it, & it rose vp no more. And then she let goe, and then shee did seath the wort, and when it was sodden it stancke in suche sorte, as that they were compelled to put ye same in the swill tubbe.

Richard Harrison Clerk, person of Beamõd saith, that he and his late wife did dwell at little Okely, in a house of his said wife, & that hee the said Richard Harrison had also the personage of Okeley in farme, and about Sommer was tweluemonth, he being at London his wife had a Ducke sitting on certaine egges vnder a Cherrie tree in a hedge, and when the saide

F 2   ducke

The apprehension

Duck had hatched, his said wife did suspect one Annis Herd a light womā, and a common harlot to haue stolen her duckelins, & that his said wife went vnto the said Annis Herd & rated her and all too chid her, but she could get no knowledge of her ducklins, and so came home & was very angry against the said Annis, & within a short time after, the said Richard Harrison went into a chamber, and there did reade on his bookes for the space of 2. or 3. houres bidding his said wife to goe to bed w̄the childrē, and ȳ he would come to her, and she so did: and being awhile laid downe in her bed, his wife did crie out: Oh Lord Lorde, helpe me & keepe me, and he running to her, asked her what she ailed: and she said, Oh Lord I am sore afraid, and haue bin diuers times, but that I would not tell you, and said, I am in doubt husband, that yonder wicked harlot Annis Herd doth bewitch me, and ȳ said Richard, said to his wife, I pray you be content and thinke not so, but trust in God and put your trust in him onely, and he will defend you from her, and from the Diuell hīselfe also: and said moreouer, what will the people say, that I beeing a Preacher shoulde haue my wife so weake in faith.

This examinat saith, ȳ within two moneths after his said wife said vnto him, I pray you as euer there was loue betweene vs, (as I hope there

of certaine whitches.

there hath been, for I haue v. pretie children (by you I thanke God) seeke som remedie for me against yonder wicked beast (meaning the saide Annis Herd). And if you will not I will complaine to my father, and I thinke he wil see som remedie for me, for (said she) if I haue no remedie, she will vtterly consume me, whereupō this examinat did exhort his said wife as hee had before, & desired her to pray to God, and ỹ he wold hang her the said Annis Herd if he could proue any such matter, and after he went to the personage, and there he saith he gathered plummes: and the said Annis Herd then came to the hedge side and Anwicks wife with her, and said vnto him, I pray you giue me som plummes sir: and this examinat said vnto her, I am glad you are here you vield strumpet, saying, I do think you haue bewitched my wife, and as truly as God doth liue, if I can perceiue ỹ she be troubled any more as she hath been, I will not leaue a whole bone about thee, & besides I will seeke to haue thee hanged: and saith, he saide vnto her that his wife would make her father priuie vnto it, and that then I warrant thee he will haue you hanged, for he will make good friends, & is a stout man of himselfe, and saith, ỹ then he did rehearse diuers things to her ỹ were thought she had bewitched, as Geese & Hogges, & as he was comming downe out of the tree, shee the said Annis

The apprehension

did sodenly depart from him without hauing any plummes.

This examinat saith, after which speeches so by him vsed vnto her, and before Christmas, his said wife was taken sore sick, & was at many times afraid both sleeping and waking, & did call this examinat her husbande vnto her not aboue two dayes before her death, and saide vnto him, husband, God blesse you and your children, and God send you good friends, for I must depart from you, for I am nowe vtterly consumed with yonder wicked Creature, naming the saide Annis Herd, which woldes hee saith were spoken by her in y presence of Iohn Pollin, & mother Poppe, and within two dayes after his said wife departed out of this world in a perfect faith, she diuers times in her sicknesse and before, repeating these wordes, Oh Annis Herd, Annis Herd shee hath consumed me.

Iohn Pollin saith, he was at maister Harrisons when his wife lay sicke, & neere y departing out of this world, & that her husband gaue her good counsell for her saluation, and that she then said, O Annis Herd, Annis Herd.

Bretts wife saith, shee heard mistres Harrison say, that the said Annis Herd had consumed her euen to the death, & that she cryed out vpon her to the houre of her death.

of certaine witches.

The enformation of Annis Dowsing base daughter of Annis Herd, taken before mee Brian Darcey Esquire, one of her Maiesties Iustices, the xviii. day of March.

THe said Annis saith, that shee is of the age of vii. yeeres the Saturday before our Lady day next, and shee being asked whether her mother had any little things, or any little imps, she saith, that she hath in one boxe sixe Auices or Blackbirds: being asked of what colour, shee saith, they be white speckled, and all blacke, and she saith, that she hath in another boxe, vi. spirits like Cowes (being asked howe big) shee saith, they be as big as Rattes, & that they haue little short hornes, & they lie in the boxes vpon white and blacke wooll: and she saith, that her mother gaue vnto her one of the saide Cowes, whiche was called by the name of Crowe, which is of colour black & white, and she saith, y her mother gaue to her brother one of them, which she called Donne, & that is of colour red & white. And she being asked wherewithall she had seene her mother to feed the Auices & blackbirdes, she saith, she hath seene her feed them somtimes w wheat, barley, somtimes w otes, & with bread & cheese, & the Cowes y were like beasts, sometime w wheat straw, somtime w barley straw, otestraw, and w hay, & being asked what she gaue them to

F 4   drinke

The Apprehension

drinke, she saith, sometimes water & sometimes beere, such drinke as they drunke.

She this examinat saith, y' her brother somtimes seeing them the Auices and black birdes, to come about him, saith, that he saith they keepe a twitling and tetling, and that then hee taketh them, and put them into the boxes.

She being asked if she saw them sucke vpon her mother, saith, that the Auices & blackbirdes haue sucked vpon her hands, and vpon her mothers legges: being willed to shew the place, she said, here sucked Aues, & here sucked Aues, and heere sucked Blackbird. And being asked how one spot vpon the backe of her hande came so somewhat like the other, she saith the same was burnt.

The examination and confession of Annis Herd of little Okeley, taken by me Brian Darcey Esquire, one of her Maiesties Iustices of the peace, the xvii. day of March.

Continued in prison.

The said Annis Herd saith, that she told one of her neighbors that the churle (meaning Cartwrite) had carried away a bough which she had laid ouer a slowe in the high way, and saide that she was faine to goe vp to the anckle euery steppe, and that shee said hee had beene as good hee had not caried it away, for she would fetch as much wood out of his fieldes as that doeth

com

of certaine Witches.

come vnto. And she saith also that she remēbreth she came vnto goodman Wad, & telled him that she was presented into the spirituall court for a witch, & that thē she desired ỹ she might answere the same when the dayes were longer.

Also she confesseth ỹ Lannes wife gaue her a pinte of milk & lēt her a dish to carie it home in, & that she kept the dishe a fortnight or longer, & thē sent it home by her girle, & also that Lannes wife came to her for ii.d. which shee ought her.

Also she confesseth that she came to the house of her neighbour West, & telled him that she had bin at mille, but she could get no meale, nor yet no bread, & that he gaue her a piece of a loafe: and she confesseth the speeches that then were of the pigs: And that shee saide to ỹ boy that brought woll, ỹ his Aunt might as well haue let her haue one as Penley. She saith also, ỹ shee remēbreth ỹ she came to goodwife Osborne, & bought of her 3.peckes of aples, & confesseth ỹ shee ought vnto her iii.d. but denieth that the boye or ladde came to her for any money.

Also she remēbreth that mistres Harisō charged her to haue stollen her ducklings, & that she called her harlot & witch, & confesseth ỹ she came vnto M. Harison, he being at ỹ parsonage a gathering of plūms, & that shee prayed him to giue her some plūms: But denieth that she hath any imps *Aueses* or blacke birds, or any kine called

The Apprehension

Crowe or *Donnet.* And all & euery other thing in generall, or that shee is a witch or haue any skill therein.

The enformation of Edward Vpcher, Thomas Rice, and seuerall others of the inhabitants of Walton, taken by me Brian Darcey esquire, the xxv. day of Marche.

The said Edward saith, that he & wife being at Colchester, this last weeke, they wēt together vnto the Gaile, to speake to Ursley Kemp, & then entring into talke with her, saieth, he asked her if she could tell what sicknes or diseases his wife had, wherevnto the said Ursley thē told him, that his wife was forspoke or bewitched, he thē asked her by whom, she told him it was by a woman that dwelt in their town, saying, that the partie hath one of her eares lesse thē the other, & hath also a moole vnder one of her armes, and hath also in her yard a great woodstacke.

Ales Miles saith, that shee went to the house of Joan Robinson for a pound of sope, at which time shee the saide Joan was gone from home, And saith that her maide Joan Hewet told her, that her Dame made her nose bleed, and thē called her Catte to eate the same, saying she did maruell why her dame shoulde call the Catte to eate her blood.

Thomas Rice saith, that about viii. dayes past,

Joan

of certaine Witches.

Joan Robinson came vnto the house of this examinate, and desired to borrowe a Payer, the which his wife denyed her, saying, that she was to vse it her selfe, whereat shee departed, and presently after there arose a great winde, whiche was like to haue blowen downe their house. And the next day after one of his Kine could not calue without helpe, it being drawen from her, died, and the Cowe was in danger and did hardly escape.

And sayeth also, that his wife hath a broode Goose a sitting, that hath been as good for the bringing foorth of her broode as any goose in Walton, and sayeth, that sithence the said Joan was denied of the hayer, the goose in the night will goe from her neste, and will not suffer his wife nor none of his folke to come neare her, but shee will flie away, so as shee hath lost two of her egges.

And sayeth also, that he thinketh the same to be done by the said Joan by some witchcraft.

Margery Carter saith, that about ten yeeres past, the husbande of the sayde Joan came vnto this Examinates house, and requested this Examinates husbande to hyre a pasture for a Cowe, the whiche shee sayeth was denied him, with aunswere that hee coulde not forbeare it for feare hee might want for his owne beastes.

And

The Apprehension

and that presently after, two of his best & likliest beasts in a strãge sort brake their neckes. & saith also ỹ presẽtly after this mischance, Joans husband came vnto this examinats husbãd W. Carter, & said, God restore you your losse, nowe you may pastor me a cowe, the which then he did, and then his beasts left breaking of their necks. And saith also, ỹ about 2. yeeres since, the said Joans husband would haue bought a house and an acre of ground of W. Carter her husband, the w hee would not sell vnto him, for ỹ he would not haue him his neighbour. And ỹ next day he had a faire ambling mare, for ỹ which he might haue had 5. li. often times: The w mare of her selfe came in to ỹ stable, & presẽtly was in a great sweat, & did hold her tongue out of her head, & shooke & quaked in a strãge sort, & presẽtly died, the w whẽ it was fleed, a neighbors dog came & fed of it, and thereof presently died.

Also she saith, not aboue 14. daies past, the said Joan Robinson came vnto this examinate, & requested to borrow a Heyer, to whõ she made answere ỹ she had vowed not to lend the same: And saith, that win 3. daies after, shee had one of her best beasts drowned in a ditche where there was but a litle water.

Ales Walter saith, ỹ well nere 4 yeeres past, the said Joan came vnto her, & requested to hie a pig of her: wherto she saith she woulde lende her one,

of certaine Witches.

one, but sell her any she would not: whereto the said Joan said ỹ she would haue none except she did bye it, & so they parted. And preſētly after ỹ sowe would not let her pigs sucke, but did bite & flye at them, as though shee had bin madde, when they had sucked aboue 7. dayes very well: & shee saith ỹ she sold of the pigs, the which Joan Robinson hearing, came vnto her, and requested to bie one of them, which she had for 3. d. and telled her that her sowe did the like, & bad her giue thē milke as it came frō the Cowe and they woulde drinke, which shee approued, and they dranke.

This examinate saith, that two yeeres since, she going to the house of Joan Robinson, found her and her husband sitting by the fire, with whō after she had talked, Joan Robinson required to bye two pigs of her sowe that then was to pige: whereto shee said shee woulde see first what shee should haue her self, and would not then promise her any. And the same night her Sowe piged two piges in the cote where shee lay, and for the more safetie of them, she tooke a broome faggot and laid it close ouerwharte the dore, because the pigs should not come out, & saith the same night all the farey of pigs being ten, came out ouer thē broome sheafe, and stoode one before an other in a tract place lieke horses in a teem, beinge al dead to the number of nine, & the tenth was drowned by the pond side being about a rod frō ỹ cote.

Allen

The Apprehension

Allen Ducke saith, that about fiue or sixe yeeres past the saide Ioan came vnto this examinate, and requested to bye a Cheese of his wife, but shee made her answere, that shee coulde sell none, yet neuerthelesse shee was very desirous to haue one, the whiche shee sayeth, shee denyed her, and that shee went away in a great anger. And this examinate saycth, that the next day he went with his Cart & foure horses therein to fetch a lode of corne, & that his wife & two of her children rid in the Cart. And saith, that as he went towardes the fielde he watered his horses at a ware called the Vicarage ware, whiche horses when they had drunke, he could not gette them out of the water, but was faine to wade to the forhorse head, it beeing about a yarde deepe, and to take him by the head and to lead him out. This examinate saith, that the said Ioan came vnto this examinates wife at two seuerall times to bie two pigges, whereof hee saith she was denied, & presently after he had two pigs that died, And saith, that he assuredly thinketh ẏ the saide pigs died of some witchcraft which she the saide Ioan vsed, and the like for the staying of his horses being in the water.

John Bralper saith, ẏ about two peres since the said Ioan Robinson came vnto this examinates house, and requested to bie a sowpigge to weane, the which was a moneth old, whereunto he told

her

her he ment to weane it him selfe, and that hee woulde not let her haue it, the which being a fat and a well liking pigge aboue all the rest, the next day died.

Also this examinate saith, ỹ sithence Christmas last past, this examinates wife went vnto the sayde Ioan Robinson, to pay her money shee ought vnto her for wares which shee had beeing due vpon scores: And for that she his wife would not pay her her owne reckoning, shee fell out with his wife: And presenely after he had a cow that was drowned in a ditche not a foote deepe with water: Al which he supposeth was done by some witchcraft by the said Ioan.

The enformation and confession of Ioan Robinson, taken by me Brian Darcey esquire, one of her Maiesties Iustices of peace, the xxv. day of March.

The saide Ioan saith, shee went to the house of T. Rice to borrowe a Heyer two dayes before a flawe of winde which was denied her: but denieth that she hath any impes or caused his calfe to die, or that she hurt her brood goose.

Also shee reëmbreth that her husbãd wēt to W. carter to bie a house & an acre of groũd, & to hire a cow pastor, & to borrow a Hayer of goodwife Carter. But denieth ỹ she sẽt any impes to hurt any of his beasts, or his ambling mare, or caused any cow of his to be drowned.   Also

The Apprehension

Also this examinate saith, that shee went to bye a pigge of Ales Walter, but denieth that she required to bye any that was not pigged of her or of any other at any time, & denieth that shee sent any Impes or spirites to kill any of her pigges, and all the other matters against her enformed shee denieth in generall.

Imprinted in London at the tree Cranes in the Vine-tree, by Thomas Dawson.
1582.
(∴)

The names of xiii. Witches, and those that haue beene bewitched by them.

The Names of those persons that haue beene bewitched and thereof haue dyed, and by whome, and of them that haue receyued bodyly harme &c. As appeareth vpon sundrye Enformations, Examinations and Confessions, taken by the worshipfull Bryan Darcey Esquire, And by him certified at large vnto the Queenes Maiesties Iustices, of Assise of the Countie of Esser, the xxix. of Marche. 1582.

A. Osyth.		The Witches.		
	1	Ursley Kempe alias Grey	bewitched to death	Kempes Wife. Thorlowes Childe. Strattons wife.
Confessed by Ursley and Elizabeth.	2	Ales Newman and Ursley Kempe	bewitched to death	Letherdalles Childe and Strattons wife.
		The sayde Ales and Ursley Kempe	bewitched	Strattons Childe, Grace Thorlowe, whereof they did languish
	3	Elizabeth Bennet	bewitched to death	William Byet and Ioan his wife, and iii. of his beasts. The Wife of William Willes and William Willingale.
		Elizabeth Bennet	bewitched	William Bonners Wife, Iohn Butler, Fortunes Childe, whereof they did languish
		Ales Newman	bewitched to death	Iohn Iohnson and his Wife, and her owne husband, as it is thought.
Confessed the same.	4	Ales Hunt	bewitched to death	Rebecca Durrant, and vi. beasts of one Haywardes.
Little Clapton.	5	Cysley Celles	bewitched to death	Thomas Deathes Childe.
		Cysley Celles	bewitched	Rosses mayde, Mary Death whereof they did languish
Thorpe.	6	Cysley Celles and Ales Mansfielde	bewitched Richard Rosses horse and beasts, and caused their Impes to burne a barne with much corne.
Confessed by Ales Mansfield	7	Ales Mansfielde and Margaret Grevell	bewitched to death	Robert Cheston and Grevell husband to Margaret.
		Ales Mansfield and Margaret Grevell	bewitched the widdow Cheston and her husband v. beasts, and one bullocke, and severall brewinges of beere, and batches of bread.
Thorpe.	8	Elizabeth Eustace	bewitched to death	Robert Stannivettes Childe and Thomas Croft.
		Elizabeth Eustace	bewitched Robert Sannevet vii. milch beasts, which gaue bloud in steede of milke, and severall of his Swine vpon.
Little Oysey.	9	Annys Herd	bewitched to death	Richard Harrisons wife, and two wiues of William Dowsing, as it is supposed.
		Annys Herde	bewitched Cartwright two beasts, mare, sheepe and lambes of West, swine and pigs, Othorpe a brewing of beere, and severall other losses of milke and creame.
Walton.	10	Ioan Robynson	bewitched beastes, horses, swine and pigs of severall mens.

The sayd Ursley Kemp had foure Spyrites viz. their names Tettey a hee like a gray Cat, Iack a hee like a black Cat: Pygine a hee, like a black Toad, & Tyffyn a shee like a white Lambe. The hees were to plague to death, & the shees to punish with bodily harme, & to destroy cattell, Tyffyn Ursleys white spirit did tell her alwayes (when she asked) what the other witches had done: And by her the most part were appealed, which spirit telled her alwayes true. As is well approued by the other Witches confession.

The sayd Ales Newman had the said Ursleyes Spyrites to vse at her pleasure.

Elizabeth Bennet had two spirits, viz. their names Suckyn, a hee like a blacke Dogge and Lyerd red like a Lyon.

Ales Hunt had two spirits lyke Coltes, the one blacke, the other white.

11 Margery Sammon had two spirits like Toads, their names Tom and Robyn.

Cysly Celles had two spirits by severall names viz. Sotheons Herculus, Iack or Mercury.

Ales Mansfield and Margaret Grevell had in common by agreement iiii. spirits, viz. their names Robin, Iack, Will, Pusse, one shee and three hees, whereof two were hees, and two shees, lyke vnto black Cats.

Elizabeth Eustace had iii. Impes or spirits, of colour white, grey and black.

Annis Herd had vi. Impes or spirittes like auises and black byrdes, And vi. other like Kine, of the bygnes of Rats, with short hornes, the Auises shee fed with wheat, barly, Otes and bread, the Kine with straw and hey.

	12	Annys Glascocke Joan Pechey Joan Robinson	These haue not confessed any thing touching the hauing of spirits.
	13		

| | Annis Glascoke | bewitched to death | Michell Stevens Childe. Ge her Childe at Pages. William Pages Childe. |

G.B., *A MOST WICKED worke of a wretched Witch* (*STC* 1030.5) formerly 1028 is reproduced by permission of the Trustees from the unique copy at Lambeth Palace Library (shelfmark ZZ.1597.15.05). The text block of the original measures 157mm × 87mm (including page no. and catchword but excluding marginal glosses).

Hard-to-read passages in the original:
A4v: [marginalia] Witches ar the most unprofitable crraturs [sic] in the world
A4v.20:   Many and sundry like actions of extreame rage and cru-
A4v.25:   veth of almes and good peoples charitie) she found him bu-

Close me carefully.
Secret train

A MOST VVICKED

worke of a wretched Witch, (the like whereof none can record these manie yeeres in England.)

Wrought on the Person of one Richard Burt, Seruant to Maister *Edling* of Woodhall in the Parrish of *Pinner* in the Countie of *Myddlesex*, a myle beyond Harrow.

Latelie committed in March last, An. 1592 and newly recognised according to the truth, by G. B. maister of Arts.

Printed by R. B. for William Barley, and are to be sold at his shop in Gratious streat.

Hexasticon.

Of wrathfull witches this same pāphlet tels,
How most of all on simple folke they worke.
What woonders to they may atchiue by spels,
God weede them out in euery cell they lurke,
God weeds them out, but satan stil doth hatch,
fresh Impes, whereby of al sorts he may catch.

Leuit. 20. 6.

If any turne after such as worke vvith spirits, and after soothsaiers, to goe a whoring after them, then will I set my face against that person, and will cutte him off from amoug his people.

A most wicked worke of a wretched Witch, wrought on the Person of one Richard Burt.

SO long (righte Gentle and courteous Reader) as wee liue heere in this wretched vale of miserie, and myserable estate of our Probationership, we are all euen the best of vs all, to account no better of our selues, then that we liue in a perpetuall warrefare, and most dangerous and deadlie combat.

Our enimies that we are to fight against are in number three: The world, the Flesh, and the Dyuell: two whereof notwithstanding (such is our blinde perseuerance) the moste parte esteeme their entire friends, whereas indeed they are the hande-mynisters of our Archenimie, all vnder colourable frendship deceiuing their familiars, and seeking their death both of bodie and soule. *The three dedlie enimies of mākind.*

Our graund foeman Sathan Architect of all mischiefe, in scripture hath many proper names, to explaine his malitious nature: Of his crueltie hee is called Abaddon, a Destroier, bicause that not like a common enimie hee is contented with the death and downefall of our bodies, but imagineth vtter destruction of the soule also, and intollerable tormentes ioyntlie to them both: Of his crafte hee is tearmed a Theefe, bicause he inuenteth by what meanes he may stile and vnwittinglie set vpon the godlie. Of his malice he is called Diabolus, an accuser, bicause euermore day and night he is busie, accusing the consciences of the righteous. *Reuel.9.11.* *Iohn.12.6.* *Iob.1.10. and 2.5.*

He is named a Dragon of his pollicie, bicause that since

A 2   the

the time of Adam, among so many thousands, in so many yeares, there hath beene founde none so wise or warie, that could withstand his stratagems, but he hath wounded and poisoned them well nighe vnto death.

He hight a Lion also of his power, bicause that as the solide bodie of the Lion is powerfull: so especiallie consisteth great strengthe and power in his taile.

We doubt not but this aduersarie, or Apollyon of ours of himselfe is mightie, puissant, & strong enough againste such faintie cowards, and wilfull slo-backs as we are, yet to make his victorie more sure, and not to faile of his purpose, he vseth also the force of his tayle: that is, his inthraled bondslaues, whom he hath sealed to execute his wil and pleasure vppon the harmelesse, which is perfourmed many times diuers and sundry waies: neyther dooth he so vsually shew his pollicie, puissance and power by anye his officers, as he dooth by subtle sædemen of false doctrine, and inchanting sorcerers: the one in stead of instruments to inueigle the mind and soule, the other to assaile the mortall bodie, and beguile and vntrappe the sences.

I speake nothing of those pseudosedmen, but I purpose (God willing) to treat of damnable Wytches, of their spight and spelles, odious in the sight of God, detested of the good, and moste hurtfull to themselues, manifesting what power and preeminence through Gods permission, that Father of sinne Sathan hath ouer sinfull worldlings.

About Shrouetide last, one Richard Burt, seruant to a Gentleman, named M. Edling, dwelling at Woodhall in the parishe of Pinner in Middlesex, a myle beyond Harrow on the Hill, going to his maysters Barne, standing at the Townes ende, accompanied with a great mastiue dogge, suddenly espied an Hare start before him, and thinking to haue set his dogge at her, missed of his purpose: for the dogge not onely refused to follow, but in stead of following began to faint, and runne rounde about his maister,

and

and to whine pittifully, as who shoulde say that kinde of game was not for them: The man taking heartie grace himselfe, followed so nighe, that he saw her take in at one Mother Atkyns house, whome before that time he knew to be a notorious witch: Wherevpon blessing himselfe, & mindful of the name of God, he boldly said, auant witch.

This was the first occasion (namely the tearming of hir a with) of al poore Richard Burts future tragedie: but to go forward. It hapned the said Richard Burt a month after, meeting hir neere to his maisters barne, and giuing hir the time of the daye, like a peruerse woman, like a perillous waspe, like a pestiferous witch, incensed with hate at the sight of him held downe hir head, not daigning to speake. *Vnspeakable is the malice of a wicked woman.*

The next day which was on wednesday the 8. of march going againe to his maisters barne to thrash, & serue certaine beasts, bicause he would not trudge too and fro for letting his work, carried his dinner with him, which was bread, butter, cheese and applepy, & a bottle of the best beer: being come to the barne he laide his prouision, and setled close to his busines, labouring hard til twelue of the clock, at which time hunger assailing and custome preuailing, he went to dinner, wherin he had not long continued, but ther was opposite to his view a monstrous blacke Cat among the straw, which began to shake the strawe, and to make a wad thereof. The fellow being agast start vp with his applepie in his hande (for it had byn pittie a poore hungrie thresher should haue lost so good a repast) suddenly hearing a voice that commanded him, come away: Away quod he, whither shal I come? The spirit answering againe, sayde: Come and leaue thy vittels behind thee and thy knife also. Poore simplicity keeping his applepy stil in his hand, came to the barne dore, where suddenly hee was hoised vp into the aire, and carried ouer many fields, by the way espyeng his mai. plow a plowing, but not able to cal vnto them, although he seemed to haue his memorie most perfect: thence passing ouer to Harrow, where on the side of the hill there

A 3   is

is a greate ponde was drawne through it, & ther left his hat which was a token of that torture) because he could stay in no place, but was violentlie rapt vp the hill, and ouer the tops of the trees at Harrow Church, so farre he absolutelie remembreth, but being haled further, he was taken (as he sæmeth) into a place which was all fire, where was heard such lamentable howling and dolefull crieng, as if all the damned fiends of hell had bæne tortured, and tormenten in that Limbo.

You heare into how strange and passionate a place this Richard Burt was translated, now it remaineth to shewe with what Symtomes the place was furnished.

First therefore (he affirmeth) it was exceeding hot, replenished with more than Cymmerian darkenesse, plentiful in filthy odors and stinches, ful of noise and clamours, insomuch that hee seemed to heare infinite millions of discrepant noises, but saw nothing saue onelie the fire which caused such an vnquenchable drouth in his stomache, that presentlie minding a pennie hee had in his purse: looked round about for an Alehouse where he might spend it.

Hearing therefore these foresaid voices, and thinking some of them had spake vnto him, he answerd sayeng, hær is no worke for me to doo: immediatlie it was reanswered, coast away with him, but with this prouiso thou passest, that thou be secret, and say nothing when thou commest home: but he replied, and said, my maister will aske me where I haue bæne: with that he was not suffered to speak any further, but his tong was doubled in his mouth, his legs burnt, hands and armes scorched, his coat pincht of his backe, and throwne into the fire, immediatly soring ouer hedges and ditckes, sowsed in mire and durt, scratched with thornes and briers, so singed and disfigured, that it is both lamentable and terrible to behold him.

Being brought againe to Pinner where his Mayster doth dwell, he first repaired to a ditch to drinke, and afterwards

wards in this pickle visited one of his acquaintance, whoe sometime serued M. Edling also: but whether hee sorted thither for that his friends house was nighest, or would not go home for shame that hee had béene absent foure whole daies togither, I cannot shew you: Onlie this, being sunday morning his maister chanced (as his custome was) to passe by that way to Church at the same instant, whoe not knowing poore Richard Burt his lost shape, demanded of his quondam seruant if he had gotten him a man: a man sir quod he, why it is your man Richard: my man quoth the Gentleman, that cannot bee, and therewithall béeing halfe amazed made a pause and earnestlie beheld him, at length willing him in the name of God to tel where he had bin though he could not speake, yet hauing memory made signes and euermore pointed toward the house where mother Atkins did dwell, looking so gristie and fiercelie that waie, that he tore and rent al that came in his hands.

In the meane while it was thought requisite, that the Parson of the towne named M. Smith, and mai. Burbidge of Pinner parke gentleman should be sent for, whoe comming to the dumbe man and pittieng his plight, the Parson charitably and like himselfe laboured about him, wrinched open his teeth got open his mouth, indented his finger vnder his toong, and with much adow got it vnfoulded, the first wordes he spake were these: Woe worth mother Atkins, woe worth mother Atkins, for she hath bewitched me: wherupon he would not be quiet, but euer requested that he might speak with hir.

The dutie of a good minister.

Maister Burbidge and M. Smith caused hir to bee sent for, who being present, he neuer ceased til he had scratched and drawne bloud on hir, perswading himselfe that was a remedy sufficient vnder God, that would make him well: neither was it or is it any Capital error, experience testyfies: for since that he hath mended reasonablie, and nowe goeth to the Church.

A 4   Thus

Thus haue you heard briefly the cares and crosses, that poore Richard Burt sustained (as they say) in summo gradu, the eighth, the ninth, tenth and eleuenth daies of march last past, what time hee was absent from his maister the foresaid whole daies, and vsed (as ye haue heard) after the foresaid manner.

Thus then leaue we Richard Burt, but with mother Atkins we must prosecute a little further.

It is credibly reported in Pinner, that the saide mother Atkins on a time resorting to the house of M. Burbidge for milke (at what time the maids were busie at the dairy and not obtaining hir desire, immediatly vpon hir departure out of doores, the Creame beganne to swel and rise in the cherne, that it burst open the top of the Cherne, and runne about the kitchen and forth at the sinke-hole, and all their huswiferie for that day went to wracke, that al was quite lost, and nothing could possiblie be well ordered. O rebels towards God: enemies to mankinde: catterpillers of a common wealth, the fire is to good to consume them.

Witches ar the moste vnprofitable creaturs in the world.

Many and sundry like actions of extreame rage and crueltie are imputed to her, only we will conclude, and shut vp these clauses, with this that followeth.

Not long since the forenamed witch entring the groūd of one Gregorie Coulson, to craue some releefe (for she lyueth of almes, and good peoples charitie) she found him busilie imploied about some countrie affaires, Radling hys lambs (I thinke it was) and framing hir petition to him, because he did not straight waie leaue al and accomplish it she flung forth in a fume: But it was not longe after her departure, but he had finished his labour also, and letting forth two Lambs into a yard, suddenly they began so nimbly to skip and friske to and fro, that they neuer ceased after til they died.

FINIS.

BIBLIOTHECA LAMBETHANA

'A report Contayning a brief Narration' (pp. 92–103), numbered by an unknown hand, from *The Triall of Maist. Dorrell* (*STC* 6287) is reproduced by permission of the Trustees from the best available copy at Lambeth Palace Library (shelfmark ZZ.1599.14.01). The text block of the original measures 111mm × 60mm.

Hard-to-read passages in the original:

93:	[marginalia] Joh. ⟨ ⟩ston, Anthony ⟨ ⟩dam g⟨ ⟩, Will. C⟨ ⟩bolde ⟨ ⟩, Constabl⟨e⟩ of Ho⟨ ⟩, M. Ra⟨ ⟩vic⟨ ⟩, Jo. Shoe⟨ ⟩,⟨ ⟩gym ⟨ ⟩ and ⟨ ⟩ oth⟨ers⟩.
96.1:	fore I brought her out againe. Then Tom
97:	[marginalia] Of who⟨m⟩ 4. were Si⟨r⟩ Nicolas B⟨a⟩cons men sent of p⟨ur⟩pose to bring tru⟨e⟩ report.
100:	[marginalia] To trie ⟨be⟩like if ⟨sh⟩e coun⟨ter⟩feited. ⟨D⟩welling ⟨on⟩ the ⟨Ba⟩nkside.
101:	[marginalia] Fo⟨r as?⟩ yet t⟨hey⟩ did n⟨ot⟩ suspect Anne ⟨ ⟩.
103.28:	Who is wise that he may observe these thinges? The righ-
103.29:	teous shall see and reioyce, and all iniquity shall stop
103.30:	her mouth. Psalm. 107.43 [sic].42.

The 12 9 29
Triall of Maist. Dorrell,

Or
6
A Collection of Defences against Allegations not yet suffered to receiue convenient answere.

Tending
To cleare him from the Imputation of teaching *Sommers* and others to counterfeit possession of Divells,

That
The mist of pretended counterfeiting being dispelled, the glory of Christ his royall power in casting out Divels (at the prayer and fasting of his people) may evidently appeare.

Iohn 7. 51.
Doeth our Law iudge a man before it heare him, and know what he hath done?

Proverb. 14. 15.
The foolish will beleeue every thing, but the Prudent will consider his steppes.

BIBLIOTHECA
LAMBETHANA

A Report,

Contayning a brief Narration of certain diuellish and wicked witcheries, practized by Oliffe Barthram alias Doll Barthram of Stradbrook in the County of Suffolke, vpon Ioane Iorden the Servant of Symon Fox of the same Towne: For which, she was arraigned before the right Ho the L chief Iustice of England condemned and executed at S. Edmondsbury in Suffolke the 12. of Iulye. 1599.

About midsomer last, the said *Doll Barthram*, falling out with the said *Ioane Iorden* for refusing to giue her of her maisters goods, practised and devised, to afflict the said *Ioane* by witcheries: as, through Gods permission by the meanes of Satā it came to passe; which in briefe was thus.

First the said Doll Barthrā sent 3. Toads to trouble her in her bed, not suffering her to rest. The first, being thrown out into the middest of the chamber, returned, and sat croaking on her beds side: which being thrown out of the window; another within fewe dayes after came and vexed her againe; which was taken and burnt. After that within a while came the 3ᵈ. which

Ioane

Ioane was counselled to burne her selfe; and going downe stayres to doe so, she was violently thrown to the stayers foot, there lying (a while) for dead. And when this Toade began to burne, (which *Simon Fox* had put into the fire,) a flame arose at the stayers foote where the toade lay when Ioane fell, & grew so great, that it seemed to them to indanger the house, yet no hurt was don.

After this, On Satterday the 9. of Iune, in the sense of * many of good accoumpt and credit, A Spirit (which had ben there the night before, and said then, beeing asked, that his name was *Gyles*, & that he came down the chimney in the likenes of a cat) came nowe againe about eleven a clock at night; first scraping on the wals, then knocking, after that shufling in the rushes: and then (as his vsuall maner was) he clapped the maide on the cheekes about halfe a skore times as to awake her; and, (as oft times els he did) he kissed her 3.or 4.times and slauered on her: and, (lying on her brest) he pressed her so sore that she could not speake; at other times hee held her handes that she could not stirre, and restrayned her voice that she could not answer.

* Ioh. Throckmorton, Anthony Adam will. bold Comfort of Iho. M. East victuall. Showe syrie, and others.

The

The shape which they sawe the Spirit then to haue, was a thick darke substance about a foote high; like to a sugar lofe, white on the top. And, (being charged) he did shoote vp in all their sightes as high againe as he shewed himselfe before.

As this spirit had a shape, so had he also an audible voyce: by which he spake and vttered many thinges. This voyce was not the maides, neither from her, nor yet of any other saue of the spirit it selfe. For; (besides that the maide denyed it,) she & the spirit were heard speak both at once; also, her lips were seene not to moue, when the spirit spake; and, some standing neerer to th'one then to th'other, did sensibly discerne and distinguish both their voyces. Neither was this the voyce of any counterfait confederate; for, (to put this out of doubt) the house was searched, the parties in the maides presence (except Io. Sheereman, M. Randall, and Sy. Fox) were strangers, the roomes vnder and adioyning to her, were full of people, and the house was besett with divers who came to see and heare these strang accidents, which indeed they did; for the voyce was easily heard to them all.

This Spirit being demanded diverse questions,

tions, returned answers; saying, (among diverse other things,) *Ioane, Ioane, I come for thy life; I will haue it, I am a Boy, a Boy; my name is Gyles; an old woman that dwells in the streete gaue mee that name, to witt, Doll Barthram; She sent me; I haue serued her* 10. *yeares, yea* 20. *yeares; She is now in prison*, (as indeede she was); *Nan Barthram sent me now; I will kill Ioane to morrow night; I will teare her in peeces; She hath giuen her life and soule to mee* (which Ioane in parte acknowledging, viz. that she had given him her life, hee laughed *Ho, Ho, Ho.*) To this whē *Iohn Sheereman* defying him) replyed, that he should not haue her life, he said, *I wil haue thine then; I come to thee, I como*; & with that, offered towards him, to the great astonishment & feare of him and the rest present. And yet thus for that time he vanished away.

But, not long after, he returned againe, in maner as at the first (except scraping the wals.) When, vpō occasion of talke touching one *Cavers* wife, in the presence of many, he said: *Tom,* (which was another of the Spirites of the said *Doll,*) *and I, at Doll Barthrams commandement, did hang her. But first I led her into a ditch vp to the chyn and could not drowne her, and therefore*

fore I brought her out againe. Then Tom brought a rope and put it vnder her chaps, and I pulled her vp and hung her. Which seemeth to haue ben so, because of the strangnes of it. For, the rope werewithall *Cauers* wife was hanged, was but put vnder her chaps, not about her neck: and the noose was so bigge, that three mens heds might haue slipt through it at once.

Moreover, this Spirite then declared, That he, (at *Doll Barthams* comandment) had killed a child, in the womb of the mother, by nipping out the braines; and that hee entred into another partie and killed him, by tearing his heart in peeces. Both which seeme to be true also: for, the woman was deliuered of a dead child, & the man did dye in a very strange maner; and both at the same time that the Spirit declared. Then, after many speaches vsed by the spirit, as, *that hee would kill Ione, and teare Iohn Sheereman in pieces; that he was their God; and that he would not be content with the life of Ioane only, but would haue also the liues of Fox, his wife, children, and cattell*, and that by the commaundement of *Doll Bartharm*, hee went away for that night.

But Satan and the Witch, nothing contented

mted with that which as yet had ben don, returned againe in more grieuous sort then before. For, in the presence of* many credible persons, there was seene a lump to arise in her body as big as a mans fist; which ascended vpwardes in her body till it came to her throate, & there setled as big as a mans arme. With this the maide was somewhat vnruly, and therefore was bound in a chaire with a long towell, very fast. But she (or rather the Divell in her) strugled and strained so sore, that it brake in pieces. Being againe bound in the chair, sixe stronge men leaned with their whole strength thereon, each also setting one foote on the rounde of the chaire to keepe it down. But she, (though so bound) notwithstāding all their strength, remoued the chaire round about the house, a yard at a time, they hanging thereon.

After this fit ended, the maide was had to bed: And about eleauen a clock the Spirit came; not after his vsuall maner, but with a great stroke on the bordes, like the fall of a greate stone. Wherewith, the people awoke, and the maide cried, *Helpe, Helpe*: & then a thicke shadow was seene to goe vp to the maides bed. Shortly after which, the maide was take out, & throwne so violetly against the wall, as if it would haue driven out the

* Of whi 4. were S Nicolas cons men sent of p pose to bring reporte.

G

side of the chamber. Then search being made for the maid, she was found lying vnderneath the standing bed: From whence it was as much as fower men could doe to pluck her. Neither was this great throw, and heavy waight, the only strange thinges in this her fit: For, her eyes were sunck into her head an inch. Her head and body were bent backwards, almost to her hips. She lay as it were dead. Her teeth were so fast closed, that a man could not opē them, though with all his strength he assayed it with his dagger and a key. And, (that which strang is,) a stiffe dry Rush being put into her nostrels, so far, as it might touch her braines in the iudgment of them that were present, yet she moved nothing thereat; neither at the violent bending of her fingers; nor yet at a great quantity of *Aqua-vitæ*, which was powred into her mouth.

In which case she having lyen halfe an hower, at last she opened one of her eyes gazing there with very strangly; then th'other, crying, ô *Barthram, thou hast killed mee*. Then, being layed in her bed, she so strived to get out, that all there present (which were not a few for such a purpose,) could scant hold her therein. And this is the summe that wᶜʰ happened to this maide bewitched

Another Report of like Argument.

IN Castle Alley neere Broken wharfe in *London*, there dwelt a witch called *Anne Kerke*; who for her notorious mischievous witcheries heereafter in brief described, was arraigned in *London* the 30. of November 1599. before the right honorable the Lorde *Anderson* & other of her Maiesties Iustices, and then condemned, and executed at *Tyburne* the 4. of December following.

To let passe the Evidence; that of long time she had ben suspected for a witch; I will set downe the summe of th'other evidences giuen in against her.

First, this witch falling out with a woman in the streete, said she would bee meete with her, or hers. Wherevpon the woman going home and sitting by the fire with her child in her lap, it gaue a great skreeke, and was suddenly changed; and after that continually pined away till it dyed.

After whose death, her other child going vp *Bredstreet Hill*, met with this witch; who asked her how her sister did. But before she could make answer, she was stricken downe in a very strange maner; her mouth beeing drawne aside like a purse, her teeth gnashing togeather, her mouth foming, and her eyes

G 2 staring

staring the rest of her body being strangely disfigured. When the witch was gon, she recouered out of this trance; howbeit she was still oftimes cast into the like. This, the maide her selfe deposed: who being willed by the Lorde *Anderson*, to " shew how she was tormented; she said she could not shew it, but when the fit was on her.

To ᴅie like if ᴇ counꜰited.

Another time, this Witch taking displeasure with a woman for not bidding her to her childes Christening, tormented the child twice or thrice a day in strange maner, vntill the Father with others went to mother *Gillams*; who tolde them, that the childe was forespoken, and that the witch had ben (as indeed she was) twice with the mother of the child before they came home; and that, for the childes recouery they should cut of a piece of the witches coate with a payre of sheeres, & burne it togeather with the childs vnder cloth: which they did, and the childe accordingly was healed.

ᴡelling the ɪnᴋside.

Againe, at another time, this witch fell out with an Inkeeper; and in revengement, bewitched his only childe so strangely, as that by no means of Physik which he could get, it could be recouered; but still it was from time to time tormented, till it dyed. But before the death, the Father (finding no help by Physicke) went to a cuning man (as they call them;) who told him, that the cauſer of his childes torments was one that was conuerſant in his houſe: and (after promiſe made of not reuealing the partie) he ſhewed him in a glaſſe this witch, *Anne Kerke*. After this, this man the Father of the childe, met this witch comming out of his neighbours dore, and making ſtay till ſhe was gon, tolde his neighbour that ſhe was a witch, and that ſhe had bewitched his childe to death. Whereuppon he going home, fell ſick and dyed.

Beſides all theſe, among other miſchiefes don by Satans inſtrument in the houſe of one M. *Nayler* dwelling in Thames ſtreet neere Broken wharf, ſhe tormēted his ſonne *George* in ſuch grievous maner that he dyed. So alſo did ſhe torment his daughter *Anne* till ſhe dyed: who was oftimes vexed wth a frenzines: and with an evill ſpirit, to which this maide in her Fathers hearing did often talke. And being demaunded who was the cauſer of theſe her torments, the ſpirit which was within her ſaid, that one would come after who ſhould "diſcouer the cauſer, and the truth of all; as afterwardes it came to paſſe by *Ione Nayler*, another of the ſaide M. *Naylers* daughters.

For ſo it was, That money being giuen to poore

poore at the buriall of the said *Anne Nayler*. This witch was vexed that she had none, being a parishioner; and therefore practised against the said *Ioane Nayler* also. Who the next night after her sisters buriall, was tormented with an evill spirit, which spake in her oftimes in the hearing of her Parents, saying, *Giue me thy liuer, thy lights, thy heart, thy saule, &c; then thou shalt be released, then I will depart frō thee*: also; *Goe, take thy lace & hang thy selfe: Go into the next roome and hang thy self in the sack rope, and so thou shalt be released*. She was oftimes grievously tormented and in a traunce, during which her mouth was turned to th'one side, her ioyncts so shrunke vp that the soles of her feete did beate togither, her shoulder bones did strike one against another, so, as that they were heard to rattle, to the terror of them present. And (according to the wordes of the spirit in her sister *Anne*) she oft said, that mother *Kerke* had bewitched her. And when the maide (according as some had willed her to doe) did reach forth her hands to scratch the mother *Kerke*, they were so fast closed that none could open thē. Wherupon, her Father suspected this *Anne Kerke* of witchcraft, procured a warrant from Sir *Richard Martin* to fetch her before him, he being thē in the hou house of the said M. *Nayl*. & in the presence of the maide. But so soone as the witch came to the dore, she fel into her former trauce, her handes being againe so closed as they could not be opened, Sir *Rich. Martin* himselfe assaying it. Into the like traunce the maide did also fal being in the houses of Sir *Iohn Hart*, & Sir *Steph. Slaney* (or *Some*) so soone as the witch (being by thē sent for,) was entred into their dores: And the like also did she fal into, being in the fields, at the same instant when the witch was bayled forth of prison: as also being in the Sessions house, when the iury were departing to cōsider of the matter. But that of Sir *R. Martin* is not heere to be omitted: who having heard that a witches hayre could not be cut, sent for the said *An. Kerke*, & cōmanded a Seriant to pull from her head 10. or 12. of her haires, & try if he could cut them. The Seriant did so; and offering to cut thē with a paire of Barbers Sissers, they turned round in his hand: and the edges were so battered, turned, & quite spoiled, as that they would not cut any thing. Then the Seriant tooke the haire, and did put it into the fire to burne it; but the fire flew from it, and the haire in the middest thereof vnburnt.

Who is wise that he may observe these thinges? The righteous shall see and reioyce, and all iniquity shall stop her mouth. Psalm. 107. 43. 42.

Witches Apprehended, Examined and Executed (*STC* 25872) is reproduced by permission from the fine copy at the Bodleian Library, Oxford University (shelfmark 4 ° E.17[11]Art). The text block of the original measures 135mm × 74mm (including running head and catchword).

Hard-to-read passages in the original:
B4.4:   throat by faith, hee would have to trample him
B4v.4: to make proofe thereof.
C3.16: up and downe to make her sinke, but could not.

Witches Apprehended, Examined and Executed, for notable villanies by them committed both by Land and Water.

With a strange and most true triall how to know whether a woman be a Witch or not.

Printed at London for *Edward Marchant*, and are to be sold at his shop ouer against the Crosse in Pauls Church-yard. 1613.

The seuerall and damnable
practises of Mother *Sutton*, and *Mary*
Sutton *her daughter of Milton Milles*,
in the Countie of Bedford : who
were lately arraigned con-
uicted, and exe-
cuted.

Linie writes
of some kinde
of Serpentes
that dare not
approach the
wild Ashtree,
nay the sight
of it is so ter-
rible to them,
they flie from
it, and will
not draw néer
the shadowe
thereof, but if they be walled round with fire,
they will rather runne through to the confusion

A 3   of

of themselues then endure it. If it were so with vs which professe our selues Christians, & should be Christes sonnes to imitate our Father, and Sauiour in his life, which hee left as a lesson to mankinde his children to learne, we should then hauing reason, (part of the inheritance of Angels) be more prouident of our proper good then Serpents are, who to auoid the persecution of their minde, will endure the affliction of their bodie, and to shunne the verie shadow of the Ashtree, will thrust themselues into torment of fire: So should men, who seeing sinne like a wild Ashtree grow in the world, and that to lurke vnder the shadow thereof is a whippe to their conscience, when to feed on the sappe is damnation to their soules, in this onely like Serpents auoid it for the reliefe of their mindrs, though with the painefull dissolution of their bodies: but such is the deafnesse of our eares, that though heauen it selfe speak in thunder to remember vs a day shall come when we must giue account for our wilfull transgressions, wee not regard it, and such the hardnesse of our hearts, that neither treasons, murthers, witchcrafts, fires, flouds, of all which the impetuous course hath béene such in this age, that we haue cause to looke our day of summons is to morrow, if not this houre, yet we are vnprepared of our account, and as if it were lawfull that euils should grow, many from one, and one from another, are as corne is fruitfull from one séede to seuerall eares. So from one sinne ws

mul-

and executed.

multiply to diuers, not dreading vengeance till our iniquities be numberlesse. As shall appeare by this following discourse.

At a place called Milton some three miles from Bedford, was lately dwelling one Mother Sutton, who being a widow, and of declining yeares, had her daughter called Mary Sutton, (as it was thought by the neighbours thereabouts) resident with her as a stay and comfort to her age, when she kept her, but as a furtherer to her diuellish practises, nay indeed to make her a scholler to the Diuell himselfe.

This widow Sutton hauing béene dwelling a long time in the foresaid, towne of Milton, and not suspected as then to haue béene a practiser in this diuellish exercise of witchcraft, was by the townsmen (being held but poore) for her better reliefe chosen to be the Hogheard, or Hog-kéeper. In which seruice she cõtinued long, not without commendations for her dutifull care had therein. And though many cattell oftentimes miscarried, and were taken with staggerings, frensies, and other diseases to their confusions, and impouerishing of the owners, yet she not till of late suspected to be a cause thereof, though since it hath euidently béene proued against her.

Continuing thus almost for the space of twentie, or one and twentie yeares, and in that time had brought her daughter to be as perfect in her diuellish charmes as her selfe, there grew some difference betwéene a Gentleman of worship called

Witches lately arraigned,

led Maſter Enger dwelling at Milton Milles, and this mother Sutton, On whom ſhe had vowed to take a ſtrange and actuall reuenge, for the diſcontent ſhe had conceiued againſt him, which rancour of hers ſhe thus proſecuted: His horſes that were left well in his ſtable ouer night, ſhe cauſed them to be found dead in the morning, ſome ſtrangled, ſome hauing beaten out their braines, others dead, and no cauſe perceiued how. Beſides this loſſe, which for the ſtrangeneſſe bred ſome amazement in him, for that it happened not once, but often, this alſo did ſecond it: when his Swine were in the fields at their troughes eating their meat, ſome of them would ſodainly fall madde, and violently fall to tearing out the guts, and bowels of their fellowes: others by ten and twentie in a company, as if they had béen carried with one deſire, would leaue their féeding, and run headlong into the Mill dammes, and drowne themſelues. So that not by accidentall meanes, but the helliſh and moſt damnable witchcrafts of this Mother Sutton, and her daughter, many theſe harmeleſſe cattell and Oxen, made as nédſull reliefes to the neceſſitie of man, were thus perplexed, and an honeſt and worſhipful Gentleman Maſter Enger, from whom ſhe had oftentimes both fóode and cloathing, damnified by her meanes to the value of two hundreth pounds in leſſe then two yeares.

 In the time of theſe aforeſaid loſſes happened to Maſter Enger, one Henry Sutton, the baſtard ſon

of

and executed

sonne of Mary Sutton (for it is to bee noted, that although she was neuer married, yet she had three bastards) comming to play himselfe about the Mill damme, fell to throwing in of stones, dirt, and filth, with other such vnhappinesse incident to children: Of which hauing béene often fore-warned by an ancient seruant of Master Engers, who was then about the Milles, and finding the boy notwithstanding his admonishment rather to perseuer then to desist from his knauerie, he came to him, and giuing him a little blow or two on the eare, the boy went home crying, and the ancient fellow went backe to his labour.

This Henry Sutton comming home beganne to tell his mother how a man of Master Engers (naming him) had beaten him. Whose venomous nature being soone enkindled, though hee had receiued no hurt, she vowed to take reuenge, and thus it followed.

This ancient seruant with another of his masters men were on the morrow being Market day at Bedford, appointed by their master to carry a Cart load of corne for the furnishing of the Market. Being on their way at Milton Townes end they espied a goodly faire blacke Sow grazing, who as they draue their Teame still kept pace with thē till they came within a mile of Bedford. Where on a sodaine they perceiued her to turne twice or thrice about as readily as a Windmill sayle at worke: And as sodainly their horses fell to starting and drawing some one way, some

B another,

another: At last the strongest preuailing, they drewe away the Cart, and corne, and left the Wheeles, and Axeltree behinde them. The horses they ranne away with their loade, as if they had beene madde, and the two fellowes after the horses, the horses being affrighted halfe out of their strength, and the fellowes as much madde to see them, downe went one sacke on this side the Cart, and another on that: The horses they ranne as if they would haue swelted themselues, and the fellowes after them breathlesse, and sweating to make the wilde Iades stay. All which till the Diuell and the Witch had plaide their partes would not serue turne.

At last this Tragicke-Comedie drawing to an end, they made a stand, when the seruants bringing them backe, and finding their Axeltrœ, pinnes, and all things vnbroken, tooke vp their Corne, made fit their Cart againe, & the horses drewe as formally as could be: And they went forthwards towards Bedford, mistrusting nothing, though they saw the Sow following and grazing, as they did before.

Being come to Bedford, and hauing vnloaden the Cart, and made sale of the Corne, the one fell to driuing the Teame home againe, leauing his ancienter fellow behind him at Bedford who happening into company, fell a carowsing with boone companions like himselfe, and in the height of their cuppes, they as desirous to heare,

as

and executed.

as he to tell, he related vnto them the manner and forme how his Cart and Wheels were diuorct' as hee was comming to Towne: some wondered, all laughed: the company brake vp, and this ancient seruant tooke his horse with purpose to ouertake his fellow, who was gone before with the Cart: Who no sooner was out of Bedford Townes end, but he might behold the same Sow (as neere as he could iudge,) grazing againe, as if the Diuell and the Witch had made her his footman to waite vpon him. But the fellow not mistrusting any thing, made his Nagge take a speedie amble, and so to ouertake the Cart, while the Sow side by side ranne along by him. When he ouertaking his fellow, and had scarce spoken to him, but the horses (as before) fell to their old contention running one from another, onely the horses were better furnished then before, for where at first they left both Wheeles and Axeltree behinde them, they now had the Axeltree to take their part, leauing the Wheeles in the high way for the seruants to bring after. The horse in this manner comming home, draue all the beholders into amazement, and the seruants beginning to haue mistrust of the blacke Sow, they watcht whither she went, whom they found to goe into Mother Suttons house, of which they told their master, and of all the accidents aforesaid, who made slight of it to them whatsoeuer he conceiued of it himselfe: and saying he supposed they were drunke, they departed.

The

Witches lately arraigned

The same old seruant of Master Engers within few daies after going to plough, fell into talke of Mother Sutton, and of Mary Sutton her daughter, of what pranckes hee had heard they had plaide thereabouts in the Countrey, as also what accidents had befallen him and his fellow, as they had passed to and from Bedford. In discoursing of which a Béetle came, and stroke the same fellow on the breast: and hee presently fell into a trance as he was guiding the Plough, the extremitie whereof was such, as his senses altogether distract, and his bodie and minde vtterly distempered, the beholders déemed him cleane hopelesse of recouerie, yea his other fellow vpon this sodaine sight was stricken into such amazement, as he stood like a liuelesse trunke deuided from his vitall spirits, as farre vnable to helpe him, as the other was néedfull to be helpt by him. Till at length being somewhat recouered, and awaked from that astonishment, hee made hast homeward, and carried his master word of what had happened.

Upon deliuerie of this newes (for hee was a man highly estéemed by him for his honest and long seruice) there was much moane made for him in the house, and Master Enger himselfe had not the least part of griefe for his extremitie, but with all possible speed hasted into the field, and vsed helpe to haue him brought home. After which he neglected no meanes, nor spared any cost that might ease his seruant, or redéeme him from the

misrey

and Executed.

misery he was in, but all was in vaine: for hyr extasies were nothing lessened, but continued a long time in as grieuous perplexitie as at first, yet though they suspected much, they had no certaine proofe or knowledge of the cause: Their meanes were therefore the shorter to cure the effect. But as a thiefe, when hee entereth into a house to robbe, first putteth out the lights, according to that, Qui male agit, odit lucem, he that doth euill, hateth light, so these Impes that liue in the gunshot of diuellish assaults, goe about to darken and disgrace the light of such as are toward, and vertuous, and make the night the instrument to contriue their wicked purposes. For these Witches hauing so long, and couertly continued to doe much mischiefe by their practises, were so hardened in their lewde and vile proceeding, that the custome of their sinne had quite taken away the sense and feeling thereof, and they spared not to continue the perplexitie of this old seruant both in bodie and minde, in such sort that his friends were as desirous to see death ridde him from his extremitie, as a woman great with childe is euer musing vpon the time of her deliuerie: For where distresse is deepe, and the conscience cleare, Mors expectatur absque formidine, exoptatur cum dulcedine, excipitur cum deuotione. Death is looked for without feare, desired with delight, and accepted with deuotion. As the actes and enterprises of these wicked persons are darke and diuellish: so in the perseue-

rance

rance of this fellowes perplexitie, hee being in his distraction both of bodie and minde, yet in bed and awake, espied Mary Sutton, (the daughter) in a Mooneshine night come in at a window in her accustomed and personall habite, and shape, with her knitting worke in her hands, and sitting downe at his beds feete, sometimes working, and knitting with her needles, and sometimes gazing and staring him in the face, as his griefe was thereby redoubled and increased. Not long after she drewe neerer vnto him, and sate by his bedde side (yet all this while he had neyther power to stirre or speake) and told him if hee would consent she should come to bedde to him, hee should be restored to his former health and prosperitie. Thus the Diuell striues to enlarge his Kingdome, and vpon the necke of one wickednesse to heape another: So that *Periculum probat transeuntium raritas, pereuntium multitudo*: In the dangerous Sea of this world, the rarenesse of those that passe the same ouer safe, and the multitude of others that perish in their passage, sufficiently proue the perill wee liue in: In the Ocean Sea, of foure shippes not one miscaries. In the Sea of this world, of many sowers, not one escapes his particular crosse and calamitie: yet in our greatest weaknesse and debilitie when the Diuell is most busie to tempt vs, and seduce vs from God, then is God strongest in the hearts of his children, and most readie to bee auxiliant, and helping to

saue

and Executed.

saue and vphold them from declining, and falling. Gods liberalitie appeares more, then his rigour, for whom hee drawes out the Diuels throat by faith, hee would haue to trample him downe by vertue, least he should onely haue fled, not foyled his enemie.

This is made showne in his miraculous working with this fellow: for hee that before had neither power to moue, or speake, had then presently by diuine assistance free power and libertie to giue repulse to her assault, and deniall to her filthie, and detested motion: and to vpbraide her of her abhominable life and behauiour, hauing before had three bastards and neuer married. She vpon this (seeing her suite cold, and that Gods power was more predominant with him then her diuellish practise, vanished, and departed the same way shee came.

She was no sooner gone, but as well as hee could, hee called for his master, told him that now hee could tell him the cause of this vexation: That Mother Suttons daughter came in at the window, sate knitting and working by him, and that if hee would haue consented to her filthinesse, hee should haue beene freede from his miserie, and related all that had happened.

His master was glad of this newes, for that the meanes found out, the matter and manner of his griefe might bee the easier helped, and redressed:

sed, yet was he distrustfull of the truth, and rather esteemed it an idlenesse of his braine, then an accident of veritie: Neuerthelesse he resolued to make proofe thereof.

The next morrow hee tooke company along with him, and went into the fields, where hee found her working, and tending her hogges. There Master Enger speaking to her, she was a verie good huswife, and that shee followed her worke night and day: No sir, said she, My huswifery is very slender, neyther am I so good a follower of my worke as you perswade mee: with that, he told her that she was, and that she had béene working at his house the night before. She would confesse nothing, but stood in stiffe deniall vpon her purgation: Insomuch as the Gentleman by fayre entreaties perswaded her to goe home with him, to satisfie his man, and to resolue some doubts that were had of her. She vtterly refused, and made answere she would not stirre a foote, neyther had they authoritie to compell her to goe without a Constable: Which Master Enger perceiuing, and séeing her obstinacie to be so great, fell into a greater dislike, and distrust of her then he did before, and made no more adoe, but caused her to bee set vpon an horse-backe to be brought to his house. All the company could hardly bring her away, but as fast as they set her vp, in despight of them shee would swarue downe, first on the one side, then the other, till at last they were faine by maine

forces

and executed

force to ioyne together, and hold her violently downe to the horsebacke, and so bring her to the place where this perplexed person lay in his bed. Where being come, and brought by force to his bed-side, he (as directions had beene giuen vnto him) drew blood of her, and presently beganne to amend, and bee well againe. But her assiduitie and continuall exercise in doing mischiefe, did so preuaile with her to doe this fellow further hurt, that watching but aduantage, and opportunitie to touch his necke againe with her finger: It was no sooner done, and she departed, but he fell into as great or farre worse vexation then he had before.

The report of this was carried vp and downe all Bedford-shire, and this Marie Suttons wicked and lewde courses being rumored as well abroad, as in Master Engers house, at last it came into the mouth of Master Engers sonne, (being a little boy of seuen yeares old) who not long after espying old Mother Sutton going to the Mill to grinde corne, and remembring what speeches he had heard past of her and her daughter followed the old woman, flinging stones at her, and calling her Witch, which shee obseruing conceited a rancour, and deadly hatred to this young childe, and purposed not to suffer opportunitie passe to bee reuenged. As soone therefore as she had dispatcht at the Mill, she hasted homewards, and could not be quiet till she had grumbled to her daughter what had happened, and

C how

how the childe had serued her; Then conferring how Master Enger had vsed Mary Sutton the daughter, and how hir little sonne had vsed the Mother, they both resolued, and vowed reuenge. This conference and consultation of villanie was had, and concluded in the presence, and hearing of Henry Sutton, (the Bastard of Mary Sutton) little thinking that his fortune should be to giue in euidene to breake the necke of his owne Mother and Grandmother.

To effect their diuellish purpose to the young childe of Master Enger, they called vp their two Spirits, whom she called Dicke and Iude: and hauing giuen them sucke at their two Teats which they had on their thighes (found out afterwards by enquirie, and search of women) they gaue them charge to strike the little boy, and to turne him to torment. Which was not long in performing, but the childe being distract, was put to such bitter and insupportable misery, as by his life his torments were augmented, and by his death they were abridged. For his tender and vnripe age was so infeebled and made weake by that diuellish infliction of extremitie, as in fiue daies, not able longer to endure them, death gaue end to his perplexities.

The Gentleman did not so much grieue for the losse and hinderance hee had in his cattell, (which was much) nor for the miserable distresse that his seruant had endured (which was more) as that the hopefull daies of his young sonne

and executed.

sonne were so vntimely cut off : (which touched his heart most of all.) Yet did his discretion temper his passions with such patience, that he referred the remembrance of his wrongs to that heauenly power, that permits not such iniquitie to passe vnreuealed, or vnreuenged.

As hee was thus wrapt in a Sea of woes, there came a Gentleman a friend of his forth of the North, that trauelling towards London soiourned with him all night. Hee perceiuing Master Enger to be full of griefe, was desirous to know the cause thereof, and hee was as vnwilling by the discourse of his misfortunes to renewe his many sorrowes, till at last his friends vrgent importunacie perswaded him not to passe it ouer with silence. Upon Master Engers relation of what had happened : the Gentleman demaunded if hee had none in suspition that should doe these wronges vnto him : Yes, (quoth Master Enger) and therewithall hee named this Mary Sutton and her mother, and told him the particulars of his losses and miseries. His friend vnderstanding this, aduised him to take them, or any one of them to his Mill damme, hauing first shut vp the Mill gates that the water might be at highest, and then binding their armes crosse, stripping them into their Smocks, and leauing their legges at libertie, throw them into the water, yet least they should not bee Witches, and that their liues might not be in danger of drowning,

C 2

ning, let there be a roape tyed about their middles, so long that it may reach from one side of your damme to the other, where on each side let one of your men stand, that if she chance to sinke they may draw her vp and preserue her. Then if she swimme, take her vp, & cause some women to search her, vpon which, if they finde any extraordinarie markes about her, let her the second time be bound, and haue her right thumbe bound to her left toe, and her left thumbe to her right toe, and your men with the same rope (if néed be) to preserue her, and bee throwne into the water, when if she swimme, you may build vpon it, that she is a Witch, I haue séene it often tried in the North countrey.

The morrow after Master Enger road into the fields where Mary Sutton (the daughter) was, hauing some of his men to accompany him, where after some questions made vnto her, they assayed to binde her on horse-backe, when all his men being presently stricken lame, Master Enger himselfe began to remember, that once rating her about his man, he was on the sodaine in the like perplexitie, and then taking courage, and desiring God to bee his assistance, with a cudgell which he had in his hand, he beate her till she was scarce able to stirre. At which his men presently recouered, bound her to their Masters horse, and brought her home to his house, & shutting vp his Mill gates did as before the Gentleman had aduised him: when being throwne in the first time

she

and Executed.

shee sunke some two foote into the water with a fall, but rose againe, and floated vpon the water like a planke. Then he commanded her to be taken out, and had women readie that searched her, and found vnder her left thigh a kind of Teat, which after the Bastard sonne confest her Spirits in seuerall shapes as Cats, Moales, &c. vsed to sucke her.

Then was she the second time bound crosse, her thumbes and toes, accoording to the former direction, and then she sunke not at all, but sitting vpon the water, turned round about like a wheele, or as that which commonly we call a whirlepoole. Notwithstanding Master Engers men standing on each side of the damme with a roape tossing her vp and downe to make her sinke, but could not.

And then being taken vp, she as boldly as if she had beene innocent asked them if they could doe any more to her: When Master Enger began to accuse her with the death of his cattell, the languish of his man, who continued in sorrow both of bodie and mind from Christmasse to Shrouetide, as also the death of his sonne: All which she constantly denied, and stood at defiance with him, till being carried towards a Iustice, Master Enger told her it was bootlesse to stand so obstinately vpon deniall of those matters, for her owne sonne Henry had reuealed all, both as touching her selfe and her mother, and of the time and manner of their plotting to torment his little boy: when she heard that, her heart misgaue her, she confessed

C 3   all,

Witches lately arraigned,

all, and acknowledged the Diuell had now left her to that shame that is reward to such as follow him. Upon which confession, the mother also was apprehended, and both being committed to Bedford Gaole, many other matters were there produced against them, of long continuance (for they had remained as before, about twentie yeares) in the prosecute of these lewd and wicked practises. But for this matter of Master Enger at the last Assises, the euidence of the Bastard son, and the confessions seuerally taken both of old Mother Sutton & her daughter Mary, found them guiltie in al former obiections. So that arraigned at Bedford on Munday the thirtieth of March last past, they had a iust conuiction, and on Tuesday the next day after they were executed.

FINIS.

Damnable Practises Of three Lincolne-shire Witches (*STC* 11106) is reproduced from the unique copy at the Pepys Library, Magdalen College, Cambridge University (shelfmark Pepys Ballads I:132 [Pl 2505]), by permission. The text block on page one measures 220mm × 180mm and on page two 250mm × 135mm (approximately).

Hard-to-read words in the original
1.1.9:   ‹Si?›nce
1.1.11: ‹B›y
1.1.13: ‹Y?›e
1.1.14: ‹do›th
1.1.15: ‹And?›

1.1.16: ‹Amo›ngst
1.1.17: ‹th›at
1.1.19: ‹a›nd
1.1.20: ‹Whi›ch
1.1.21: ‹an›d
1.1.22: ‹Th›at
1.1.23: ‹rec›eived

1.1.24: ‹And?› eke
1.1.25: ‹as?›
1.1.26: ‹But?›
1.1.27: ‹y›e
1.1.28: ‹She?›
1.1.29: ‹Unt?›o
1.1.30: ‹at?›
1.1.31: ‹Wo›uld

1.1.32: ‹Which wh?›en
1.1.33: ‹And of?›
1.1.34: ‹They grie?›ved

Damnable Practises

Of three Lincolne-shire Witches, *Joane Flower*, and her two Daughters, *Margret* and *Phillip Flower*, against *Henry* Lord *Rosse*, with others the Children of the Right Honourable the Earle of Rutland, at Beauer Castle, who for the same were executed at Lincolne the 11. of *March* last. To the tune of the Ladies fall.

Of damned déeds, and deadly dole,
  I make my mournfull song,
By Witches done in Lincolne-shire,
  where they haue liued long:
And practisd many a wicked déed,
  within that Country there,
Which fills my brest and bosome full,
  of sobs, and trembling feare.

The Beauer Castle is a place,
  that welcome giues to all,
By which the Earle of Rutland gaines
  the loues of great and small:
His Countesse of like friendlinesse,
  doth beare as frée a mind:
And so from them both rich and poore,
  helps and succour find.

Amongst the rest were Witches thrée,
  that to this Castle came,
Margaret and Phillip Flower,
  with Ioane their Mothers name:
Which Women dayly found reliefe,
  and were contented well:
And at the last this Margret was,
  receiued there to dwell.

And put vnto such houshold charge,
  vnto her belongd,
Who possest with fraud and guile,
  her place and office wrongd;
And secretly purloyned things,
  vnto her mother home:
At vnlawfull howers from thence,
  she nightly goe and come.

When the Earle & Countesse heard,
  her dealings knew,
And proued much that she should proue,
  so vntrue.

And so discharg'd her of the house,
  therein to come no more:
For of her lewd and filching prankes,
  of proofes there were some store.

And likewise that her Mother was,
  a woman full of wrath,
A swearing and blaspheming wretch,
  forespeaking sodaine death:
And how that neighbours in her lokes,
  malitious signes did sée:
And some affirm'd she dealt with Sprits,
  and so a Witch might be.

And that her Sister Phillip was
  well knowne a Strumpet lewd,
And how she had a young mans loue,
  bewitched and subdued,
Which made the young man often say,
  he had no power to leaue
Her curst inticing company,
  that did him so deceaue.

When to the Earle and Countesse thus,
  these iust complaints were made,
Their hearts began to breed dislike,
  and greatly grew affraid:
Commanding that she neuer should,
  returne vnto their sight,
Nor back into the Castle come,
  but be excluded quite.

Whereat the old malitious fiend,
  with those her darlings thought:
The Earle and Countesse them disgrac't,
  and their discredits wrought:
In turning thus despightfully,
  her daughter out of dores,
For which reuengement, in her mind
  she many a mischiefe stores.

Heereat the Diuell made entrance in,
  his Kingdome to inlarge.
And puts his executing wrath,
  vnto these womens charge:
Not caring whom it lighted on,
  the Innocent or no,
And offered them his diligence,
  to flye, to run, and goe.

And to attend in pretty formes,
  of Dog, of Cat, or Rat,
To which they fréely gaue consent,
  and much reioyc't thereat:
And as it seemd they sould their soules,
  for seruice of such Spirits,
And sealing it with drops of blood,
  damnation so inherits.

These Women thus being Diuels growne
  most cunning in their Arts:
With charmes and with inchanting spells,
  they plaid most damned parts:
They did forespeake, and Cattle kilo,
  that neighbours could not thriue,
And oftentimes their Children young,
  of life they would depriue.

At length the Countesse and her Lord,
  to fits of sicknesse grew:
The which they deemd the hand of God,
  and their correctiones due:
Which crosses patiently they bore,
  misdoubting no such déeds,
As from these wicked Witches here,
  malitiously procéeds.

Yet so their mallice more increast,
  that mischiefe set in foote,
To blast the branches of that house,
  and vndermine the roote:
Their eldest sonne Henry Lord Rosse,
  possest with sicknesse strange,
Did lingring, lye tormented long,
  till death his life did change.

Their second sonne Lord Francis next,
  felt like continuing woe:
Both day and night in grieuous sort,
  yet none the cause did know:
And then the Lady Katherin,
  into such torments fell:
By these their deuilish practises,
  as grieues my heart to tell.

The second Part. To the same tune.

Yet did this noble minded Earle,
  so patiently it beare:
As if his childrens punishments,
  right natures troubles were:
Suspecting little, that such meanes,
  against them should be wrought,
Untill it pleas'd the Lord to haue
  to light these mischiefes brought.

For greatly here the hand of God,
  did worke in iustice cause:
When he for these their practises
  them all in question drawes.
And so before the Magistrates,
  when as the yongest came,
Who being guilty of the fact
  confest and told the same.

How that her mother and her selfe,
  and sister gaue consent:
To giue the Countesse and her Lord,
  occasions to repent
That ere they turnd her out of dores,
  in such a vile disgrace:
For which, or them or theirs should be,
  brought into heauy case.

And how her sister found a time,
  Lord Rosses gloue to take:
Who gaue it to her mothers hand
  consuming spels to make.
The which she prickt all full of holes,
  and layd it deepe in around:
Whereas it rotted, so should he,
  be quite away consum'd.

All which her elder sister did,
  acknowledge to be true:
And how that she in boyling blood,
  did oft the same imbrew,
And hereupon the yong Lord Rosse,
  such torments did abide:

That strangely he consum'd away,
  vntill the houre he died.

And likewise she confest how they,
  together all agreed:
Against the children of this Earle,
  to practise and proceed.
Not leauing them a child aliue,
  and neuer to haue more:
If witchcraft so could doe, because,
  they turnd them out of dore.

The mother as the daughters told,
  could hardly this deny:
For which they were attach'd all,
  by Iustice speedily.
And vnto Lincolne Citty borne,
  therein to lye in Iayle:
Untill the Iudging Sizes came,
  that death might be their bayle.

But there this hatefull mother witch,
  these speeches did recall:
And said, that in Lord Rosses death,
  she had no hand at all.
Whereon she bread and butter tooke,
  God let this same (quoth she)
If I be guilty of his death,
  passe neuer thorough me.

So mumbling it within her mouth,
  she neuer spake moe words:
But fell downe dead, a iudgment iust,
  and wonder of the Lords.
Her Daughters two their tryalls had,
  of which being guilty found,
They dyed in shame, by strangling twist,
  and layd by shame in ground.

Haue mercy Heauen, on sinners all,
  and grant that neuer like
Be in this Nation knowne or done,
  but Lord in vengeance strike:
Or else conuert their wicked liues
  which in bad wayes are spent:
The feares of God and loue of heauen,
  such courses will preuent.

FINIS.

There is a booke printed of these Witches, wherein you shall know all their examinations and confessions at large: As also the wicked practises of three other most Notorious Witches in *Leceister*-shire with all their examinations and confessions.

Printed by *G. Eld* for *Iohn Barnes*, dwelling in the long Walke neere Christ-Church 1619.

Henry Goodcole, *The wonderfull discouerie of ELIZABETH SAWYER* (*STC* 12014) is reproduced by permission from the fine copy at The British Library (shelfmark C.27.b.38). The text block of the original measures 142mm × 84mm. The British Museum stamp and marks on the verso of the title page are illegible.

C. 27. 4. 38.

The wonderfull dif-
couerie of ELIZABETH SAVVYER
a *Witch*, late of Edmonton, her
conuiction and condemnation
and Death.

Together with the relation of the Diuels
acceſſe to her, and their conference together.

Written by HENRY GOODCOLE Miniſter of the
Word of God, and her continuall Viſiter in the
Gaole of Newgate.
Publiſhed by Authority.

London, Printed for VVilliam Butler, and are to be ſold at his Shop in Saint
Dunſtons Church-yard, Fleetſtreet, 1621.

The Authors Apologie to the *Christian Readers*, who wisheth to them all health and happinesse.

He *Publication of this subiect whereof now I write, hath bin by importunitie extorted from me, who would haue beene content to haue concealed it, knowing the diuersitie of opinions concerning things of this nature, and that not among the* ignorant, but among some of the learned. For my part I meddle heare with nothing but matter of fact, and to that ende produce the Testimony of the liuing and the dead, which I hope shall be Authenticall for the confirmation of this Narration, and free mee from all censorious mindes and mouthes. It is none of my intent here to discusse, or dispute of Witches or Witchcraft, but desire most therin to be dispensed with

A 3   all,

To the Readers.

all, knowing, that in such a little Treatise as this is, no matter that can be effectuall therein can pe comprised; especially, in so short a time of deliberation, as three or foure dayes. And the rather doe I now publish this to purchase my peace, which without it being done, I could scarse at any time be at quiet, for many who would take no nay, but still desired of me written Copies of this insuing Declaration. Another reason was to defend the truth of the cause, which in some measure, hath receiued a wound already, by most base and false Ballets, which were sung at the time of our returning from the Witches execution. In them I was ashamed to see and heare such ridiculous fictions of her bewitching Corne on the ground, of a Ferret and an Owle dayly sporting before her, of the bewitched woman brayning her selfe, of the Spirits attending in the Prison: all which I knew to be fitter for an Ale-bench then for a relation of proceeding in Court of Iustice. And thereupon I wonder that such lewde Balletmongers should be suffered to creepe into the Printers presses and peoples eares.

And so I rest at your opinions
and iudgements

Your well-wisher in the Lord Iesus,

HENRY GOODCOLE

A true declaration

of the manner of proceeding againſt ELIZABETH SAVVYER *late of Edmonton Spinſter, and the euidence of her Conuiction.*

Great, and long ſuſpition was held of this perſon to be a witch, and the eye of Mr. *Arthur Robinſon*, a worthy Iuſtice of Peace, who dweleth at *Totnam* neere to her, was watchfull ouer her, and her wayes, and that not without iuſt cauſe; ſtil hauing his former long ſuſpition of her, by the information of her neighbours that dwelt about her: from ſuſpitiō, to proceed to great preſumptions, ſeeing the death of Nurſe-children and Cattell, ſtrangely and ſuddenly to happen. And to findeout who ſhould bee the author of this miſchieſe, an old ridiculous cuſtome was vſed, which was to plucke the Thatch of her houſe, and

The wonderfull discouery of the

and to burne it, and it being so burnd, the author of such mischiefe should presently then come: and it was obserued and affirmed to the Court, that *Elizabeth Sawyer* would presently frequent the house of them that burnt the thatch which they pluckt of her house, and come without any sending for.

This triall, though it was slight and ridiculous, yet it setled a resolution in those whom it concerned, to findeout by all meanes they could endeauour, her long, and close carried Witchery, to explaine it to the world; and being descried, to pay in the ende such a worker of Iniquity, her wages, and that which shee had deserued, (namely, *shame* and *Death*) from which the Diuell, that had so long deluded her, did not come as shee said, to shew the least helpe of his vnto her to deliuer her: but being descried in his waies, and workes, immediately he fled, leauing her to shift and answere for her selfe, with publike and priuate markes on her body as followeth.

1. Her face was most pale & ghoast-like without any bloud at all, and her countenance was still deiected to the ground.

2. Her body was crooked and deformed, euen bending together, which so happened but a little before her apprehension.

3. That tongue which by cursing, swearing, blaspheming, and imprecating, as afterward shee

the Witch of Edmonton.

cōfessed, was the occasioning cause, of the Diuels accesse vnto her, euen at that time, and to claime her thereby as his owne, by it discouered her lying, swearing, and blaspheming; as also euident proofes produced against her, to stop her mouth with Truths authority: at which hearing, she was not able to speake a sensible or ready word for her defense, but sends out in the hearing of the Iudge, Iury, and all good people that stood by, many most fearefull imprecations for destruction against her selfe then to happen, as heretofore she had wished and indeauoured to happen on diuers of her neighbours: the which the righteous Iudge of Heauen, whom she thus inuocated, to iudge then and discerne her cause, did reueale.

Thus God did wonderfully ouertake her in her owne wickednesse, to make her tongue to be the meanes of her owne destruction, which had destroyed many before.

And in this manner, namely, that out of her false swearing the truth whereof, shee little thought, should be found, but by her swearing and cursing blended, it thus farre made against her, that both Iudge and Iurie, all of them grew more and more suspitious of her, and not without great cause: for none that had the feare of God, or any the least motion of Gods grace left in them, would, or durst, to persume so im-
B   pudent-

the Witch of Edmonton.

pudently, with execrations and false oathes, to affront Iustice.

On Saturday, being the fourteenth day of Aprill, *Anno Dom.* 1621. this *Elizabeth Sawyer* late of *Edmonton*, in the County of *Middlesex* Spinster, was arraigned, and indited three seuerall times at Iustice Hall in the Old Baily in *London*, in the Parish of Saint *Sepulchers*, in the Ward of Farrington without: which Inditements were, *viz*.

That shee the said *Elizabeth Sawyer*, not hauing the feare of God before her eyes, but moued and seduced by the Diuell, by Diabolicall helpe, did out of her malicious heart, (because her neighbours where she dwelt, would not buy Broomes of her) would therefore thus reuenge her selfe on them in this manner, namely, witch to death their Nurse Children and Cattell. But for breuities sake I here omit formes of Law and Informations.

She was also indited, for that shee the said *Elizabeth Sawyer*, by Diabolicall helpe, and out of her malice afore-thought, did witch vnto death *Agnes Ratcleife*, a neighbour of hers, dwelling in the towne of *Edmonton* where shee did likewise dwell, and the cause that vrged her there-vnto was, because that *Elizabeth Ratcliefe* did

stricke

The wonderfull discouerie of

strike a Sowe of hers in her sight, for licking vp a little Soape where shee had laide it, and for that *Elizabeth Sawyer* would be reuenged of her, and thus threatned *Agnes Ratcleife*, that it should be a deare blow vnto her, which accordingly fell out, and suddenly; for that euening *Agnes Ratcleife* fell very sicke, and was extraordinarily vexed, and in a most strange manner in her sicknesse was tormented, Oath whereof, was by this *Agnes Ratcleifes* Husband, giuen to the Court, the time when shee fell sicke, and the time when shee died, which was within foure dayes after she fell sicke: and further then related, that in the time of her sicknesse his wife *Agnes Ratcleife* lay foaming at the mouth, and was extraordinarily distempered, which many of his neighbors seeing, as well as himselfe, bred suspition in them that some mischiefe was done against her, and by none else, but alone by this *Elizabeth Sawyer* it was done; concerning whom the said *Agnes Ratcleife* lying on her death-bed, these wordes confidently spake: namely, that if shee did die at that time shee would verily take it on her death, that *Elizabeth sawyer* her neighbour, whose Sowe with a washing-Beetle she had stricken, and so for that cause her malice being great, was the occasion of her death.

The wonderfull discouery of

To proue her innocency, she put her selfe to the triall of God and the Countrey, and what care was taken both by the honourable Bench and Iury, the iudicious standers by can witnesse: and God knowes, who will reward it.

The Iury hearing this Euidence giuen vpon oath by the husband of the aboue named *Agnes Ratcliefe*, and his wiues speeches relating to them likewise an oath, as she lay on her death-bed, to be truth, that shee had said vnto her husband; Namely, that if she dyed at that time, shee the said *Elizabeth Sawyer* was the cause of her death ; and maliciously did by her Witchery procure the same.

This made some impression in their mindes, and caused due and mature deliberation, not trusting their owne iudgements, what to doe, in a matter of such great import, as life, they deemed might be conserued.

The Foreman of the Iury asked of Master *Heneage Finch* Recorder, his direction, and aduice, to whom hee Christianlike thus replyed, namely, *Doe in it as God shall put in your hearts*.

Master *Arthur Robinson*, a worshipfull Iustice of Peace dwelling at *Totnam*, had often & diuers times, vpon the complaints of the neighbours against this *Elizabeth Sawyer*, laboriously and carefully examined her, and stil his suspition was strengthened against her, that doutlesse shee was

a Witch

the Witch of Edmonton.

a Witch. An Information was giuen vnto him by some of her Neighbours, that this *Elizabeth Sawyer* had a priuate and strange marke on her body, by which their suspition was confirmed against her, and hee sitting in the Court at that time of her triall, informed the Bench thereof, desiring the Bench to send for women to search her, presently before the Iury did goe forth to bring in the verdict, concerning *Elizabeth Sawyer*, whether that shee was guilty or no : to which motion of his, they most willingly condescended.

The Bench commanded officers appointed for those purposes, to fetch in three women to search the body of *Elizabeth Sawyer*, to see if they could finde any such vnwonted marke, as they were informed of : one of the womens names was *Margaret Weauer*, that keepes the Sessions House for the City of *London*, a widdow of an honest reputation, and two other graue Matrons, brought in by the Officer out of the streete, passing by there by chance, were ioyned with her in this search of the person named, who fearing and perceiuing shee should by that search of theirs be then discouered, behaued her selfe most sluttishly and loathsomely towards them, intending thereby to preuent their search of her, (which my pen would forbeare to write these

The wonderfull discouery of
these things for modesties sake; but I would not vary in what was deliuered to the Bench, expresly & openly spoken) yet neuerthelesse, nicenesse they laid aside, and according to the request of the Court, and to that trust reposed in them by the Bench, they all three seuerally searched her, and made seuerally their answer vnto the Court being sworne thereunto to deliuer the truth. And they all three said, that they a little aboue the Fundiment of *Elizabeth Sawyer* the prisoner, there indited before the Bench for a Witch, found a thing like a Teate the bignesse of the little finger, and the length of halfe a finger, which was branched at the top like a teate, and seemed as though one had suckt it, and that the bottome thereof was blew, and the top of it was redde. This view of theirs, and answere that she had such a thing about her, which boldly shee denied, gaue some insight to the Iury, of her: who vpon their consciences returned the said *Elizabeth Sawyer*, to be guilty, by dibolicall help, of the death of *Agnes Ratcliefe* onely, and acquitted her of the other two Inditements. And thus much of the meanes that brought her to her deserued death and destruction.

I will addresse to informe you of her preparation to death, which is alone pertinent to my function, and declare vnto you her Confession *verbatim*,

the Witch of Edmonton.

batim, out of her owne mouth deliuered to me, the Tuseday after her conuiction, though with great labour it was extorted from her, and the same Confession I read vnto her at the place of her execution, and there shee confessed to all people that were there, the same to be most true, which I shall here relate.

And because it should not bee thought that from me alone this proceeded, I would haue other testimony thereof to stop all contradictions of so palpable a verity, that heard her deliuer it from her owne mouth in the Cappel of *Newgate* the same time.

In testimony whereof, the persons that were then present with mee at her Confession, haue hereunto put to their hands, and if it be required, further to confirme this to be a truth, will bee ready at all times to make oath thereof.

A true

A true Relation of the confession of Elizabeth Sawyer *spinster*, after her conuiction of Witchery, taken on *Tuesday the* 17. *day of* Aprill, Anno 1621. in the Gaole of Newgate, where she was prisoner, then in the presence and hearing of diuers persons, whose names to verifie the same are here subscribed to this ensuyng confession, made vnto me Henry Good-cole *Minister of the word of God*, Ordinary *and* Visiter *for the Gaole of Newgate*. *In Dialogue manner are here expressed the persons that she murthered, and the cattell that she destroyed by the helpe of the Diuell*

In this manner was I inforced to speake vnto her, because she might vnderstand me, and giue vnto me answere, according to my demands, for she was a very ignorant woman.

Question.

BY *what meanes came you to haue acquaintance with the Diuell, and when was the first time that you saw him, and how did you know that it was the Diuell?*

Answere.

The first time that the Diuell came vnto me was, when I was cursing, swearing and blaspheming

C

ming

The wonderfull discouery of

ming; he then rushed in vpon me, and neuer before that time did I see him, or he me: and when he, namely the Diuel, came to me, the first words that hee spake vnto me were these: *Oh! haue I now found you cursing, swearing, and blaspheming? now you are mine.* A wonderfull warning to many whose tongues are too frequent in these abhominable sinnes; I pray God, that this her terrible example may deter them, to leaue and distaste them, to put their tongues to a more holy language, then the accursed language of hell. The tongue of man is the glory of man, and it was ordained to glorifie God: but worse then brute beasts they are, who haue a tongue, as well as men, that therewith they at once both blesse and curse.

A Gentleman by name Mr. Maddox standing by, and hearing of her say the word blaspheming, did aske of her, three or foure times, whether the Diuell sayd haue I found you blaspheming, and shee confidently sayd, I.

Question.

What sayd you to the Diuell, when hee came vnto you and spake vnto you; were you not afraide of him? if you did feare him, what sayd the Diuell then vnto you?

Answere.

I was in a very greate feare, when I saw the Diuell, but hee did bid me not to feare him at all, for hee would do me no hurt at all, but would do for mee whatsoeuer I should require of him; and as he promised vnto me, he alwayes did such mischiefes as I did bid him to do, both on the bodies of Christians and beastes: if I did bid him vexe them to death, as oftentimes I did

so

so bid him, it was then presently by him so done.

Question.
Whether would the Diuell bring vnto you word or no, what he had done for you, at your command; and if he did bring you word, how long would it bee, before he would come vnto you againe, to tell you?

Answere.
He would alwayes bring vnto me word what he had done for me, within the space of a weeke, he neuer failed me at that time; and would likewise do it to Creatures and beasts two manner of wayes, which was by scratching or pinching of them.

Question.
Of what Christians and Beastes, and how many were the number that you were the cause of their death, and what moued you to prosecute them to the death?

Answere.
I haue bene by the helpe of the Diuell, the meanes of many Christians and beasts death; the cause that moued mee to do it, was malice and enuy, for if any body had angred me in any manner, I would be so reuenged of them, and of their cattell. And do now further confesse, that I was the cause of those two nurse-childrens death, for the which I was now indited and acquited, by the Iury.

The wonderfull discouery of

Question.
whether did you procure the death of Agnes Ratcliefe, for which you were found guilty by the Iury?

Answere.
No, I did not by my meanes procure against her the least hurt.

Question.
How long is it since the Diuell and you had acquaintance together, & how oftentimes in the weeke would hee come and see you, and you company with him?

Answere.
It is eight yeares since our first acquaintance; and three times in the weeke, the Diuell would come and see mee, after such his acquaintance gotten of me; he would come sometimes in the morning, and sometimes in the euening.

Question.
In what shape would the Diuell come vnto you?

Answere.
Alwayes in the shape of a dogge, and of two collars, sometimes of blacke and sometimes of white.

Question.
What talke had the Diuel and you together, when that he appeared to you, and what did he aske of you, and what did you desire of him?
Answere.

the Witch of Edmonton.

Answer.

He asked of me, when hee came vnto me, how I did, and what he should doe for mee, and demanded of mee my soule and body; threatning then to teare me in peeces, if that I did not grant vnto him my soule and my body which he asked of me.

Question.

what did you after such the Diuells asking of you, to haue your Soule and Body, and after this his threatning of you, did you for feare grant vnto the Diuell his desire?

Answer.

Yes, I granted for feare vnto the Diuell his request of my Soule and body; and to seale this my promise made vnto him, I then gaue him leaue to sucke of my bloud, the which hee asked of me.

Queston.

In what place of your body did the Diuell sucke of your bloud, and whether did hee himselfe chuse the place, or did you your selfe appoint him the place? tell the truth, I charge you, as your will answere vnto the Almighty God, and tell the reason if that you can, why he would sucke your bloud.

Answer.

The place where the Diuell suckt my bloud was a little aboue my fundiment, and that place chosen by himselfe; and in that place by continuall drawing, there is a thing in the forme

I demanded this question of her to confirme the womens search of her, concerting, that she had such a marke about her, which they vpon their oathes informed the court, that truth it was, she had such a marke.

C 3

The wonderfull discouery of

forme of a Teate, at which the diuell would
sucke mee. And I asked the Diuell why hee
would sucke my bloud, and hee sayd it was to
nourish him.

This I asked of her very earnestly, and shee thus answered me, without any studying for an answer.

Question.

Whether did you pull vp your coates or no when the Diuell came to sucke you?

Answer.

No I did not, but the Diuell would put his head vnder my coates, and I did willingly suffer him to doe what hee would.

Question.

How long would the time bee, that the Diuill would continue sucking of you, and whether did you endure any paine, the time that hee was sucking of you?

Answer.

He would be suckinge of me the continuance of a quarter of an howre, and when hee suckt mee, I then felt no paine at all.

I asked this question because she sayd that the Diuell did not alwayes speake to her

Question.

What was the meaning that the Diuell when hee came vnto you, would sometimes speake, and sometimes barke.

Answer.

It is thus; when the Diuell spake to me, then hee was ready to doe for me, what I would bid him to doe: and when he came barking to mee he then had done the mischiefe that I did bid him to doe for me.

Question.

The witch of Edmonton.

Quest.

By what name did you call the Diuell, and what promises did he make to you?

Answ.

I did call the Diuell by the name of *Tom*, and he promised to doe for me whatsoeuer I should require of him.

Quest.

What were those two ferrets that you were feeding on a fourme with white-bread and milke, when diuers children came, and saw you feeding of them?

Answ.

I neuer did any such thing.

Quest.

What was the white thing that did run through the thatch of your house, was it a spirit or Diuell?

Answ.

So farre as I know, it was nothing else but a white Ferret.

Quest.

Did any body else know, but your selfe alone, of the Diuells comming vnto you, and of your practises? speake the truth, and tell the reason, why you did not reueale it to your husband, or to some other friend?

Answ.

I did not tell any body thereof, that the Diuel came vnto me, neither I durst not; for the Diuell charged me that I should not, and said, That if I did tell it to any body, at his next comming to

I asked this of her, because that some children of a good bignesse, and reasonable vnderstanding, informed the Court, that they had diuers times seene her feed two white ferrets with white bread & milk.

I asked this questiō of her because her husband testified to the Bench, he saw such a white thing runne thorow the thatch of the house, and that he catcht at it, but could not get it, and hee thought it was a white ferret;

The wonderfull discouery of

to me, he then would teare me in pieces.
Quest.

Vpon my generall suspitio I asked of her this question.

Did the Diuell at any time find you praying when he came vnto you, and did not the Diuell forbid you to pray to Iesus Christ, but to him alone? and did not he bid you pray to him the Divell, as he taught you?

Answ.

I doe here relate the selfe-same wordes vpon this question propounded vnto her, what prayer the Diuell taught her to say.

Yes, he found me once praying, and he asked of me to whom I prayed, and I answered him, to Iesus Christ; and he charged me then to pray no more to Iesus Christ, but to him the Diuell, and he the Diuell taught me this prayer, *Santibicetur nomen tuum.* Amen.

Quest.

Were you euer taught these Latine words before by any person else, or did you euer heare it before of any body, or can you say any more of it?

Answ.

No, I was not taught it by any body else, but by the Diuell alone; neither doe I vnderstand the meaning of these words, nor can speake any more Latine words.

Quest.

Did the Diuell aske of you the next time he came vnto you, whether that you vsed to pray vnto him, in that manner as he taught you?

Answ.

Yes, at his next comming to me hee asked of me, if that I did pray vnto him as he had taught me; and I answered him againe, that sometimes

I

the Witch of Edmonton.

I did, and sometimes I did not, and the Diuell then thus threatned me; It is not good for me to mocke him.

Quest.
How long is it since you saw the Diuell last?
Answ.
It is three weekes since I saw the Diuell.
Quest.
Did the Diuell neuer come vnto you since you were in prison? speake the truth, as you will answer vnto almighty God.

Answ.
The Diuell neuer came vnto me since I was in prison, nor I thanke God, I haue no motion of him in my minde, since I came to prison, neither doe I now feare him at all.

I asked this question because it was rumoured that the diuel came to her since her conuiction and shamelesly printed and openly sung in a ballad, to which many giue too much credite.

Quest.
How came your eye to be put out?
Answ.
With a sticke which one of my children had in the hand: that night my mother did dye it was done; for I was stooping by the bed side, and I by chance did hit my eye on the sharpe end of the sticke.

The reason why I asked this was because her father and mothers eye, one of theirs was out.

Quest.
Did you euer handle the Diuell when he came vnto you?
Answ.
Yes, I did stroake him on the backe, and then he would becke vnto me, and wagge his tayle as being therewith contented.

I asked of her this question because some might thinke this was a visible delusion of her sight only.

Quest.

D would

The wonderfull discouery of, &c.

would the Diuell come vnto you, all in one bignesse?

Answ.

No; when hee came vnto mee in the blacke shape, he then was biggest, and in the white the least; and when that I was praying, hee then would come vnto me in the white colour.

Quest.

why did you at your triall forsweare all this, that ou now doe confesse?

Answ.

I did it thereby hoping to auoyd shame.

Quest.

Is all this truth which you haue spoken here vnto me, and that I haue now written?

Answ.

Yes, it is all truth, as I shall make answer vnto almighty God.

Quest.

what moues you now to make this confession? did any vrge you to it, or bid you doe it, is it for any hope of life you doe it?

Answ.

No: I doe it to cleere my conscience, and now hauing done it, I am the more quiet, and the better prepared, and willing thereby to suffer death; for I haue no hope at all of my life, although I must confesse, I would liue longer if I might.

A

A Relation what shee said at the *place of Execution, which was at Tiborne,* on Thursday, the 19. day of Aprill. 1621.

ALl this beeing by her thus freely confessed after her conuiction in the Gaole of New-gate, on Tuesday, the 17. day of Aprill, I acquainted Master Recorder of *London* therewith; who thus directed mee, to take that her confession with me to the place of Execution, and to reade it to her, and to aske of her whether that was truth which shee had deliuered to me in the prison, on Tuesday last, concerning what she said; and how shee dyed I will relate vnto you.

Elizabeth Sawyer, you are now come vnto the place of Execution; is that all true which you confessed vnto mee on Tuesday last, when that you were in prison? I haue it here, and will now reade it vnto you, as you spake it then vnto me, out of your owne mouth: and if it be true, confesse it now to God, and to all the people that are here present.

Answer.

This confession which is now read vnto me, by Master *Henry Goodcoale* Minister, with my owne mouth I spake it to him on Tuesday last at *New-gate*, and I here doe acknowledge, to all

The wonderfull Discouery of

all the people that are here present, that it is all truth, disiring you all to pray vnto Almightie God to forgiue me my greeuous sinnes.

Question.

By what meanes hope you now to bee saued?

Answer.

By Iesus Christ alone.

Question.

Will you now pray vnto Almightie God to forgiue vnto you all your misdeedes?

Answer.

I, with all my heart and minde.

This was confirmed, in the hearing of many hundreds at her last breath, what formerly shee in prison confessed to me, and at that time spake more hearti'y, then the day before of her execution, on whose body Law was iustly inflicted, but mercy in Gods power reserued, to bestow, when and where hee pleaseth.

My labour thus ended concerning her, to testifie and auouch to the world, and all opposers hereof, this to be true; those that were present with me in the prison, that heard her confession, I haue desired here their testimonies, which is as followeth.

We whose names are heere subscribed, doe

the Witch of Edmonton.

doe thereby testifie, that *Elizabeth Sawyer* late of *Edmonton* in the Countie of *Midds.* Spinster, did in our hearings, confesse on Tuesday the 17. of *Aprill,* in the Gaole of *Newgate,* to Master *Henry Goodcoale* Minister of the word of God, the repeated foule crimes, and confirmed it at her death the 19. of *Aprill* following, to be true: and if wee be thereunto required, will bee ready to make faith of the truth thereof, namely that this was her confession being aliue, and a litle before her death;

Conclusion.

Deare Christians, lay this to heart, namely the cause, and first time, that the Diuell came vnto her, then, euen then when she was cursing, swearing, and blaspheming. The Diuell rageth, and mallice reigneth in the hearts of many. O let it not doe so, for heere you may see the fruites thereof, that it is a playne way to bring you to the Diuell; nay that it brings the Diuell to you: for it seemed that when shee so fearefully did sweare, her oathes did so coniure him, that hee must leaue then his mansion place, and come at this wretches commande and will, which was by her imprecations. Stand on your guard and watch with sobrietie to resist him, the Diuell your aduersary, who waiteth on you continually,

The Conclusion

to subuert you, that so you that doe detest her abhominable wordes, and wayes, may neuer taste of the cup nor wages of shame and destruction, of which she did in this life: from which and from whose power, Lord Iesus saue, and defend thy little flocke.

Amen.

A MOST Certain, Strange, and true Discovery of a WITCH (Wing M2870) is reproduced by permission from the fine copy at The British Library (shelfmark E.69 [9]). The text block of the original measures 144mm × 90mm.

Hard-to-read passages in the original:
A2.16:   learning done, Adam by temptation toucht and tasted
A2.17:   the deceiving apple, so some high learnd & read by the
A2.18:   same temp[t]or that deceived him hath bin insnared to
A2.19:   contract with the Divel; as for example, in the instan-
A2.20:   cing a few, as English Bacon of Oxford, Vandermast of
A2.21:   Holland, Bungy of Germany, Fostus of the same, Francis-
A2.22:   cus the English Monke of Bury, Doctor Blackleach,
A2v.24: being there adiacent, a tall, lean, slender woman, as he

A MOST
Certain, Strange, and true Discovery of a
VVITCH.

Being taken by some of the Parliament Forces, as she was standing on a small planck-board and sayling on it over the River of *Newbury*:

Together with the strange and true manner of her death, with the propheticall words and speeches she used at the same time.

Printed by John Hammond, 1643.

(3)

A TRUE RELATION OF THE
WITCH
in the Army.

Many are in a belief, that this silly sex of women can by no means attaine to that so vile and damned a practise of sorcery, and Witch-craft, in regard of their illiterate-nesse and want of learning, which many men have by great learning done, *Adam* by temptation toucht and tasted the deceiving apple, so some high learnd & read by the same temptor that deceived him hath bin insnared to contract with the Divel; as for example, in the instancing a few, as *English Bacon* of *Oxford*, *Vandermast* of *Holland*, *Bungey* of *Germany*, *Fastus* of the same, *Franciscus* the *English Monke* of *Bury* Doctor *Blackleach*,

A 2   and

(4)

divers others that were tedious to relate of, but how weake women should attain unto it many are incredible of the same, and many too are opposite in opinion against the same, that giving a possibility to their doubtings, that the malice, and inveterate malice of a woman entirely devoted to her revengefull wrath frequenting desolate and desart places, and giving way unto their wished temptation, may have converse with that world roaring Lyon, and covenant and contract upon condition; the like hath in sundry places, and divers times been tried at the Assises of Lancaster, Carlile, Buckingham, and else where, but to come to the intended relation of this Witch or Sorceresse, as is manifest and credibly related by Gentlemen, Commanders, and Captains, of the Earle of Essex his Army.

A part of the Army marching through Newbury some of the Souldiers being scattered by the reason of their loytering by the way, in gathering Nuts, Apples, Plummes, Blackberries, and the like, one of them by chance in clambring up a tree, being pursued by his fellow or Comrade in waggish merriment, jesting one with another, espied on the river being there adjacent, a tall, lean, slender woman, as he supposed, to his amazement, and great terrour treading of the water with her feet, with as much ease and firmnesse as if one should walk or trample, on the earth, wherewith he softly calls, and beckened to his fellowes to behold it, and with all possible speed that could be to obscure them from her sight, who as

conveniently

as they could they did observe, this could be no little amazement unto them you may think to see a woman dance upon the water, nor could all their sights be deluded, though perhaps one might but coming neater to the shore, they could perceive there was a plank or deale overshadowed with a little shallow water that she stood upon, the which did beare her up, anon rode by some of the Commanders who were eye witnesses, as well as they, and were as much astonished as they could be, still too and fro she fleeted on the water, the board standing firm bout upright, indeed I have both heard and read of many that in tempests and on rivers by casualty have beene shipwracked, or cast over board, where catching empty barrells, rudders, boards, or planks have made good shift by the assisting providence of God to get on shore, but not in this womans kind to stand upon the board, turning and winding it which way she pleased, making it pastime to her, as little thinking who perceived her tricks, or that she did imagine that they were the last she ever should show, as we have heard the swan sing before her death, so did this divellish woman, as after plainly it appeared make sport before her death, at last having sufficiently been upon the water, he that deceived her alway did so then, blinding her that she could not at her landing see the ambush that was laid for her, coming upon the shore she gave the board a push, which they plainly perceived, and crossed the river, they searched after her but could not find her she being landed the Commanders beholding her, gave order to lay

hold

hold on her and bring her to them ftraight, the which fome were fearfull, but fome being more venturous then other fome, boldly went to her & feized on her by the armes, demanding what fhe was? but the woman no whit replying any words unto them, they brought her to the Commanders, to whom though mightily fhe was urged fhe did reply as little: fo confulting with themfelues what fhould be done with her, being it fo apparently appear'd fhe was a *Witch*, being loth to let her goe, & as loth to carry her with them, fo they refolved with themfelues, to make a fhot at her, and gave order to a couple of their Souldiers that were approved good marks-men, to charge and fhoot her ftraight, which they prepared to do, fo fetting her boult upright againft a mud banke or wall; two of the Souldiers according to their command made themfelues ready, where having taken aime gave fire and fhot at her as thinking fure they had fped her, but with a deriding and loud laughter at them fhe caught their bullets in her hands and chew'd them, which was a ftronger teftimony then the water, that fhe was the fame that their imaginations thought her for to be, fo refolving with themfelues if either fire or fword or halter were fufficient for to make an end of her, one fet his Carbin clofe unto her breft: where difcharging, the bullet back rebounded like a ball, and narrowly he mift it in his face that was the fhooter: this fo enraged the Gentleman, that one drew out his fword & manfully run at her with all the force his ftrength had power

to

to make, but it prevailed no more then did the shot, the woman still though speeechlesse, yet in a most contemptible way of scorn, still laughing at them, which did the more exhaust their furie against her life, yet one amongst the rest had heard that piercing or drawing bloud from forth the veines that crosse the temples of the head, it would prevail against the strongest sorcery, and quell the force of Witchcraft, which was allowed for triall: the woman hearing this, knew then the Devill had left her and her power was gone, wherefore she began alowd to cry, and roare, tearing her haire, and making pitious moan, which in these words expressed were; And is it come to passe, that I must dye indeed? why then his Excellency the Earle of Essex shall be fortunate and win the field, after which no more words could be got from her; wherewith they immediately discharged a Pistoll underneath her eare, at which she straight sunk down and dyed, leaving her legacy of a detested carcasse to the wormes, her soul we ought not to iudge of, though the evills of her wicked life and death can scape no censure.

FINIS.

This Book is not Printed according to Order.

THE EXAMINATION, CONFESSION, TRIALL, AND EXECUTION (Wing E3712) is reproduced by permission from the fine copy at The British Library (shelfmark E.303.[33]). The text block of the original measures 155mm × 100mm.

THE EXAMINATION, CONFESSION, TRIALL, AND EXECUTION,

Of *Joane Williford, Joan Cariden*, and *Jane Hott*:

Who were executed at *Feversham* in *Kent*, for being Witches, on Munday the 29 of September, 1645.

Being a true Copy of their evill lives and wicked deeds, taken by the Major of *Feversham* and Jurors for the said Inquest.

With the Examination and Confession of *Elizabeth Harris*, not yet executed.

All attested under the hand of ROBERT GREENSTREET, *Major of Feversham*.

LONDON,
Printed for *J. G.* October 2. 1645.

(1)

The Confession of *Joan Williford*, Septemb. 24. 1645. made before the *Major, and other Jurates*.

Shee confessed:

That the divell about seven yeeres agoe did appeare to her in the shape of a little dog, and bid her to forsake God and leane to him: who replied, that she was loath to forsake him. Shee confessed also that shee had a desire to be revenged upon *Thomas Letherland* and *Mary Woodrufe* now his wife. She further said that the divell promised her, that she should not lacke, and that she had money sometimes brought her she knew not whence, sometime one shilling, sometimes eight pence, never more at once; shee called her Divell by the name of *Bunne*. She further saith, that her retainer *Bunne* carried *Thomas Gardler* out of a window, who fell into a backside. She further saith, that neere twenty yeeres since she promised her soule to the divell. She further saith, that she gave some of her blood to the Divell, who wrote the covenant betwixt them: She further saith that the Divell promised to be her servant about twenty yeeres,

A 2 and

and that the time is now almost expired. She further saith that *Iane Hot*, *Elizabeth Harris*, *Ioan Argoll* were her fellowes. She further saith that her Divell told her that *Elizabeth Harris* about six or seven yeeres since curst the Boat of one *Iohn Woodcott*, and so it came to passe. Shee further saith, that the Divell promised her that shee should not sinke being throwne into the water. She further said Goodwife *Argoll* cursed Mr. *Major*, and also *Iohn Mannington*, and said that he should not thrive, and and so it came to passe. She likewise saith, that the Divell sucked twice since she came into the prison, he came to her in the forme of a Muce.

She being brought to the Barre, was asked, *Guilty or not guilty*, she answered, *guilty*.

When she came to the place of execution Mr. Major asked her if she thought she deserved death? to whom she answered, that she had; and that she desired all good people to take warning by her, and not to suffer themselves to be deceived by the Divell, neither for lucre of money, malice, or any thing else, as she had done: but to sticke fast to God, for if she had not first forsaken God, God would not have forsaken her.

The Examination of Joan Cariden *widdow, taken Septemb.* 25. 1645.

THis Examinant saith, that about three quarters of a yeere agoe, as she was in the bed about twelve or one of the clocke in the night there lay a rugged soft thing

thing upon her bosome which was very soft, and she thrust it off with her hand; and she saith that when she had thrust it away she thought God forsooke her, for she could never pray so well since as she could before; and further saith, that shee verily thinkes it was alive.

The second Examination of the said Joan Cariden, *alias* Argoll, *taken the same day before the Major.*

THis Examinant saith, that in the same yeere that this Major was formerly Major the Divell came to her in the shape of a blacke rugged Dog, in the night time, and crept into the bed to her, and spake to her in mumbling language; The next night it came to her againe, and required this examinant to deny God and leane to him, and that then he would revenge her of any one she owed ill will to, and thereupon this examinant promised him her soule upon those conditions; And that about that time the Divell sucked this examinant, and hath divers times since sucked her, and that it was no paine to her.

September 27. 1645.

COnfest upon the examination of *Ioan Carriden* before Master Major, that Goodwife *Hott* told her within these two daies that there was a great meeting at Goodwife *Panterys* house, and that Goodwife *Dadson* was there, and that Goodwife *Gardner* should have been there, but did not come, and the Divell sat at the upper end of the Table.

The

The Examination of Jane Hott *widdow, taken before the Major and Jurates the* 25 *of September,* 1645.

THis examinant confesseth that a thing like a hodg-hog had usually visited her, and came to her a great while agoe, about twenty yeares agoe, and that if it sucked her it was in her sleep, and the paine thereof awaked her, and it came to her once or twice in the moneth and sucked her, and when it lay upon her breast she strucke it off with her hand, and that it was as soft as a Cat.

At her first comming into the Goale she spake very much to the other that were apprehended before her, to confesse if they were guilty; and stood to it very perversely that she was cleare of any such thing, and that if they put her into the Water to try her she should certainely sinke. But when she was put into the Water and it was apparent that she did flote upon the water, being taken forth, a Gentleman to whom before she had so confidently spake, and with whom she offered to lay twenty shillings to one that she could not swim, asked her how it was possible she could be so impudent as not to confesse herselfe, when she had so much perswaded the other to confesse: to whom she answered, That the Divell went with her all the way, and told her that she should sinke; but when she was in the Water he sate upon a Crosse-beame and laughed at her.

These three were executed on Munday last.

The Examination of Elizabeth Harris *the* 26 *of September,* 1645. *before Master Major.*

THis examinant saith, that about 19 yeeres agoe the Divell did appeare to her in the forme of a Muse: she further saith, that she had a desire to be revenged, and the divell told her that she should be revenged; she called the Divell her Impe. She further saith, Goodman *Chilman* of Nueuham said that she stole a Pigge, then she desired that God would revenge her of him, and the man pined away and dyed, and she saw it apparent that her Impe was the cause of that mans death; she further saith, that the Divell bid her to forsake Christ and leane to him, whereupon she saith that she scratched her selfe with her nailes and fetched blood from her breast, and she wiped it with her finger and gave it to her Impe who wrote the covenant with it: she further saith, that a fortnight after the divell sucked her, but she felt no paine. Being demanded how many Witches were in Town? she answered, that were a heavy sentence. She further saith that Goodwife *Dadson,* Ioan Argoe, William Argos *wife,* Goodwife Cox have very bad tongues; She further saith that her Impe did sucke her every three or foure nights; she further saith that her sonne being drowned in Goodman *Woodcots* High she wished that God might be her revenger, which was her watchword to the Divell, and this High was cast away, and she conceives that her wish was the cause of its being cast away: she further saith, that *Ioan Williford* told her, that her Impe said on Wednesday laſt, that though the Boate, (ſhe not knowing what Boat,) went chearfully out, it ſhould not come ſo chearfully home; She ſaith further, that Goodwife *Pantery* did many times make meetings with Goodwife *Williford* and with Goodwife *Hott*; She further ſaith, that Goodwife *Gardner* hath a very ill tongue.

ALL theſe are true coppies of Examination, one whereof is not yet executed, and were taken before me,

Robert Greenſtreet, Major.

FINIS.

Mary Moore, *Wonderfull News from the North* (Wing M2581) is reproduced by permission from the fine copy at The British Library (shelfmark E618.[10]). The text block of the original measures 150mm × 105mm.

Hard-to-read passages in the original

B.24:	the Lord, They being three miles off, in the Holy Island, were sent
B3.28:	up ready to burst, shrinking with her head, as if she feared blowes
B3.29:	then would she be drawne, as in conlvusion fits, till she got that wri-
B3.30:	ting from them that had it, and either burne it in the fire, or chew it in
B3.31:	her mouth, till it could not be discerned. Let any one snatch the paper
B3.32:	from her and hide it as private as he could, she would have gone to the
B3.33:	party and place, still in torment till she got it, and either burne it, or
B3.34:	chewed it, that none could discerne one word she had wrote, then im-
B3.35:	mediately she would have ease: Thus for a moneth or six weekes, eve-
B3.36:	ry other day, with severall torments, and such like expressions conti-
B3.37:	nued; her good things, as she called them, came still and saved her
B3v.6:	first afflicted; ‹but› I
B4.1:	hearing many strange passages, which cannot halfe be remembred. But
B4.8:	her, with her eyes fixt on her objects, wrote this againe, Jo. Hu. Do.
B4.9:	SWI. hath been the death of one deare friend, consumes [an?]other deare
B4.10:	friend, and torments me; for three dayes they have no power, but the
B4.11:	fourth they will torment me: two drops of his or her bloud would
B4.12:	save my life, if I have it not I am undone, for seven yeares to be
B4.13:	tormented before death come. Whilst she was writing the teares
B4.22:	So when this servant told him his message, another being by to wit-
B4.23:	nesse his answer, which was thus: WILLIAM HALL, your Mrs.
B4.24:	knowes as well who hath wrong's her child as I: for the party that
B4.25:	with a troubled minde your Mrs. had concealed all this time, and at
B4.26:	Newcastle in her chamber all alone told you is she that hath done her all
B4.27:	this wrong. The servant answered, God blesse me, could he tell what
B4.28:	his Mistresse said to him, no living soule else present, bidding him re-
B4.29:	veale the party? the Rogue sayd, a great stone is not easily lifted, and
B4.30:	he had one foot in the grave already; repeating many old sayings:
B4.31:	but sayd, DOROTHY SWINOW wife then to Colonell SWINOW,
C4.29:	Lords sake, for Jesus Christs sake; saying I ought to command Justice
Ev.1–Ev.7:	[Northumberland General Sessions of the Peace held at Alnwick, 24 April 1650, before William Selby, George Fenwick and Henry Ogle and others, Justices of the Peace for the county, etc. The names of the jurors...]
Ev. 8:	Johannes Alderton, Ar.

Wonderfull News from the North.

OR, A TRUE
RELATION
OF THE SAD AND
GRIEVOVS TORMENTS,

Inflicted upon the Bodies of three Children of Mr. *George Muschamp*, late of the County of *Northumberland*, by Witch-craft:

AND HOW MIRACULOUSLY IT pleased God to strengthen them, and to deliver them:

As also the prosecution of the sayd Witches, as by Oaths, and their own Confessions will appear, and by the Indictment found by the Jury against one of them, at the Sessions of the Peace held at *Alnwick*, the 24. day of *April*, 1650.

Novemb. 25. 1650.
Imprimatur, JOHN DOVVNAME.

LONDON,
Printed by *T. H.* and are to be sold by *Richard Harper*, at his shop in Smithfield, 1650.

A Preface to the Reader.

Courteous Reader:

With a sad heart I present unto thee the ensuing Discourse, not out of malice to the person of any, but to shew the great mercy of Almighty God, and to magnifie his glorious Name for preservation of Me and my Children, and for delivering us from those extreame torments and miseries wherewith by Diabolicall meanes we have beene afflicted. In prosecution of which sad Story, I have delivered nothing but Truth, as is testified by very many people of great Ranke and Quality, as also by Divines, Phisitians, and numbers of other people, who have beene sad Spectators of our Miseries. Beseeching the Almighty God to deliver thee and all good Christian People from the like Miseries, and Torments, which have happened unto Me, and my poore innocent Children.

Thine, Mary Moore.

A briefe Description of Mr. GEORGE MUSCHAMPS *Childrens unnaturall Tryalls, from the Yeare of our Lord,* 1645. *Untill Candlemas,* 1647. *The time of their Releasement.*

Irst in Harvest, some two Moneths before MI-CHAELMAS, about four or five of the Clock in the afternoone, Mistris MARGARET MUSCHAMP suddainely fell into a great Trance, her Mother being frighted, called Company, and with much adoe recovered her; as soone as the childe looked up, cryed out, deare Mother, weepe not for me; for I have seene a happy Sight, and heard a blessed sound; for the Lord hath loved my poore soule, that he hath caused his blessed Trumpet to sound in my eares, and hath sent two blessed Angels to receive my sinfull soule. O weepe not for me, but rejoyce, that the Lord should have such respect to so sinfull a wretch as I am, as to send his heavenly Angels to receive my sinfull soule, with many other divine expressions: Calling good Mother send for my deare Brother, and honest Mr. HUET, perhaps the Lord will give me leave to see them; that faithfull man may helpe my soule forward in praying with me, and for me; for we know the prayers of the faithfull are very powerfull with the Lord. They living three miles off, in the Holy Island, were sent

B for,

for, and with what speed might be, came; she all this while in her Heavenly Rapture, uttering such words as were admirable to the beholders, her Brother and the Minister came to her, which heard her expresse much joy. The Minister exhorting her, to whom she gave such satisfaction, that he blessed God in shewing such mercy to a childe of eleaven yeares old. All that night she continued, apprehending these Heavenly Visions, the Minister praying with her, and for her, as she desired him. After she fell into a little rest, and when she awaked, remembred not any thing she had sayd or done.

Witnesses to this first,
Mr. HURT. Minister.
Mrs. KENADY, her two Brothers, and two Sisters, with her Mother.
GEORGE ROBINSON, and his Wife.
KATHERINE GRAME.

ODNEL SELBY, and his Wife.
MARGARET DIKSON, with divers others in the house then present.

After this she continued well till Candlemas.

ON Candlemas Eve, betwixt the houres of one and two in the afternoone, being the Sabboth, her mother with most of her servants being at Church, onely her two Brothers, and two Sisters with her, she was saddainely striken with a great deale of torment, called for a little beere, but ere they cou'd come with it, the use of her tongue was gone, with all her limbs, pressing to vomit, and such torments, that no eyes could looke on her without compassion: Her mother comming home with a sad heart, beheld her childe, using what meanes could be, but no ease, till eleaven or twelve a Clock at night she fell into a slumber and slept till six in the morning; as soon as Berwick gates were opened her mother sent for Phisitions, both of soule and body, with the Lady SELBY, Colonell FENVVICKS Widow, with other friends, who forthwith came to behold this sad sight, with many others that came to the childe waking out of her sleepe, which was without present torment, but had lost the use of both limbs, tongue, stomacke, onely smiled on them, and signed, that we could understand she had all her other senses very perfect, but would let nothing come within

within her mouth of any nourishment, for her Jawes were almost closed: Physitians gave their advice, with other friends; and what could be had, was gotten for her: but her signes from the beginning were, away with these Doctors Drugs, God had layd it on her, and God would take it off her.

She beg'd that Mr. BALSOM, Mr. STROTHER, and Mr. HUET, wou'd be her Doctors in their earnest prayers to the Lord for her; for she was confident there was no helpe for her, but from Heaven: yet her mother to her great expences neglected no lawfull meanes that could be used. About 12. a clock she had a tormenting fit before all the company; but it was not above an houre: but from that time till Whitson Eve, being 16. weekes, she slept as well in the nights, as any one, but as soone as she awaked in the morning begun her torment: First three or foure houres every day, encreasing till it came to eight houres, every houre a severall torment, such strong cruell ones that cannot be exprest, as many with weping eyes beheld it, that Ministers would pray by her till the sad object would make them leave her to the Lord, expecting nothing but death. Sir WILLIAM SELBY his Lady, the Comtesse LENDRIK, the Lady HAGGARSTON, with many others, would look, till sorrow would mak them forbeare: Yet as soone as these torments were over, the child would instantly smile, and make signes she felt no paine at all: so lying quietly till the next morning, onely we wet her lips with a little milke and water; for nothing she would let come within her jawes, but would smile and shew her Armes and breast, and say God fed her with Angels food: for truely all the 16. weekes fast, did not appeare to diminish her fatnesse or favour any thing at all.

On Whitson Eve in the morning she had eight hours bitter torment, in the afternoone her mother being abroad, left her Husbands Brothers Daughter Mrs ELIZABETH MUSCHAMP with her, who made signes to her to carry her into the Garden, in her mothers absence; her Cozen casting a mantle about her, gave her her desire, and sate in the Garden with her on her knee, who in the bringing downe had so little strength in her neck, that her head hung wagging downe; but was not set a quarter of an houre, till shewing some signes to her Cozen, bolted off her knee, ran thrice about the Garden, expressing a shrill voyce, but did not speake presently: she that was brought down in this sad condition came up staires on her owne legs, in her Cozens hands: Captaine FALSET, his Wife and his Daughter being then in the house, did behold this miraculous mercy of the Lord done to this child: her mother being at Berwick, three miles off, was sent for, and imparted her joyfulnesse unto the Lady SELBY, and good Mr. BALSOME, whose prayers with the rest (as the child sayd) had prevailed with God for mercy. When her mother came home, her Daughter which she left in so bad a condition, came with her cloathes on, down to the gate, calling Mother, Mother welcome home. Now the Mothers joy may be imagined, but not expressed; desiring her mother presently to send many thanks to Mr. BALSOME, and Mr. STROTHER for that the Lord had answered their prayers for her. The next day being the Sabbath, she beg'd on her mother to returne thanks to the glorious God, who never failed any that trusted in him, and her self would ride into the Holy Iland and joyne in thanks and prayers to the Lord, with Mr. HUET, Sir THOMAS TEMPEST, Captaine SHAFT, with the rest of the parish that feared God; She by Gods power did it the next Thursday, being a Lecture in Berwick, her selfe, and with Mr. BALSOME and Mr. STROTHER gave glory to the Lord for his never forgotten mercy to her; though her flesh did not diminish, yet her strength was but weake, and her stomack by degrees came to her again, and for seven or eight weeks was very well: then her mother removed to Berwick, where the Garison being kept, the discharge of a Musket would cause her to fall into very great extasies, being there severall times for 24 hours space, she would be suddenly taken with her former torments. For three weeks space she lost her stomack, and all her limbs, and of a sudden recoverd all again, not remembring what she had either done or suffered. To avoyd this inconvenience, her mother removed from Berwick, and carried her in one of these sad conditions one mile off Berwick, where she continued seven weekes more in these afflictions.

Her eldest Brother upon S. Johns day at night in the Christmas following betwixt the houres of 1. and 2. was taken exceedingly ill, that it was thought he would not live: the next morning he was a little eased of his extremity and pain, but both his stomack and the use of his legs taken from him, so that he was forced to have help to put on his cloathes, was lifted into a chaire where he sat all day long, but could

neither

neither eate nor drinke any thing, but a little milke or water, or sowre milke. He consumed away to nothing, yet not heart-sicke; but would reason, talke and laugh with any friend as if nothing ayled him. His mother now being prest downe with sorrow, sent to the Doctors both at Newcastle, Durham, and Edenborough, not doubting or suspecting any unnaturall Disease; the Physitians all agreed by the course of nature he could not live a month to an end, which was sad newes to his sorrowfull Mother, God knowes.

After two or three weekes she had another fit of her former torments: after she had lyen three or foure weekes in her extremity, begun, and cryed the Rogue, never till then, offering a word in her torments, but as if some were striking at her; she seemed to save her selfe with hands and bedcloaths from blowes, deciphering a wretched creature as we all after knew by her description: Sometimes he would fight with her in the shape of a Dragon, of a Bear, a Horse, or Cow: Many fancies she did expresse; and good things, she sayd, fought for her, and still got the better of him: The enemies Weapons were a Club, a Staffe, a Sword, and Dagger; her good things got them all, as she thought, and after the wretch, she thought, got the Dagger againe.

Now when she fixt her eyes upon her objects, no action you could use would move either eyes or gesture, till she came out of her fits, then did not remember any thing she either did or sayd: After a while she would make her hand goe on her brest, as if she would write, with her eyes fixt on her object; they layd paper on her brest, and put a pen with inke in her hand, and she not moving her eyes, writ, Jo. Hu. Do. Swo. have beene the death of one deare friend, consume another, and torment mee; whilst she was writing these words, she was blowne up ready to burst, shrinking with her head, as if she feared blowes: then would she be drawne, as in convulsion fits; till she got that writing from them that had it, and either burne it in the fire, or chew it in her mouth, till it could not be discerned. Let any one snatch the paper from her and hide it as private as he could, she would have gone to the party and place, still in torment till she got it, and either burne it, or chewed it, that none could discerne one word she had wrote, then immediately she would have ease: Thus for a moneth or six weekes, every other day, with severall torments, and such like expressions continued; her good things, as she called them, came still and saved her from her enemies.

These

(6)

These words written, and her other expressions, caused her sad mother to have very contradictive thoughts: So that one day her Neece MUSCHAMP that had been her Companion in most of these sad conditions, being troubled to thinke what this childs writing should mean; sayd to her Aunt, there is one that I have ever feared since my cousin MARGARET was first afflicted; but I dare not name her whom I have suspected: Her Aunt answers, and onely one I suspect: And these Letters make me tremble to thinke on it; but the Lord pardon our thoughts, if we thinke amisse: So revealing our thoughts one to another, and pitcht both on DOROTHY SVVINOVV. Her Neece saith, Mrs. SVVINOVV came to see the childe when you were away, and spake harshly of you, and besides the childes looking on her, which she never did on any else, makes me feare her: Her Aunt answered, if she could doe me hurt, and not her owne soule, I feare her more then any else, but that cannot bee; so Lord pardon us, if we thinke amisse, and let us not speake any further of her.

This childes mothers occasions called her to Newcastle, which journey was not pleasant, leaving so sad a house at home, and her childes writing, and her Neeces thoughts, and her owne, made her very sad, that her servant wondering to see such a change, presumed to aske the cause of it. she knowing her servant to be trusty, revealed the suspected party to him, no living soule being by; her occasions being dispatched returned home.

But in her absence her Daughter had beene quite distracted, run up and downe with a staffe in her hand, saying she would kill the Rogue: in this rage she apprehended her good things (for so she called them) in the likenesse of a Dove, and a Partridge, and begun and sung, *Judge and revenge my cause O Lord*: Next, *How long wilt thou forget me Lord; shall I never be remembred?* And concluded, *Behold and have regard, ye servants of the Lord*; and so came out of her fit, not remembring any thing, either done or sayd; she never having any of these Psalmes by heart, or any booke by her, nor as yet any voice to sing them to this day.

By her at that time was my Neece MUSCHAMP, Mr. MOORES six sonnes, and his Daughter, with my owne children and servants, and divers neighbours. After my comming home, she fell into another of these strange fits; the Minister of Tweedmouth being by, seeing and

hearing

hearing many strange passages, which cannot halfe be remembred. But part of her discourse was; that if she had two drops of his blood or hers, within ten dayes, it would save her life; if not death long comming, but torment perpetually.

Divers of these fits she had, in every one expressing their bloud would save her life; from ten dayes to six, from six to three, which was on a Saturday, being heavily tormented, her tongue taken from her, with her eyes fixt on her objects, wrote thus againe, Jo. Hu. Do. SVVI. hath been the death of one deare friend, consumes another deare friend, and torments me; for three dayes they have no power, but the fourth they will torment me: two drops of his or her bloud would save my life, if I have it not I am undone, for seven yeares to be tormented before death come. Whilest she was writing the teares comming downe her face, still saving her selfe in this bitter agony, as it were, from her enemies blows.

As soone as her mother came from Newcastle, she sent (that servant she revealed her minde to at Newcastle) to one JOHN HUTTON, he was one it was suspected that could do more then God allowed of; bidding him confesse who had wrong'd her child, or she would apprehend him: her child in her extremity writing the two first Letters of his name, with anothers.

So when this servant told him his message, another being by to witnesse his answer, which was thus: WILLIAM HALL, your Mrs. knowes as well who hath wrong'd her child as I: for the party that with a troubled minde your Mrs. had concealed all this time, and at Newcastle in her chamber all alone told you is she that hath done her all this wrong. The servant answered, God blesse me, could he tell what his Mistresse said to him, no living soule else present, bidding him reveale the party? the Rogue sayd, a great stone is not easily lifted, and he had one foot in the grave already: repeating many old sayings: but sayd, DOROTHY SVVINOVV wife then to Colonell SVVINOVV, was the party that had done all the mischiefe to her child, and was the cause of all her further crosses.

This answer being brought, and her childs last writing, three dayes they had no power, the fourth to torment; and the Sabbath being one of the three, the monday following, her mother, her Neece MUSCHAMP, her son in Law EDVVARD MOORE, GEORGE ARMORER,

RER, WILLIAM HALL, and WILLIAM BARD, rid to Etherston thinking Mr. WALTON to have beene a Justice of the Peace; but was nott then she with her company went directly to Sunderland, where Jo. HUTTON dwelt, and sent for him, who forthwith came, and though they had never seen him, but by the childes description, nor he them; he knew them all naming their names; and fell downe on his knees for to pray for the child: but her mother bidding him rise, she desired none of his prayers, but tell her how he came to know what she spake to her servant all alone, so far off, he repeated before all the company what he had formerly spoken.

She sayd her eldest son was very ill too, the Lord blesse him, not thinking that he was wronged; but the Rogue answered, one was the cause of both: she in a maze sayd, I had a sister that dyed in a restlesse sicknesse, God grant she was not wronged too: the Rogue sayd, Mistresse, Mistresse, Mistresse, one is the cause of all, envy nothing will satisfie, but death. Said she is this possible? Mistresse sayd he my life is in your hand, but I'le maintaine DOROTHY SVVINOVV was the death of the Lady MARGERY HAMBLETON, the consuming of your son, and the tormentor of your daughter, and the cause of all your evill; and if you would have my hearts bloud take it, for my life is in your power, none speaking of bloud to him. She told him the child had wrote two drops of his or her bloud would save her life; and if the Devill had left so much in him, she would (if it pleased the Lord) have it ere they parted. The wretch using still Godly words and his prayers, desired to take his bloud privately, that none should see; so the child nickt him halfe a dozen times in the forehead, but no bloud appeared; then he put forth his right arme, and that was not till her mother threatned his heart-bloud should goe before she wanted it; then he layd his thumb on his arme, and two drops appeared, which she wip'd off with a paper, the which she had writ the words in, and bid him farewell: he bid them ride softly, they had both tide and time enough, it being a fine quiet day; of a sudden as soon as they were on horse back it grew very boystrous, that they had much adoe to sit on their horses; riding fast, at Sunderland Towns end, came two white Lambs to them, and kept close with their horses till they came to Bambrough, being two long miles, neither sheep nor lambs neere them; the water was very deep, yet being venterous they rid it over.

On

On Munday night she fell into a heavenly Rapture, rejoycing that ever she was borne, for these two drops of blood had saved her life, otherwise she had beene seaven yeares in torment without any ease, or death had come: behold her two Angels (which she was bold to call them) on her right hand, and her Tormenters on her left, setting her selfe with a majestick carriage, her words so punctuall and discreet, that it was admirable to the beholders.

Saying her Angels bid her now be bold to speake out, looking on her left hand, saying, thy name is JOHN HUTTON, and hers is DOROTHY SVVINOVV, she hath beene the death of my Aunt HAMBLETON, the consumer of my Brother, and the tormenter of me; she knowing my Aunts estate was but for life, and her onely sonne had marryed FAUSETS daughter, who to enjoy the estate, he having but one sonne, was the cause of yong JAMES FAUSETS unnaturall fits: But thinking Mr. FAUSET would follow her more strictly there, then we could doe here, let him alone, to be the more vehement with us, every fit promising me ease, if I would consent to lay it on my mother; but I will never consent, but if it were possible indure more torment; since she is all that the Lord of his goodnesse hath left to take care of us five fatherlesse children; except our Father in Heaven, which protects her for our sakes.

Thus for two heures together she continued in a very heavenly religious Discourse with these Angels, rejoycing that she had got two drops of blood; saying, if her Brother had as much, it would save his life also; witnesse to these words were Mr. MOORE of Spittle, his six Sonnes and a Daughter, Mr. ELIZABETH MUSCHAMP, Mrs. MARGARET SELBY, ANNE SELBY, and GEORGE LEE, who was almost cast away comming into Barwick Harbour in a Ship by that fearfull tempest which HUTTON raised: GEORGE ARMORER, WILLIAM HALL, WILLIAM BEARD, HENRY ORDE, with divers Neighbours, all admiring the Lords great power expressed in that afflicted childe. Her mother being desirous to have some small quantity of HUTTONS blood, rode the next day to him with two servants, who brought him to her sonne, he not being able to goe to him. He acknowledged still his life was in her hands, and came riding behinde one of her servants home to the Spittle where she dwelt, and being brought before Mr. MOORE, confirmed all that he had formerly confessed,

confessed, and withall sayd, Mrs. SVVINOVV had two bad women about her, the Millers and the Websters Wives, who had beene the death of Jo. CUSTERD and his Wife, with many other things of their wickednesse: That night he desired to goe to rest, and when he pleased to call him, he would confesse further to him alone; the next day came Mr. WILLIAM ORDE, Mr. BROAD Minister, with Mr. HEBERIN, and EDVVARD SAUFIELD, who heard all this confirmed, and so the mother tooke her sonne in her armes to the place where the wretch was, and got his blood.

He stayed there seven or eight dayes, and yet Mr. MOORE had never power to examine him any more, the wretch still desiring to be gone, the mother in the presence of MARGARET SELBY, MARGARET ORDE, and WILLIAM BEARD, charged him, that although he had beene long the Devills servant, at last to be but a Bridge for Gods creatures to goe over, in confessing the truth; who answered, Mistris, Mistris, If I were a yong man, able to endure all the torments that should be layed on me, I would take my death that Mrs. DOROTHY SVVINOVV was the death of the Lady HAMBLETON, the consumer of your sonne, and the Tormentor of your Daughter, and the cause of all your other troubles.

Now whilest he was there the Girle was never troubled, but he was not past the Townes end, till she fell into a terrible fit; saying, DOROTHY SVVINOVV with two Witches more were come to torment her worse then ever HUTTON did, and the one was a yong woman, and the other an old: So that till they had Justice of DOROTHY SVVINOVV, her mother and they should never be at peace: Upon this her mother rid to Justice FOSTER of Nuham, and upon Oath gave Information against both HUTTON and Mrs. SVVINOVV, to apprehend them, who after delayes apprehended him, and sent him to Newcastle Goale, but not her, though it will appeare she was three severall times in his company after he had the Information upon Oath, whereof he gave her a Coppy, with the Coppy of HUTTONS Examination, but would never let Mrs. MUSCHAMP see it; seeing that delay, she spoke with a Durham Justice at Bellford, which not being in the County, and in haste he could not grant her a Warrant to apprehend the sayd Mrs. SVVINOVV; but bid Mr. FOSTER doe Justice, which is not yet done.

The

The Girle having many tormenting fits, in the midst of which her Angels alwayes appearing to her, banishing the Witches, which she apprehended; the Girle would cry out and relate to her Angels how she by the two Witches had been tormented, forcing her to get the information, whereof her mother kept a Coppy: so that let her mother give the paper to whom she would, or laye it any where, the child would goe to either place or party most strangely. As soone as her Angels departed, her torments leaving her, she told them that her enemies would have killed her: but justly might she sing the 35. Ps *Plead thou my cause O Lord, &c.* Repeating the first part thereof so sensibly and distinctly, that the Ministers there present admired to heare it. As likewise her declaring the death of the Rogue HUTTON in prison before it was knowne there, saying if he had been urged he would have discovered the other 2. Witches; foretelling many strange truths, appointing divers meetings with her Angels, such a day and such an houre, to consult with them what should become of her brother, and what punishment her enemies should have, bidding every one they should not so much as looke after her, for if they did it would anger her Angels, and undoe her, for there were some strange Angels besides her owne to meet her; this being the fourth meeting with them, and it would declare all, saying she must have all cleane cloathes about her; for this day or to morrow she must meet them under such a tree in the Garden: After comming out of her fit, she remembred not any thing what was done or sayd.

Her mother observing her words, which hitherto had beene so remarkable, clothed her childe all in white, and freely commended her to the Lord, watching his glorious time in the afternoone, being in a walk under a tree with her Brothers and sisters; suddenly she gave a great shrike, and skipt over a double ditch and another, and run to the Garden doore. Her eldest sister came to her mother saying, MARGRET is gone to her Angels meeting, who with hast ran with the key of the Garden doore, where her childe was standing, beating at it, saying, I come, I come: she opened the doore and left her to her protector, and hastily went to the other side of the house to secure that part of the Garden: but (alas) ere she came, a wicked creature set on by the enemies instigation, had been looking after her, and her childe wringing her hands, weeping bitterly, as if she could have torne her flesh from the bones, or haire off her head, saying who was here? what wicked creature had stayd her blessed Angels from her; and for three houres together tooke on grievously, her mother weeping with her, begging of the Lord not to punish the innocent for the wickeds fault. After some time the child went into the Garden againe, where finding one of her Angels, she sayd, Lord, it was not my fault: but well is me that you will come unto me! but (alas) where are the rest? Her mother being within, hearing these words, A quarter of a yeare (a long time to be without comfort) still weeping: Then she had this Answer from her Angels, that for twelve weeks they would not visibly appeare to her. This she remembred for three dayes, and related to her brothers and sisters, and the rest of the houshold the shape of those Angels: which were bodyed like Birds, as big as Turkies, and faces like Christians, but the sweetest creatures that ever eyes beheld: one of the strange ones came flying over the trees with a sweet voyce, and gave her notice the rest were come; which she found most true. Two or three lighted upon the ground, and the rest with the heavenliest voyces that ever were heard, with a resolution to declare the truth of all. And if the Justices, and Judges at the Assizes would not doe justice, her owne two Angels (who were alwayes to her like a Dove and a Partridge) would visibly, to the admiration of all the beholders, appear like a man and a woman, and justifie the truth, if the wicked wretch had not scared them away. But now the one of her Angels bid her have a care she were neither frighted nor angred for twelve weeks, in which time they would not come to her; but in the meane time her enemy wou'd make every third fit a terrible one, which was most true.

In the meane time Colonel SVVINOVV dyed, and she comes into the Countrey, and because FOSTER would doe no justice, I got her apprehended in Berwick; she made such friends that it was a greater freedome to her then she had formerly from all other Lawes, and went at pleasure. The Girle with her mother being one Sabbath day at Berwick Church, comming along the Bridge with her Husbands son, and daughter; DOROTHY SVVINOVV being at the farther end thereof, the Girle never seeing her but in her fits, knew her and was ready to fall downe in her mothers hand, crying yonder is the wofull thiefe; her mother knowing it true, sayd now to the Girle it is not she, who
answered

answered, I have seen her a hundred times to my smart, it is she: her mother troubled much at the sight too, would have had the Girle back, but her desire was to be at home, who was no sooner come in, but she fell Into a terrible fit, for two houres long; sometimes her tongue drawne in within her throat, other whiles hanging over her chin on her breast. Sad and heavy sights were seen in her afflictions, still bidding all that were by her see the wicked Wretch DOROTHY SVVINOVV with the two Witches at her back, saying she would not let her goe back to Berwick, lest the Justices should have been witnesses themselves; but let her come home, where she knew all their hearts were hardened: for alas, she sayd I have two weeks and two dayes yet before my Comforters come, which made her enemies thus cruell, that if it were in her power to take their lives she would but the Lords preserving power would never leave them who suffered these torments for his owne glory and their soules health) saying, ours were but the corrections of a loving Father to shew his great power in his weakest children, rejoycing exceedingly that he thought her (a sinfull creature) worthy so much happinesse, accounting it more joy to see her blessed Angels then all the world could afford, thanking God especially for making her a watch over her mother, brothers, and sisters, and would foretell strange things before they happened.

When her 12. weekes were past, the very day and houre came divers to see the Event, and waited with patience her appoynted time, which was the very minute of the houre of the day 12. weekes, they were scared from her, Mr. BROAD, Minister, Mr. STEVENS, Physitian, Mrs. MUSCHAMP, and Mrs. HAGARSTON, besides their owne Neighbours were Witnesses, hearing her expresse much joy to meete with those long absent deare friends, relating the intention some had to looke after them againe; so apprehending them in the Chamber, where the Spectators heard her for two houres, most divinely and heavenly discourse with them, answering and replying to that religious discourse, praying for her enemy DOROTHY SVVINOVV, with the teares running downe her face, that if the Lord had mercy in store to grant her it, lamenting the sad condition she had run her soule into, for satisfying her malice to lessen her hope of eternity, making such a description betweene hell torments and heavenly joyes, as that no Divine on earth could have gone beyond her: Crying out for Justice, saying, if she

C 3   were

were in hold as a Fellon ought to be, her power would be gone, and their torments eased; but now with much joy she blest God her Angels would never leave her againe, whilst they were in affliction; saying, she would go to the Judges (and desired to carry her brother there to) and begge for Justice; if she got it, her brother should come home as well as ever he was, she no more tormented, and there should be no more hard heartednesse against her mother, which the Lord knowes was such without any just cause, that her passion is by Gods power beyond imagination: Every fit she spake to this effect, till the Sizes came: in her fit her brother asked her if it were possible that he could ride that could neither go or stand; she answered that the Lord would inable him, therefore he should goe, and her Angels would goe along with them, and bring them safe back againe.

So their Mother not daring to disobey such divine commands, whose confidence doth wholly depend upon Gods providence from Heaven, rid behinde her sonne, and came to the Judge, relating her sad condition; he heard her, but being falsely informed, did not resent it: she went to the Justices to remove DOROTHY SWINOWS body to the County where the act was committed: they pretended ignorance, the childrens mother went with them to a Counsellour to instruct them, whose answer was he would not meddle in it: Yet these dejectments did not drive her from an undoubted confidence in an all sufficient God; the next day betweene one and two of the Clock in the afternoone the Girle suddainely had a fit and after her torments her Angels appeared unto her, to them she complaines, saying, no Justice abroad, no Peace at home, what should become of her mother? for that Godlesse thiefe DOROTHY SWINOW, by the instigation of the Divell, had hardned the heart of both Judges and Justices against her, and now at this instant (sayd she) is using meanes to harden her husbands heart against her too (which she knowes will be cruellest to her of all) and withall begun to consume her eldest sister, and that she would this night, or to morrow morning go to the Judge, begge once more for Justice; if she got it, her Brother with the rest should be well, if not, worse then ever; saying, if the Judge denyed her it, it would not be well with him; this was part of her two houres discourse.

Witnesse

Witnesses the Chamber full, amongst which was,

Colonel SIPTHORP, and his Wife.
Colonel RODDAM.
Captain TOMPSON, his Brother and two Sisters.
Mr ANDERSON, and Mr. SWADWELL.
Mrs. CLETHER.
Mrs. ALLGOOD.
Dr. GENISON.

BEfore she was out of her fit came Dr. GENISON, who invited the mother with her children to his house, being the next house to the Judges Chamber, in regard the Girles first appoyntment was alwayes kept ; so after her supper sent to see if it were more convenient to waite upon the Judge that night, or the next morning: the answer was returned that night was fittest : So Dr. CLETER and his wife, with Dr. GENISON and his, went along with the mother and their children thither, there was a great many spectators to see the Event.

Thus being set downe in the chamber, her mother began her former suit, in begging Justice : his answer was, that that which belonged unto the County Palatine of Durham, belonged not unto him : So she requested him in his returne back, either to doe it, or else give order to the Justices in the County to apprehend her ; of a suddaine the Girle fell into a fit, relating before them all DOROTHY SWINOWS malice from the beginning, the cause of the troubles that broke Sir Ro. HAMBLETONS heart, the death of his Lady, and how she sought still by evill meanes to take away her mothers life, when the Lord would not permit that, got leave first to torment her, then to consume her brother, and now hath begun to consume her eldest sister, and harden her Father in Lawes heart, to make her mothers life more sorrowfull, with her hands up, and eyes fixed upon her objects, begged Justice for the Lords sake, for Jesus Christs sake ; saying I ought to command Justice by the Lawes of the Realme, in the name of our Sov-raigne Lord the King, but I beg not in the name of any mortal man, but in the name of the King of Kings, Justice for Christs sake, Justice for his mercies sake, if we have but ordinary Justice; which ought not to be denyed to the poorest creature who demands it, my brother that sits there shall goe home as well as ever he did, I no more tormented, my mother no

more

more afflicted, and my sisters torments at an end: if we have no justice my torments shall be doubled, my brother worse then ever he was, and my sister (which she hath this day begun to torment) worse then any of us, and my mothers afflictions, by the hardning of folks hearts against her will be unsufferable; but the Lords preserving mercy will never leave them who depend upon his providence; but it will be worse for them who deny us justice then for us. These words with many more significant expressions, that the Judge thought she feigned: but as soon as she was out of her fit, did not know what was past, as all the beholders did see, onely an innocent bashfull Girle, without any confidence at all when she was out of her fits. So her mother returned home with them, where she found her other Girle began to consume.

That night she came home the Girle fell into a fit, pressing to vomit, but nothing came up but a piece of Fir-stick full of crooked pinnes: after her Angels came, she cryed out of the Judges injustice, saying, now the enemy when she sees she can have no justice, strived to choake her with these things, being stones, coles, brick, Lead, straw, quills full of pins, with straw full of pins, tow, and Virginall wire, all full of pins; one great stone for three weekes together came alwayes to her throat and went back again, till at the last the Lord brought it up. She bid watch with her brother three weeks; for they would if they could either cut his throat in the night, or else burne him with fire; therefore let the Watchers be very wakefull, and carefull, so blessed be God they were, and did heare as it were knives sharpning on the staires, and 3 severall times fire was found in the roome one night, like to have burnt them, but by Gods mercyes were saved. She sayd now DOROTHY SWINOW was seeking a new way to take away her mothers life; for she was consuming the child within her, and withall bad them watch with her brother and sister that night twelve month they began to torment him (which was Saint Johns day at night) betwixt the houres of 1. and 2. in the morning, and that very moment of the houre they would seek to take his life and the use of his sisters legs, if Christians prayers and diligent watching did not prevent them; so it pleased the Lord to move the hearts of good friends to watch with them till the houre came.

The Girle then had her fit; and cryed out, the Grand Witch Meg is come to the doore with a lighted Candle in each hand, pray on one halfe houre longer, and their power will be gone, who observed her request, there was a suddaine smell of brimstone, but nothing seene by any; but here are some of their names that were witnesses to most of her tryalls, and first them that prayed by her.

Mr. BROAD.	Mr. EDVVARD MOORE'S six
Mr. EDVVARD ORDE.	Sonnes, and one Daughter.
Mr. GEORGE ATHERLONY.	With divers others, which were too tedious to relate.

After this her Brother and Sister continued still consuming, and she every other day falling into her fits, and after torment her Angels alwayes appearing unto her, she still declares that DOROTHY SVVINOVV hardened the hearts of all that her mother had to deale with, sayd, it should be worse and worse, till of an instant the Lord should make her greatest enemies her greatest friends; declaring how that if she were in hold her paine were gone, as well as HUTTONS was for telling her owne releasement a quarter of a yeare before it came; saying, it was neither for her owne desires or her owne ease, that the Lord released her, but to helpe her mother when she could not helpe her selfe, which was most true to her great griefe and sorrow, but much joy to thinke that the Lord should not onely foretell it, but inable her own to helpe her: She still expecting justice, sent these strange things the Girle cast off her stomack to Durham, which could scarce be believed; yet by chance one being by at the casting of them, which was there present, got a Warrant to apprehend DOROTHY SVVINOVV, and served it her owne hands, with many contradictions ere it was done: Where DOROTHY SVVINOVV came into a chamber in the Constables house, which afterwards she confessed was for feare of taking her blood, which was never in the others thoughts: Yet obeyed not that Warrant, till a second, then went but onely and put in bayle, as though it had beene for an ordinary fault, which the Girle in her fits cryed out of, saying, that still gave her further power to worke her wickednesse. Still all this quarter the Girl in her fits desired them to watch with her, on Candlemas Eve, and they should not thinke their labour lost, and

D   betwixt

betwixt the houres of one and two the next day the glory of God should appeare, her mother being confident of the Lords mercy, gave notice to all that came nigh her; so some that feared God came to see the Event, which releasement being writ from her owne mouth, will confirme these warnings of her former trialls, which have all with much patience beene gone thorow, that the preserving mercies of the most glorious God, who never failes those that depend upon his most firme promises was never more declared on earth then in the weakest of his creatures, preserved by a gratious God, to whom let all that read and heare these unexpressible mercies, give all Glory, Honour, Laud, and Praises.

The Expressions of MARGARET MUSCHAMP *when she was in her last extreame fit, upon the second day of* FEBRUARY, 1647.

THey thought because their time was but short, to have tormented me worse then ever, but I defie them.

I have reason to blesse God more for his mercies to me, then I thinke ever sinfull creature had.

Both my torments are at an end, and those fearefull sights I doe not now see, though it hath pleased God to suffer and let them have power to torment me, yet I was never without comfort.

My time was sad when I had no comfort; but I thanke God who hath given me patience.

I blesse God who never suffered the Devill to have so much power, as to cause me blaspheme his name, or to speake words to offend him.

It is a great mercy that he granted me patience to endure my payne; if it had pleased God I should have beene content as well with torment as releasement.

To her Angels.

Because I shall have no more torment, shall not I see your faces againe? That's sad to me, that's more griefe to me, I had rather endure my paine; that's more griefe ten thousand times; but since it's Gods will, I am as well content with the one as the other, I still trust in God

he

he will send you to protect and watch over us.

I have endured my paines a great while, it is two yeares agoe yesterday; yet I blesse God for it, alwayes with much patience, my paine hath beene very vehement for the time, yet I blesse God I did never speake wordes to offend him: I confesse I doe not deserve it, I deserve no such thing, rather Judgement, not such Godly Chasticement: since he granted them power, he never left me to my selfe.

Is this the last farewell? If it had been Gods will, I had rather indured all the torments could be put to a creature.

But since it hath pleased God it should be so, I am content, the thing that's his will, the Lord grant that it never be sorrowfull to me, but make his will my will, that we may never repine.

He knowes the secrets of all hearts.

As for that wicked woman, if she had had any fear of God, she would have thought that though she had done it never so secretly, yet God would finde it out: She should have thought no such thing; but where the Divell gets entrance, his temptations are very strong.

These torments are more welcome to me, then if I had been in my perfect health; if I had not knowne what torments had been, what pain had been, I should never have seen such joyfull sights: these are more joyfull to me then all the paine.

Our paine, what's all our pain? what's all the pain on earth? Gods mercy is above the Divels power.

Their time is limited.

They sought my mothers life, but could not get it.

Oh! to think of Hells torments which she hath run her soule into, that's more torment then all ours. It's comfort for me, joy for me, that God hath showne his power, that God hath given the Divell power to torment, I care not what the Divell can doe; I defie all the Divels in Hell, for where the Divell hath any power, he triumphs as much as he can, though he triumph and we are weake, God is strong, his power is not lessened.

That wicked woman DOROTHY SVVINOVV was the cause of the death of my Aunt MARGERY HAMBLITON, she was the cause of those troubles, which she thought should have broke my Aunts heart, but they broke Sir ROBERTS, that the estate might fall to her sonne: She was the cause of JAMES FAUCETS unnaturall fits, but the let him alone, because she knew that if he came to London he would follow her more strictly then we can here.

She set two Witches more to torment us: Jo. HUTTON, that dyed in prison was my great tormenter, these Witches have begun my sisters torment, though our torments have been more long, yet her time hath been most sad, because she wanted comfort: though I have had my paines, I never wanted comfort.

She hath entred into the Divels service, ought she not to think of the torment of her soule?

If it had not been thus with us, we should have despised the merceyes of God, our comfort is for joy in heaven, thats more comfort for us, thats more happinesse to thinke of, then all our paines and torments; if our bodyes were torne at horse heeles, and dragged with wild Beares, yet all were nothing to heavens joyes.

Our souls are a precious jewell, we ought all to looke after them; our bodies are but dust and ashes: if our bodies were tortured with all torments, one blinke of heavens joyes will sweeten all.

Now my torments are at an end, I care not though they were longer: the torment of my body is nothing, but to thinke of the torment she hath hazarded her soule into, is the torment of Hell fire.

Wee confesse wee all deserve that, but not by that meanes she hath.

None will believe it, she sets such a faire face upon it: where the Divell tempts, delusions are strong.

The Divell hath gotten power to harden all hearts.

Those that are to do us justice, will not: though they deny us justice, yet God can and will in his due time, grant us justice over them all.

Though God hath suffered the Divell to have power to torment us; they now have their times: certainly our times are in a better life; we have no pleasure here, all our pleasure is in the world to come.

I have cause to blesse God, who doth send these blessed Angels to watch over me: my paynes were always with joy, never sorrowfull, and when I had no comfort, yet I had hopes that God who layed them on me, would take them off me in his due time.

Have not I reason to blesse God? none hath reason more: the Lord
grant

grant I never forget his mercies: he hath been very mercifull to us, in granting us patience to endure more then wee could expect at his hands.

What is this they have run their soules into? the Lord grant them hearts to repent them of their sinns; the Lord grant us penitent hearts to repent us of our sinnes: we have all done as much as deserves hell, where is gnashing of teeth, paines, fire and brimstone for ever.

We have cause to blesse God that hath not suffered us to go neither to Witches, nor any of the divels servants, but to looke to God.

No creature thought we could have indured, what can we indure of our selves? No, without God we can doe nothing, what cannot God inable us to indure? There is nothing that can be done, but we can do it by Gods assistance, we cannot say we can doe any thing of our selves, no not the least thing in the World, seeing our helpe is in an able God, we can do any thing.

I know the Lord will never suffer the divell to have any further power over our bodies; though they hurt our bodies, they shall not hurt our soules, they shall not come neare our soules.

Our soules are all the comfort we can expect, what are our bodies? Our bodies are nothing; I blesse God that would have his glory tryed on our weake bodies, which no creature thought could have indured such torment.

We have reason my brother, sister, and all of us to blesse God; yea, all creatures that behold it have reason to blesse God, and to thinke that he is a mercifull God to us, it is his mercy we know, it is his promise that all those that repent with penitent hearts, he is still ready to forgive them, we acknowledge it is Gods mercy, not our deserts.

They have tormented my brother a yeare a gone St. JOHN's day at night, and they have tormented me two yeares agone yeasterday, my sister is pined away, they began with her since Lammas, she hath lesse comfort then we have had.

She from the beginning hath had great paine without comfort, and though my paine have beene sorest, yet I have had great comfort.

Since God hath granted this day to be my releasement, have I not reason to blesse this God? My brother and sister are still under their burthen: Let them not thinke it a burthen, but rather beg patience to indure it.

D 3   If

If ever God give them health, we have all reason to have thoughts of eternity, and never to forget the word of God.

My sister is worse then my brother, or then ever I was, my torments were vehement, sometimes a day, sometimes eight houres, sometimes shorter, sometimes longer; and though my time was sore and vehement, yet still I had ease after it, but my sister hath no ease.

Now when I am released, what shall become of my brother and sister, if it please God to give them so much power as to torment them? If that God make me a watch over them, that I may declare their grief, it is a great mercy.

They thought to have choaked me, once they made me cast up pins, and stones, and things that creatures would not thinke possible should have come out of my mouth, yet God inabled me to indure that not any creature thought I could.

They thought to have done the like to my Brother, but God did not suffer the Divell to have so much power, but they have striven so to do.

For my Brother GEORGE he had neede to have a care of himselfe, he by the sight of me I saw consumed; we have reason to blesse God he is away.

If you love my sister BETTYES life, bring her not home, you may as well take a knife and cut her throat, as be the cause of her torments.

If they love my sister and brothers life, bring them not in sight one minute, by looking on them doth them more hurt then we thinke of.

If my sister had gone away to and not looked so much on my Brother as she hath done it had beene better for her.

She hath done her selfe more wrong then us, in setting these two more against us, though it hath pleased God to let them have so much power over our bodies, yet they never had power over our soules.

They are trying all ways in the world to have power to torment my Mother, they are seeking to torment her by an unnaturall way, if we have not a care of our selves, and one of another by Gods mercies.

Shall they never have more power to torment me?

They thought this last night to have made me more passionate then ever I was; I blesse God though they made me somewhat passionate, yet stil God inabled me with patience not to be much extravagant much after their desires, those Justices all of them have denyed us Justice: Let them take heede of themselves; Let them take heede of a heavy

burthen

burthen that may fall upon themselves: Though our Mother be loving unto us; yet let them take heede of a heavy burthen may fall on them: I wish to God it be not so, that the innocent doe not suffer, the Lord grant they may have a sensiblenesse of the wrong they have done us, and suffer not the innocent to indure for them.

Now after this, when they cannot get power to torment me, will they ever be more vehement with my brothers and sisters?

Whensoever she is put in hold till she come to her tryall she should not have her liberty; for if she come abroad amongst her company, she will be as cruel as ever.

If these two Witches were catcht and in hold, she would goe to death to the utmost to make them more vehement then ever: though they torment the rest, yet they shall never have power to torment me.

It is sayd in the word of God, you shall not suffer a Witch to live; yet she consults with Witches, and consults with their wayes, which by the Lawe of God deserves death.

Shall I never behold your faces againe? If it were so it would be more sad to me then all my paine: Though you be not in my sight, yet I trust in Gods mercy so much, as that you will still watch over us, and protect us.

God grant we never forget Gods mercies, to be impatient, seeing we have rest in torment.

What mercies can be showne unto a creature, but it hath pleased God to shew it to me? that it hath pleased him to grant mee so much patience, though of my selfe I was not sensible of my torments, that was a mercy and much comfort to my soule, that though they tormented my body, they never had power to cause me speake unbefitting words to hazzard my soule.

But had it not pleased God to have sent you to me that time, what have would become of me? I had beene distracted and like a mad body.

When the Divell was strong and had most power, God still crossed him of his opportunity.

Those that are so malicious, seldome any thing satisfies their mindes, save this extravagant way, that is a sore thing: many times malice is never satisfied without life: shall I never see you with my eyes here? yet ye will reveale this, either by me, or by some other means

It shall be more strange before it be all declared. Now after this

time

time shall I never have more torment by any Witch, nor none I hope. Shall I meet you in such a place, at such a time? I will.

Seeing you have set mee that time of appoyntment, I hope you will put me in minde of it: I will, if it be Gods will to make me do it.

M^r. FRANCIS BROAD, and Mr. GEORGE ATHERLONY two Ministers, with Doctor STEPHENS a Physitian, were with her in divers of her last tormenting fits.

These words were spoken in the hearing of two Ministers, and at least a hundred others. And taken by Mr. Edward Ord.

MARGARET WHITE of CHATTON, *her owne Confession of her selfe.*

Confesseth and saith, That she hath beene the Divels servant these five yeares last past, and that the Divell came to her in the likenes of a man in blew cloaths, in her owne house, and griped her fast by the hand, and told her she should never want, and gave her a nip on the shoulder, and another on her back; And confesseth her Familiar came to her in the likenesse of a black Grey-hound, and that the Divell had carnall knowledge of her in her owne house two severall times.

Likewise the sayd MARGARET WHITES *Confession upon Oath of others, as followeth, viz. Mrs.* DOROTHY SVVINOVV *of* CHATTON, *and* JANE MARTIN *of the same, and sister to the sayd* MARGARET WHITE *of* CHATTON, *aforesayd,*

Confesseth upon Oath that Mrs. SVVINOVV, and her sister JANE, and her selfe were in the Divels company in her sister JANES house, where they did eate and drinke together (as by her conceived) and made merry.

And

And Mrs. SVVINOVV, and her the sayd MARGARETS sister with her selfe, came purposely to the house of Mr. EDVVARD MOORE of Spittle, to take away the life of MARGARET MUSCHAMP and MARY, and they were the cause of the Childrens tormenting, and that they were three severall times to have taken away their lives, and especially upon St. Johns day at night gone twelve moneths; And sayth that God was above the Divell, for they could not get their desires perfected; and saith, that Mrs. SVVINOVV would have consumed the childe that Mrs. *Moore* had last in her wombe, but the Lord would not permit her; and that after the childe was borne Mrs. *Swinow* was the occasion of its death, and Mrs. *Swinow* came riding on a little black Nag to the Spittle with a riding coat, and that she and her sister were also the occasion, and had a hand in the death of the sayd child: And further confesseth that she and her sayd sister were the death of *Thomas Yong* of *Chatton* (by reason) a kill full of Oates watched against her sisters minde; And further saith, that the Divell called her sister *Jane* (*Besse*.) She confesseth, that her sister *Jane* had much troubled *Richard Stanley* of *Chatton*, and that she was the occasion of his sore leg.

This is acknowledged and confessed to be true, before John Sleigh *Justice of Peace, and* Robert Scot *Towne Clarke of* Barwick.

MARGARET WHITE,] her Marke

This was confirmed after, in the presence of Mr. *Ogle* of *Eglingame*, Mr. *Walton* of *Ethenstone*, Mr. *Foster* of *Newham*, Justices of the Peace, being present a multitude of people at *Kinnerstone*: This same was afterward taken upon Oath at *Morpeth*, in the presence of Mr. Delavall, High Sherriffe of *Northumberland*, Mr. *Ogle*, Mr. *Fenwick*, Mr. *Delavall*, Mr. *Shafto*, Mr. *Kilinworth*, Mr. *Hall*, six Justices of the Peace. Warrants issued out after her Inditement was found, for the apprehending of her, but as yet not taken.

Northumber. *Ad Generalem Sessionem Pacis tent. apud Aln-wick pro Com. pred. die Mercurii viz. 24. die Aprilis, 1650. Coram* Gulielmo Selby *Mil.* Georgio Fenwick *Ar.* Henrico Ogle *Ar. & al. Justic. ad Pacem in Com. pred. conservand. assignat. &c. Necnon, &c.*
Nomina Jurator. ad Inquirend. &c.

Johannes Ilderton. Ar.	*Edvardus Bell,* Gen.
Will. Armorer, Gen.	*Radulphus Watson,* Gen.
Nich. Forster, Gen.	*Hugh Arrowsmith,* Gen.
Ephr. Armorer, Gen.	*Jo. Creswel.* Gen.
Franc. Alder. Gen.	*Joh. Ord,* Gen.
Richard. Widhouse, Gen.	*Georgius Craw,* Gen.
Georgius Lisle, Gen.	*Franc. Forster,* Gen.
Alex. Armorer, Gen.	*Henricus Johnson,* Gen.
Christoph. Ogle, Gen.	

Qui quidem Jurator. putant ut sequitur.

Jur. *pro Custod. libert. Angl. Authoritat. Parliamenti super sacram suam presentant. quod* Dorotheo Swinow *nuper de* Chatton *in Com.* Northumber. *Vid. 24 die Martii Anno Dom. millesimo, sexcentesimo, quadragesimo, octavo, ac divers. al. dict. & vicibus tam antea quam postea Deum pre oculis non hab. sed instigatione Diabolica seduct. quosd. malas & Diabolicas Artes Angl. vocat* Witchcrafts, Inchantments, Charmes, and Sorceries, *nequit Diabolic. ac Felonice apud* Spittle *in Com. Palatin.* Dunelm. *die & Anno supradict. usa fuit & exercit. ratione quarundum malarum & Diabolicarum Artium quidem* Sibilla Moore *de* Spittle *pred. in Com. Palatin. Dunelm. pred. infans existen. & ad tunc in Pace Dom. R. ad tunc existen. a pred.*

pred. vicesimo quarto die Martii supradict. usq; primam diem Aprilis Anno supradict. languebat. & pred. Sibilla apud Insulam Sacram in Com. Palatin. pred. ad mortem suam devenit & vitam suam dimisit & sic Jur. pred. super sacr. suum pred. dicunt quod Vid. Dorothea pred. Sibilla ratione practitionibus & exerii Diabol. Artiū pred. apud Insul. sacr. pred. in Com. Palatin Dunelm. pred. modo & forma pred. Felonice & Diabolice interfecit Contr. Pacem Publicam nunc.

Copia. Ex. per Crow. Cl. Pa.

Northumber.   *Ad Generalem Sessionem Pacis tent. apud Aln-wick pro Com. pred. die Mercurii, viz. vicesimo quarto die Aprilis* 1650. *Coram* Gulielmo Selby *mil.* Georgio Fenwick *Ar. &* Henrico Ogle *Ar. & al. Justic. ad Pacem in Com. pred. concernant. assignant. &c. Necnon &c.*

WHereas *Dorothy Swinow* of *Chatton* Widdow, doth stand indicted at this Sessions of divers *Witchcrafts, Inchantments, Charmes,* and *Sorceries,* and especially for useing and practising the sayd Diabolicall Arts upon *Sibilla Moore* an Infant and Child of Mrs. *Mary Moore* Widdow: It is therefore Ordered by the Court, and the High Sheriffe of the sayd County, his Bayliffes and Officers, and all others whom it may concern, are hereby required forthwith to apprehend the body of the sayd *Dorothy Swinow,* & her to carry & convey unto the Goal of the said County, there to remain untill she shall be thence delivered by due course of Law.

Crow, Cl. Pac.

To the High Sheriffe of the sayd County,
   and to all Constables and Officers,
   whom it may concerne.

Northumber.

Northumber. Ralph Delaval *Esquire*, *High Sheriffe of the sayd County*, to all Bayliffes of Liberties, Sheriffes, Bayliffes, Constables, and whomsoever else it may concerne, greeting; By vertue of an Order from the Sessions of the Peace to me directed, these are to charge and command you, and every of you, that immediately upon sight hereof, you attach and apprehend the body of Dorothy Swinow of Chatton *Widdow*, and her safely convey to the Common Goale at Morpeth, there to remaine untill she shall be from thence delivered by due course of Law; hereof faile not, as you will answer the contrary at your utmost perills. Given under the Seale of my Office this 26. day of *April*, Anno Domini, 1650.

Per eundem Vic.

FINIS.

The fine copy of Francis Bragge, *WITCHCRAFT Farther Display'd* (ESTC T68954) is reproduced by permission of The British Library (shelfmark 8631.aaa.42). The text block of the original measures 159mm × 88mm.

Hard-to-read passages in the original:
B3.38:   at least 30 Pins
B3.39:   they would cry out upon *Amy Duny*
B3.40:   *Rose Cullender*, saying they saw
B3.41:   as before. That they saw
B3.42:   the House
C3v.34: House
C3v.36: of the
C4.35:   The Woman in the Veil here
C4.36:   cannot but
C4.37:   Hood
C4.40:   is almost
C4.42:   out
Ev.35:   her Fits
Ev.36:   pray by her
Ev.37:   Devotion and Trust... in her
Ev.38:   There
Ev.39:   her as... Sight
Ev.40:   Longdon
Ev.41:   accounted
Ev.42:   worse at
F4.25:   [The Greek phrase is from I John 3:8; it is translated by John Tillotson as 'dissolve or demolish' and in the Authorized Version as 'destroy']
F4.41:   *Posthum. Fol.*

WITCHCRAFT
Farther Display'd.

CONTAINING

I. An Account of the *Witchcraft* practis'd by JANE WENHAM of *Walkerne*, in *Hertfordshire*, since her Condemnation, upon the Bodies of ANNE THORN and ANNE STREET, and the deplorable Condition in which they still remain.

II. An Answer to the most general Objections against the Being and Power of WITCHES: With some Remarks upon the Case of JANE WENHAM in particular, and on Mr. Justice POWEL's Procedure therein.

To which are added,

The TRYALS of FLORENCE NEWTON, a famous *Irish* Witch, at the Assizes held at *Cork, Anno* 1661; as also of two WITCHES at the Assizes held at *Bury St. Edmonds* in *Suffolk, Anno* 1664, before Sir MATTHEW HALE, (then Lord Chief Baron of the *Exchequer*) who were found guilty and executed.

Now the Works of the Flesh are manifest, which are these, Adultery, Fornication, Uncleanness, Lasciviousness, Idolatry, Witchcraft, &c. Galat. Chap. V. Vers. 19, 20.

LONDON,

Printed for E. CURLL, at the *Dial and Bible* against St. *Dunstan*'s Church in *Fleet-Street*, 1712. Price 6 d. Where may be had, The TRYAL and PROCEEDINGS at large against *Jane Wenham*, at *Hertford-Assizes*. Price 6 d.

Introduction.

AFTER having, in as plain and clear a Manner as I could, given the World a full and true Account of the Proceedings against *Jane Wenham*, I was in hopes that I should have no farther Occasion to divert my Pen from some other much more important Subjects, which I was engag'd in, both by Duty and Inclination.

But being inform'd, that the *Incredulity* of the *Judge*, together with the great Proneness of the Age to *Sadducism* and *Infidelity*, had caus'd many Objections to be rais'd against that faithful and impartial Relation of *Matter of Fact*, I thought my self oblig'd, for my own Vindication, and that of the Persons principally concern'd in the Prosecution, not to remain silent, when I had so much to urge in my Defence.

In order to which, I first present my Reader with an Abstract of a famous Tryal of two Witches before the Great and Good Sir *Matthew Hale*, a Man too well known to need any *Encomiums*, either for his *Piety*, or *Knowledge in the Law*; and it is humbly hop'd, that his declar'd Opinion, that *there were really such Persons as Witches*, will be put in the Ballance with that of Mr. Justice *Powel*.

Having also, upon reading Mr. *Glanvil*'s Book, met with an Instance of a Discovery of Witchcraft, almost in every Circumstance agreeing with our Case, I thought my self oblig'd to insert it with Observations upon those parts of it which so nearly resemble our particular Case, that the one seems to be a Copy of the other.

I have also, for the Satisfaction of some honest Gentlemen, who never had any Occasion to enquire into these Matters, and disbelieve the Being and Power of Witches, upon the Prejudices of Education only, thought fit to represent fairly to them all the most material Objections that are rais'd against the Belief of such Stories, and have endeavour'd to keep my self to such a plain way of solving these Difficulties, as may be understood by ordinary Capacities. For which Reason I have industriously avoided any nice and philosophical Disquisitions relating to the

INTRODUCTION.

Nature and Being of Spirits in general, and suppose my Reader to be a Christian, and Believer of the Holy Scriptures.

But as I doubt not but those who have read my former Account, would be glad to know in what Condition the two poor afflicted Creatures are in at present, so I think the Relation of it may possibly serve to other good Ends, and convince some Unbelievers; and therefore I shall acquaint my Reader what to my own knowledge has pass'd since the printing of the abovemention'd Narrative, which, tho' not sworn yet before any Magistrate, yet I can assure him is nothing but the Truth.

Anne Thorn continues to be frequently troubl'd with the Apparition either of Jane Wenham in her own Shape, or that of a Cat, which speaks to her, and tempts her to destroy her self with a Knife that it brings along with it. On the 18th of March particularly, it came to her, and spoke as usual; upon which Anne Thorn fell into a Fit, and recovering by Prayers, she took up the Bible and fell to Reading. While the Book was in her Hands, she perceiv'd something pull it from her, and she was forc'd to let it fall. Three Persons who were then in the Room with her, took up the Bible and endeavour'd to hold it in her Hands, but all their Strength could not do it, the Book being violently taken away from them, and flung to the Ground. At the same Time Anne Thorn cry'd out, she was prick'd in the Hand, and when they look'd on her Hand, it bled, and seem'd to have been prick'd with a Pen.

Another Thing still more remarkable, happen'd to this unhappy Maid. On Thursday the 27th of March, she at first perceiv'd a strange Numbness in two of her Fingers, which was succeeded by a violent Pain in her Wrist, and in an Hour or two afterward, she could not stir her Hand, and her Wrist seem'd to be out of Joint, altho' she knew not how it was hurt. Upon which she was sent to the Bone-setter, who affirm'd that the Bone was above an Inch out of its Place, and did set it. When Anne Thorn was return'd home, this Cat came again to her, and brought her a Knife, bidding her not mind what those about said to her, but cut her Throat, and she should be well. She has several Times since seen the Cat, who brought her once a Razor, and upon her refusing to take it, the Cat said, I'll go to Nan Street, and she will take it; and it was found that exactly at that Time the Cat appear'd to Anne Street, and offer'd her a Razor.

This Anne Street continues also in a strange Condition, and is often troubl'd with the Apparition of this Cat, as also of a Dog which accompanies her. On Thursday the 27th of March, she says, this Dog came to her, bidding her come out; and upon her saying her Prayers, he went away for the present,

INTRODUCTION.

sent, but in the Afternoon, about five a Clock, she saw the Dog again, who bad her follow him to the River, and she says he ran before her, and she follow'd him, but before she got to the River, three Men met her, and brought her home, after which she fell into a Fit, and was recover'd by Prayers.

On *Saturday* following, she says, she saw the Cat again in the Yard, it spoke to her, bidding her hang her self with her Garter, or cut her Throat with a Razor; and after the Cat was gone, *Anne Street* was grievously pinch'd in the Arm, she knew not how.

The next Day also she saw the Cat, and was pinch'd; and at Night a Rapping was hear'd at the Window by all that were present; after which, a Noise was heard as of a Woman crying under the Window, for four Hours together, tho' nothing was to be seen.

On *Monday* Night, being the 31st, she saw *Jane Wenham* again in her own Shape, but she went away upon *Anne Street*'s saying her Prayers, and she has not been troubl'd since that Time, to this present Day, the 3d of *April*.

As for Mother *Wenham*, I hear she has found out a Way to get plenty of Money while she is in Prison. She says she was prosecuted out of Spite, only because she went to the *Dissenting Meetings*: And by this Means, she gets Contributions from the Party: And of a wicked old Witch, is on a sudden become a *precious Saint*. This Story put me upon enquiring of Mr. *Gardiner*, whether she had ever been counted a Dissenter, and he declares, that he never before heard that she us'd to go to any Place of Divine Worship, and that he never took her to be of any Religion at all; however, we are very willing to part with her, and wish the Fanaticks much Joy of their new Convert.

I shall only take Notice of one Thing more to the Reader, *viz.* to assure him that neither Mr. *Gardiner*, nor Mr. *Strutt*, had any Hand in writing the Narrative of the Proceedings against *Jane Wenham*, altho' they are both Witnesses to the Truth of it; so that some Gentlemen (who in Justice and Gratitude, as well as good Manners, ought to have held their Tongues) might as well have spar'd their *personal Reflections*.

Ardely-Bury, April
the 3d, 1712

F. B.

AN

An Account *of the* TRYAL *of* Amy Duny, *and* Rose Cullender, *for* Witchcraft, *at the Assizes held at* Bury St. Edmonds, *in* Suffolk, *March* 10. 1664. *before Sir* Matthew Hale, *Knight, then Lord Chief Baron of the Exchequer.*

AMY *Duny* and *Rose Cullender*, both of *Leystoff*, in *Suffolk*, were severally indicted for bewitching *Elizabeth, Anne,* and *William Durent, Jane Bocking, Susan Chandler, Elizabeth* and *Deborah Pacey*.

When the Prosecutors were giving Directions for laying the Indictment, three of the afflicted Persons, *viz. Anne Durent, Susan Chandler,* and *Elizabeth Pacey,* fell into violent Fits, screaming in a dismal Manner; so that they were uncapable of giving their Evidence; and altho' they did at length recover out of their Fits, yet they continu'd speechless till the Conviction of the Prisoners.

The first Witness at the *Tryal,* was *Dorothy Durent,* who depos'd, That about the 10th of *March, nono Car.* 2. her Business calling her from Home, she left her Child, *William Durent,* (then a sucking Infant) to the Care of *Amy Duny* for a few Hours that she was absent; but strictly charg'd the said *Amy* not to give it Suck. Being ask'd what need there was of that Caution, *Amy* being an old Woman, and uncapable of giving Suck? She answer'd, she knew she could not give Suck; but one Reason was, *Amy* had long had the Reputation of a Witch: Another was, it was usual with old Women, if they tended a sucking Child, and nothing else would please it, to give it the Breast, which must be pernicious to the Infant, who suck'd nothing but Wind. She said farther, That when she came Home, *Amy* told her, *That she had suckl'd her Child,* contrary to her Orders. That upon this, she was very angry with *Amy,* who then threaten'd her in a great Rage, saying, *She had better have done something else, than have*

have found Fault with her, and went away; and that very Night her Child was taken with strange and terrible Fits, and so continu'd for several Weeks.

The said *Dorothy Durent* farther said, That being full of Concern at her Child's Disorder, she went to one Dr. *Jacob*, who liv'd at *Yarmouth*, a Man famous for curing Persons bewitch'd. This Man advis'd her to hang the Child's Blanket all Day in the Chimney-Corner, and at Night to wrap her Child in it, advising her not to be afraid, if she saw any Thing in the Blanket, but take it and fling it into the Fire. She did so; and at Night, when she look'd into the Blanket, there fell from it a great Toad, which ran about the Floor. A young Man who was with this Examinant, catch'd this Toad, and held it in the Fire with a Pair of Tongs. Immediately it made a great Noise, to which succeeded a Flash like Gun-powder, follow'd by a Report as great as that of a Pistol; and after this, the Toad was no more seen, neither was its Substance perceiv'd to consume in the Fire.

She said farther, That a Neice of the said *Amy Duny*, came to her this Examinant the next Day, and told her, that her Aunt (meaning *Amy*) was in a sad Condition, her Face being scorch'd with Fire, and that she was sitting alone stript to her Smock, without any Fire. That she this Examinant went immediately to *Amy Duny*, and saw her Face, Legs, and Thighs much scorch'd with Fire. That she ask'd *Amy* how she came in that Condition, *Amy* answer'd, *She might thank her for it, she was the Cause of it; but she should see some of her Children dead, and go on Crutches herself.* This Examinant said farther, That since the burning the Toad, this Child was well, and is yet alive.

She said also, That about the 6th of *March*, 11 *Car*. 2. *Elizabeth Durent*, her Daughter, was taken with like Fits with the first, and cry'd out, That *Amy Duny* appear'd to her, and tormented her. That she this Examinant going to fetch some Physick for her Child, when she return'd Home, she found *Amy* there, who said, *She came to see her Child, and give it some Water.* At which this Examinant was very angry with her, and thrust her out of the House; upon which *Amy* said, *You need not be so angry, your Child will not live long*; which prov'd true, for her Child dy'd in two Days after; and this Examinant really believes,

that

that *Amy Duny* did bewitch her Child to Death, she having long had the Reputation of a Witch, and some of her Relations having suffer'd for Witchcraft.

She farther said, That soon after the Death of her Daughter *Elizabeth*, this Examinant was taken lame in both her Legs, and was forc'd to go upon Crutches; which she continu'd to do to this Time. The Court ask'd her, *Whether it were with her, when she was took lame, according to the Custom of Women?* She answer'd, It was, and always was so, but when she was with Child.

So far this Witness. It was remarkable, that altho' she had gone upon Crutches for three Years, and did so at the Assizes, before *Amy Duny* was convicted, yet then she was immediately restor'd to her Strength, and went Home without Crutches.

As for *Elizabeth* and *Deborah Pacey*, the eldest about 11 Years old, as I said before, was taken with a Fit, and continu'd speechless. While she was in her Fit, she appear'd at first without any Symptom of Life, saving that her Stomach and Belly, when she drew her Breath, would rise to a great Height. Afterwards, when she was a little better, she lean'd her Head upon a Cushion laid over the Bar of the Court, with her Apron over her Head, and her Hand upon it, and continu'd in this Posture, 'till, by Order of the Judge, *Amy Duny* was brought privately to her, and touch'd her Hand; upon which, the Child, whose Eyes had been fast clos'd all this while, flew at *Amy*, and scratch'd her, and was hardly forc'd from her, and afterwards made many Signs of Eagerness to come at her.

Deborah, the youngest, was so ill, that she could not be brought to the Assizes. The Evidence relating to these two, was as follows:

Samuel Pacey, of *Leystoff*, Merchant, (a sober good Man) being sworn, said, That on *Thursday* the 10th of *October* last, his younger Daughter *Deborah*, about nine Years old, was suddenly taken so lame, that she could not stand on her Legs, and so continu'd 'till the 17th of the same Month, when the Child desir'd to be carry'd to a Bank on the *East* Side of the House, looking towards the Sea; and while she was sitting there, *Amy Duny* came to this Examinant's House, to buy some Herrings, but was deny'd. Then she came twice more, but being as often deny'd, she went away discontented and grumbling. At

B 2 this

this Instant of Time, the Child was taken with terrible Fits, complaining of a Pain in her Stomach, as if she was prick'd with Pins, shrieking out with a Voice like a Whelp, and thus continu'd 'till the 30th of the same Month.

In the mean Time, Dr. *Feavor* was sent for, who declar'd to this Examinant, (and afterwards at the Tryal) That he could not conceive the Cause of the Child's Affliction. And farther, this Examinant saith, That *Amy Duny* having long had the Reputation of a Witch, and his Child having in the Intervals of her Fits, constantly cry'd out on her, as the Cause of her Disorder, and said, that the said *Amy* did appear to her, and fright her. He did suspect the said *Amy Duny* to be a Witch, and charg'd her with being the Cause of his Child's Illness, and set her in the Stocks. That while she was in the Stocks, *Alice Letteridge* and *Jane Buxton*, (who afterwards depos'd the same in Court) ask'd *Amy* what was the Reason of Mr. *Pacey*'s Child's Illness, telling her they heard she had a Hand in't? She answer'd, *Mr. Pacey keeps a great Stir with his Child, but let him stay 'till he has done as much by his Children, as I have done by mine.* Being ask'd what was that, she said, *She had been fain to open her Child's Mouth with a Tap, to give it Victuals.*

He farther said, That two Days after his Daughter, *Elizabeth* was taken with such strange Fits, that they could not force open her Mouth without a Tap, which they were compell'd to use; and the younger Child being in the same Condition, they us'd to her the same Remedy.

He said also, That both Children would grievously complain, that *Amy Duny*, and another Woman, whose Habit and Looks they describ'd, did appear to them, and torment them, and would cry out, *There stands* Amy Duny, *There stands* Rose Cullender, the other Person who afflicted them.

Their Fits were not alike; sometimes they were lame on the Right Side, sometimes on the Left; sometimes so sore they could not bear to be touch'd; sometimes perfectly well in other Respects, but they could not *hear*; at other Times they could not see; sometimes they lost their Speech for one, two, and once eight Days together. At times they had swooning Fits, and when they could speak, were taken with a Fit of Coughing, and vomited Flegm and crooked Pins, and once a great Two-penny Nail,

Nail, with above 40 Pins, which Nail the Examinant said he saw vomited up, and many of the Pins. The Nail and Pins were produc'd in the Court. They usually vomited a Pin towards the End of a Fit, four or five of which they sometimes had in a Day.

Thus the Children continu'd for two Months, in which Time this Examinant often made 'em read in the *New Testament*, and observ'd when they came to the Words *Lord*, *Jesus*, or *Christ*, they could not pronounce them, but fell into a Fit. When they came to the Word *Satan*, or *Devil*, they would point, and say, *This bites, but makes me speak right well*. He said, That in the Intervals of the Fits, which he thinks occasion'd by naming Lord, Jesus, or Christ, he ask'd them why they could not speak those Words, they would say, Amy Duny *saith I must not use that Name*.

He said also, That his Children would say *Amy Duny* often appear'd to 'em, with *Rose Cullender*, and threaten'd 'em, *That if they told what they saw or heard, they would torment 'em ten times more than ever they did before*. That the Children would run to the Place where they fancy'd 'em to be sometimes spinning, sometimes reeling, in various Postures, threatening them.

This Examinant saith farther, That finding his Children thus tormented, without Hopes of Recovery, he sent them to his Sister *Margaret Arnold*, at *Yarmouth*, being willing to try whether Change of Air would help 'em, and refers to her the Relation of what happen'd to them afterwards.

Margaret Arnold being sworn, saith, That about the 30th of *November*, *Elizabeth* and *Deborah Pacey* came to her House, with her Brother, who told her what had happen'd at his House, and that he thought his Children bewitch'd; but she this Examinant did not much regard it, supposing the Children had play'd Tricks, and put the Pins into their Mouths themselves. She therefore took all the Pins from their Cloths, sowing them with Thread, instead of pinning them. But notwithstanding, they rais'd at times at least 30 Pins in her Presence, and had terrible Fits; in which Fits they would cry out upon *Amy Duny* and *Rose Cullender*, saying they saw them, and heard them threatening as before. That they saw Things like Mice running about the House, and one of them catch'd one of them,

them, and threw it into the Fire, which made a Noise like a Rat.

Another Time the younger Child being out of Doors, a Thing like a Bee would have forc'd it self into her Mouth, at which the Child ran screaming into the House, and before this Examinant could come to her, fell into a Fit, and vomited a Two-penny Nail with a broad Head; and after that, this Examinant ask'd the Child how she came by this Nail, she answer'd, *The Bee brought the Nail, and forc'd it into her Mouth.*

At other times the eldest Child told this Examinant, That she saw Flies bring her crooked Pins, and then she would fall into a Fit, and vomit such Pins. One time the said Child said she saw a Mouse, and crept under the Table to look for it; and afterwards the Child seem'd to put something in her Apron, saying, *She had caught it,* and ran to the Fire and threw it in, on which did appear to this Examinant something like a Flash of Gun-powder, altho' she does own she saw nothing in the Child's Hand.

Once the Child being speechless, but otherwise very sensible, ran up and down the House, crying, *Hush, hush,* as if she had seen Poultry; but this Examinant saw nothing. At last the Child catch'd at something, and threw it into the Fire. Afterwards, when the Child could speak, this Examinant ask'd her what she saw at that time, she answer'd, *She saw a Duck.* Another time the youngest Child said after a Fit, That *Amy Duny* had been with her, and tempted her to drown herself, or cut her Throat, or otherwise destroy herself. Another time they both cry'd out of *Amy Duny* and *Rose Cullender*, saying, *Why don't you come your selves? why do you send your Imps to torment us?*

This Examinant farther saith, That she did set down these Things as they happen'd, and that she does really believe these Children are bewitch'd by *Amy Duny* and *Rose Cullender*, although at first she was not inclinable to think so.

Anne Durent was another of the Persons afflicted, and then present in Court.

Her Father, *Edmund Durent*, of *Leystoff*, being sworn, said, That towards the End of *November* last, *Rose Cullender* came to his House to buy Herrings of his Wife, who refus'd to let her have any; upon which, the said *Rose* went away seemingly angry. That afterwards, on the 1st of

December

December following, *Anne Durent*, his Daughter, complain'd of a sad Pain in her Stomach, like the pricking of Pins, and soon after fell into swooning Fits; and upon her Recovery, she cry'd out, that she had seen the Apparition of *Rose Cullender*, who threaten'd to torment her; and thus she continu'd (having vomited up several Pins, which were produc'd in Court) until the Assizes. This *Anne Durent* was then in Court, but could not give her Evidence, by Reason of strange Fits she fell into at the Sight of *Rose Cullender*.

Anne Baldwin being sworn, testify'd the same Thing, as to *Anne Durent*'s being bewitch'd.

Jane Bocking, another of the afflicted, was so ill, that she could not come to the Assizes. But as to her

Diana Bocking, of *Leystoff*, was sworn, and said, Her Daughter, *Jane Bocking*, had been formerly troubl'd with Fits, but always recover'd of them; but on the 1st of *February* last, she complain'd grievously of a strange Pain in her Stomach, as if it had been prick'd with Pins, and fell afterwards into a Fit, and had many Returns of these Fits 'till this Time, eating little or nought, and often vomited crooked Pins, particularly on *Sunday* last she brought up seven of them. When she was in her Fits, she would spread Abroad her Arms, and use Postures as if she catched at something, with her Hands open, and then would shut 'em again; and upon opening her Hands, crooked Pins were found in 'em, altho' it could not be perceiv'd how they could be brought to her. At another time she talk'd in her Fits as if to some Person, (altho' she would take no Notice of any that were present) then she held out her Hand, saying, *I will not have it, I will not have it*. Afterwards she said, *I will*, and shut her Hands close, and upon forcing her Hand open, was found in it a Lath-Nail. She often cry'd out in her Fits, *There stands* Rose Cullender *at the Bed's Feet*; sometimes she said *she saw her at the Bed's Head*, and sometimes in other Places. Afterwards she was speechless for several Days, tho' not in Fits. When she could speak, she desir'd some Meat, and being ask'd why she did not speak in so many Days, she said, *Amy Duny would not let her*. The Pins and Nail were shewn in Court.

As to *Susan Chandler*, another of the afflicted, and in Court, her Mother, *Mary Chandler*, being sworn, said, That

That about the Beginning of *February* last, she was appointed, among five other Women, by Sir *Edmond Bacon*, (who had granted a Warrant against the Prisoners upon the Complaint of Mr. *Pacey*) to search the Bodies of the Prisoners. That they went to *Rose Cullender*, and told her they had Orders to search her Body, which she consented to. That having stript her naked, they began at her Head, and toward the Bottom of her Belly, they found something like a Teat, about an Inch long. Being question'd about it, she said, *She had got a Strain by carrying Water, which was the Cause of that Excrescence.* On farther Search, they found in her Privities more of these Teats, but smaller than the other. This Examinant saith farther, That at the End of the long Teat, was a little Hole, that it seem'd to have been newly suck'd, and it being squeez'd, there came out white Milky Matter.

She said also, That her said Daughter *Susan*, then a Servant in *Leystoff*, and about 18 Years old, having Business to rise the next Morning to wash, saw *Rose Cullender* appear to her, and the said *Rose* took her by the Hand; at which she was much frighted, and came to this Examinant, and told her of it. Then she fell extreamly sick, complaining grievously of her Stomach; and that Night, being in Bed with another young Woman, she shriek'd out, crying *Rose Cullender would come to Bed to her*, and fell into grievous Fits, beating herself in a terrible Manner. In her Intervals, she said sometimes *she saw Rose Cullender*, sometimes *she saw her, and a great Dog with her*. She vomited many crooked Pins, and was sometimes stricken blind, at other times dumb, as she was for the present in Court; but being carry'd out, in half an Hour she recover'd her Speech; and being brought in again, and ask'd whether she could give her Evidence, she said she could. But being sworn, and ask'd what she could say against the Prisoners, she fell into a grievous Fit, and cry'd out, *Burn her, Burn her*; which was all she could say.

Robert Chandler being sworn, agreed with his Wife in all Parts of her Evidence, except that concerning the searching *Rose Cullender*.

This was all the Evidence relating to the bewitching these Children. At the Tryal were many eminent Persons; and among the rest, Mr. Serjeant *Keeling*, who was

unsatisfy'd

unsatisfy'd with the Evidence, which he thought not sufficient to convict the Prisoners. For supposing these Persons were bewitch'd, yet their Imagination only was not sufficient to fix it on the Prisoners; else who could be safe, since their Fancies might possibly run on an innocent Person?

The learned Dr. *Browne* of *Norwich*, being also present, was desir'd to give his Opinion of the three Persons in Court. He said he was clearly of Opinion, that they were bewitch'd; that there had lately been a Discovery of Witches in *Denmark*, who us'd the same Way of tormenting Persons, by conveying crooked Pins, Needles, and Nails into their Bodies. That he thought in such Cases the Devil acted upon Human Bodies, by natural Means, *viz.* By exciting and stirring up the super-abundant Humours, he did afflict them in a more surprizing Manner, by the same Diseases their Bodies were usually subject to. That these Fits might be natural, only rais'd to a great Degree, by the Subtilty of the Devil co-operating with the Malice of these Witches.

Besides the above-mention'd Particulars, other Tryals were made to satisfy the Court, that the Children were really bewitch'd.

At first the Prisoners were brought into Court to the afflicted, to touch them; and upon the least Touch of them, (of *Rose Cullender* in particular, tho' before they seem'd void of all Sense, and their Fists were fast clench'd, so that a strong Man could not force them open) they instantly shriek'd out, and open'd their Hands; but when any other Person touch'd 'em, they took no Notice of it; and altho' they were blinded, lest they should privately see, *Rose Cullender*'s touching them had the same Effect.

An ingenious Person that was present, objected, that this Experiment was not sufficient to find the Prisoners guilty, since the Children might counterfeit, and perceiving when she touch'd them, put themselves into those violent Motions.

It was therefore privately desir'd by the Judge, that some eminent Gentlemen in Court would attend one of the distemper'd Persons, while she was in her Fits, at the other End of the Hall, and bring one of the Witches to her, and see what would follow. They did so, and the Maid being blinded, *Amy Duny* was brought near; but another

nother Person touch'd her, and the Touch had the same Effect with that which the Witches had. Whereupon the Gentlemen return'd, and protested they believ'd the whole Business an Imposture. This put the whole Court to a Stand. At that, Mr. *Pacey* said, The Maid might be deceiv'd by a Suspicion, that the Witch touch'd her, when she did not. That he observ'd, that in all her Fits, she was sensible of what was done to her; which was afterwards confirm'd by the Maid, when she recover'd, on Conviction of the Prisoners. And in some Mens Opinion, this was rather a Confirmation that they were really bewitch'd, than a Sign of Fallacy. For it is impossible, that Children as they were, and of several Families no way related to each other, should be able all to deceive their Relations; and 'tis unreasonable to think, that they should conspire together to take away the Lives of two silly Women; and the Prisoners themselves did scarce so much as object that there was any Malice in the Case. Therefore, say they, that extraordinary Commotion of the Spirits of the Children, at the approach of these Women, and no others, shows, that they were the Persons that did bewitch 'em.

Secondly, *John Soam* of *Leystoff*, being sworn, said, That not long since he had three Harvest-Carts going into the Field to load; that one of them wrench'd the Window of *Rose Cullender*, who came out, and threaten'd him. That the other Carts went well enough, but this was overturn'd twice or thrice that Day. That they could not get it through a Gate, 'till they had cut down the Posts, altho' the Cart did not touch them; neither could they bring it to the Place where they would unload it, 'till the next Morning; and then they did it easily.

Robert Sherringham being sworn, said, That about two Years since the Axle-tree of his Cart broke down part of *Rose Cullender*'s House; upon which she threaten'd him in a great Rage, that his Horses should suffer for it. That soon after all those Horses, being four, dy'd. That he has since had great Losses in his Cattel, and was shortly after taken lame for some Days, and recover'd, but was so plagu'd with great Lice, that he was forc'd to burn two Suits of Cloaths, and then was well again.

Richard Spencer being sworn, said, That on the 1st of *September* last he heard *Amy Duny* say, *That the Devil would not let her rest, 'till she was reveng'd on* Cornelius Sandeswell*'s Wife.*

Anne, Wife to *Cornelius Sandeswell*, depos'd on Oath, That seven or eight Years ago, she having bought some *Geese*, *Amy* told her, *If she did not fetch 'em Home, they'd be destroy'd*; which happen'd accordingly. That *Amy* told her Husband, (who was her Landlord) That he must take Care of such a Chimney, or it would fall. That this Examinant repyl'd, *'Twas a new one.* Soon after the Chimney fell down, as *Amy* had said. She said farther, That having a Firkin of Fish sent to her, which lay in *Leystoff* Road, she desir'd *Amy* to go with her, to help bring it Home. *Amy* reply'd, *She would go when she had it.* Then this Examinant said, That she went to the Boat-man, and demanded the Firkin. The Men told her, *They could not keep it in the Boat from falling into the Sea, they thought 'twas gone to the Devil, they never saw the like before.* She ask'd them whether they lost any other Goods? They said, *Not any.*

This was all the Evidence. The Prisoners saying nothing material to any Thing that was prov'd against them, the Judge, in his Direction to the Jury, wav'd repeating the Evidence, to avoid any Mistake, and told the Jury, there were two Things they were to enquire into, *First*, Whether or no these Children were bewitch'd. *Secondly*, Whether these Women did bewitch them.

He said he did not in the least doubt but there were Witches: *First*, Because the Scriptures affirm it. *Secondly*, Because the Wisdom of all Nations, particularly our own, hath provided Laws against Witchcraft; which implies their Belief of such a Crime. He desir'd them strictly to observe the Evidence, and begg'd of God to direct their Hearts in the weighty Concern they had in Hand, since to condemn the Innocent, and let the Guilty go free, are both an Abomination to the Lord.

The Jury went from the Bar, and in half an Hour brought them in guilty of all the Indictments, being thirteen in Number.

The next Morning the three Children came to Sir *Matthew Hale*'s Lodgings very well: And Mr. *Pacy* being asked at what Time they were thus restor'd to their Speech and Health, he answer'd, That within half an Hour after the Conviction of the Prisoners, they were all restor'd to

Health, and slept well that Night, without Pain, except *Susan Chandler*, who complain'd, of a Pain like pricking of Pins in her Stomach.

After this, they came into Court; but *Anne Durent* was afraid to look on the Witches, and pray'd that she might not see them. But the other two declar'd in open Court, before the Prisoners, (who did not much contradict them) that all that had been sworn to, was true. After this, the whole Court being satisfy'd with the Verdict, the Witches were sentenc'd to be hang'd.

Great Endeavours were us'd to bring them to Confession, but in vain, and they were executed on *Monday* the 17th of *March*, but confess'd nothing.

Observations on the foregoing Tryal of Amy Duny *and* Rose Cullender.

IT is very probable, that Mr. Justice *Powell* had never seen this Tryal, when he said in that of Mother *Wenham*, *That he never heard, that in any Witch's Tryal before, the afflicted Persons fell into a Fit in Court.* For here the Reader sees, that three Persons disturb'd, all fell into Fits at the Sight of the Prisoners; which was exactly the Case of *Anne Thorn*. She was to all Appearance very well in the Morning, 'till she saw the wicked Author of her Torments in Court; and then she fell into a Fit, as is related, p. 24. of the *Account of the Discovery of Sorcery*, &c.

But this Circumstance is not the only one in which these two Cases agree: For 1. As *Durent*'s Child's Fits immediately succeeded upon *Amy Duny*'s threatening her, *That she had as good have done otherwise, as have found Fault with her*; so in our Case, immediately before *Anne Thorn*'s first Fit, *Jane Wenham* threaten'd Mr. *Gardiner*, as you may see p. 3. and before the second she had threaten'd *Anne Thorn* herself, *That if she told any more such Stories of her, as if she had bewitch'd her, it should be worse with her, than it had been yet*, p. 5. to say nothing of her threatening her after Condemnation, that *Anne Thorn* and *Anne Street* should not be well yet; which has exactly come to pass since.

2. These

2. These two Cases agree also in the Circumstance of the Witches appearing to the Afflicted, before a Fit, in her own Shape; and the very remarkable Passage of Pins being convey'd by invisible Means to the Hands of the Persons afflicted, is so exactly resembling the Case of *Anne Thorn*, that they seem to be the same Story. If the Reader will compare the Evidence of *Diana Bocking* in this Tryal, with p. 19 of the Account, he will find they are so very much alike, that the one seems to be a Copy of the other.

Then their starting up with great Strength and Fury upon the Touch of the Witch, is the same in both Cases; their endeavouring to get at her to scratch her; their continual crying out of her, or them: But there is this Difference in Favour of *Anne Thorn*, that she never recovered upon the Touch of any other Person, altho' she could not tell whether it was not the real Witch, her Eyes being fast clos'd; whereas one of the distemper'd Persons in this Tryal being blinded, and supposing the Witch touched her, sprung up as usual; when in Truth it was not the Witch, but another Person that touch'd her.

That part of *Margaret Arnold*'s Evidence concerning *Elizabeth* and *Deborah Pacey*, that *Amy Duny* had been *with Deborah Pacey, and tempted her to drown herself, or to cut her Throat, or otherwise to destroy herself*, is but too nearly resembl'd in the violent Temptations both *Anne Thorn* and *Anne Street* have all along since their Illness struggl'd with, to destroy themselves; and this they have been tempted to do sometimes by the Apparition of *Jane Wenham* in her own Shape, at other times by the *Cat*, which speaks to them, bidding *'em not mind what their Friends say to them, but kill themselves, and they should be well*.

When the Reader compares the Evidence given at these two Tryals, he must needs perceive a vast Superiority of Strength in that of Mother *Wenham*. That which fix'd these Witchcrafts upon *Amy Duny* and the other, was chiefly the strong Imagination of the Parties afflicted, who cry'd out in their Fits, that these Women did appear to them, and torment 'em. There were indeed other Circumstances, such as their threatening the Relations of the Afflicted, &c. but this was the most material Proof. Now, the Prosecutors of *Jane Wenham* did not only bring all these Proofs, but strengthen'd them beyond

yond Contradiction by the Confession of the Prisoner herself, which was at large attested upon Oath by two reverend and worthy Divines.

I was very well pleas'd to find, upon reading this Tryal, that Sir *Matthew Hale* declar'd himself clearly of Opinion, that there were such Creatures as Witches upon the Authority of the Scriptures, as well as the Laws of all Nations, who would not have unanimously agreed in providing proportionable Punishments for the Offence, had they not been perswaded, that there really was such a Crime as Witchcraft. I shall now subjoin another very remarkable Instance of a Tryal, which in many Circumstances comes still nearer to the Case of *Jane Wenham*. It is taken out of the Collection of *Relations* at the End of Mr. *Glanvill*'s *Sadducismus Triumphatus*; together with Observations on such Parts of it as resemble *Wenham*'s Case.

An Abstract of the Relation of the Proceedings against Florence Newton, *an* Irish *Witch of* Youghall, *taken out of her Tryal at the Assizes held for the County of* Cork, *September* 11. 1661.

*F*Lorence *Newton* was committed to *Youghall* Prison by the Mayor of the Town, *March* 24. 1661. for bewitching *Mary Longdon*, who gave Evidence against her at *Cork* Assizes, as follows:

Mary Longdon being sworn, and examin'd what she could say against the said *Florence Newton*, for any Practice of Witchcraft on herself; and being bid to look on the Prisoner, her Countenance chang'd very pale, and she was afraid to look towards her; but at last she did. Being ask'd whether she knew her? she said *she did, and wish'd she never had*. Being ask'd how long she had known her? she said, for three or four Years; and that at *Christmas* last the said *Florence* came to the Deponent, at the House of *John Pyne* of *Youghall*, where the Deponent was a Servant, and ask'd her to give her a Piece of Beef out of the Powdering-Tub. And the Deponent answering

her

her she could not give away her Master's Beef, the said *Florence* seem'd to be angry, and said, *Thou had'st as good have given it me*; and so went away grumbling.

Observation.

The Reader is desir'd to look back to p. 1. of the Account of *Jane Wenham*, where he will find something very like this in the Information of Matthew Gilston.

Mary Longdon *goes on, and saith,*

That about a Week after, this Deponent going to the Water with a Pail of Cloaths on her Head, she met the said *Florence Newton*, who came full in her Face, and threw the Pail off her Head, and violently kiss'd her, saying, *Mary, I pray thee, let thee and I be Friends; for I bear thee no ill Will, and I pray thee do thou bear me none.* And that she the Deponent went afterwards Home, and that within a few Days after, she saw a Woman with a Vail over her Face standing by her Bed Side, and one standing by her like a little old Man in Silk Cloaths; and that this Man, which she took be a Spirit, drew the Veil from the old Woman's Face, and then she knew it to be Goody *Newton*; and that the Spirit spake to this Deponent, and would have had her promise him to follow his Advice, and she should have all Things after her own Heart. To which she answer'd, *That she would have nothing to say to him, but put her Trust in the Lord.*

Observation.

How very like is this Hypocrisy of Mother Newton, who, to gain a greater Power to do Mischief, pretended a Desire to be reconcil'd to Mary Longdon, is to that Part of Susan Aylott's Information, p. 13. of the Account, wherein she saith, That *Jane Wenham* came to her House, and look'd upon a Child which was in her Lap, and strok'd it, and said, *Susan, you have a curious Child; you and I had some Words, but I hope we are Friends,* &c. Soon after which the Child dy'd strangely. The Woman in the Veil here mention'd, cannot but bring to Mind the Woman in the Riding-Hood, who appear'd to Matthew Gillton, p. 1. and Anne Thorn, p. 4. and 8. and the Spirits speaking to Mary Longdon, and tempting her, is almost the same with the Cat's speaking to Anne Thorn and Anne Street, tempting them to come out, p. 23 and 36.

Mary

Mary Longdon *proceeds, and saith,*

That within a Month after the said *Florence* had kiss'd her, she this Deponent fell very ill of Fits and Trances, which would take her on the Sudden, in that Violence that three or four Men could not hold her; and in her Fits she would often be taken with Vomitings, and would vomit up Needles, Pins, Horse-Nails, Stubs, Wooll, and Straw. And being ask'd whether she perceiv'd at these times what she vomited? She said, *She did ; for she was not then in so great a Distraction, as in other Parts of her Fits she was.* And that a little before the first Beginning of her Fits, several (and very many small) Stones would fall upon her as she went up and down, and would follow her from Place to Place, and from one Room to another, and would hit her on the Head, Shoulders, and Arms, and fall to the Ground, and vanish away. And that she and several others would see them both fall upon her, and on the Ground, but could never take them, save only some few, which she and her Master caught in their Hands. Amongst which, one that had a Hole it it, she ty'd (as she was advis'd) with a Leather Thong to her Purse, but it vanish'd immediately, tho' the Leather continu'd ty'd on a fast Knot.

That in her Fits she often saw this *Florence Newton*, and cry'd out against her, for tormenting her; for she says that she would several times stick Pins into her Arms, and some of them so fast, that a Man must pluck three or four Times to get out the Pin, and they were stuck between the Skin and the Flesh. That sometimes she should be remov'd out of her Bed into another Room ; sometimes she should be carry'd to the Top of the House, and laid on a Board betwixt two solar Beams ; sometimes put into a Chest, sometimes under a Parcel of Wooll, sometimes between two Feather Beds on which she us'd to lie, and sometimes betwixt the Bed and the Mat in her Master's Chamber in the Day-time. Being ask'd how she knew she was thus carry'd about and dispos'd of, seeing in her Fits she was in a violent Distraction, she answered, *She never knew where she was, 'till they of the Family, and the Neighbours with them, would be taking her out of the Places whither she was so carry'd and remov'd.* And being ask'd the Reason why she cry'd out so much against *Florence Newton* in her Fits? she answer'd, *Because she saw and felt her Tormenting.* And

And being ask'd how she could think it was *Florence Newton* that did her this Prejudice, she said, first, Because she threaten'd her; then, because after she had kiss'd her, she fell into these Fits, and that she both saw and felt her tormenting. And lastly, That when the People of the Family, by Advice of the Neighbours, and Consent of the Mayor, had sent for *Florence Newton* to come to the Deponent, she was always worse when she was brought to her, and her Fits more violent, than at another time. And that after the said *Florence* was committed at *Youghall*, the Deponent was not troubl'd, but was very well 'till a little while after the said *Florence* was remov'd to *Cork*, and then the Deponent was as ill as ever before. And the Mayor of *Youghall*, one Mr. *Mayre*, then sent to know whether the said *Florence* were bolted (as the Deponent was told) and finding she was not, Order was given to put the Bolts on her; which being done, the Deponent saith she was well again, and so hath continu'd ever since. And being ask'd whether she had such like Fits before the said *Florence* gave her the Kiss, she saith she never had any, but believes that with that Kiss she bewitch'd her. And the rather, because she hath heard from *Nicholas Pyne*, and others, that the said *Florence* hath confess'd as much.

Observation.

Here are also some Things in which the Fits of Mary Longdon *and* Anne Thorn *agree, particularly the great Strength of the Afflicted when in a Fit, so great that three or four Men could hardly hold 'em down. But there is one very remarkable Difference which I doubt not but my Reader has already taken Notice of, viz. That this* Mary Longdon *was always worse of her Fits whenever* Florence Newton *came into the Room; whereas* Anne Thorn *constantly recover'd of her's at the Touch of* Jane Wenham. *And yet I think these different Appearances may be both accounted for the same Way. It is not reasonable to suppose, that either of these Alterations in the Afflicted, came to pass by the Consent or Procurement of the Witches themselves, who could not but perceive that they serv'd as strong Circumstances against them; but this was done by the over-ruling Providence of Almighty God, to convict these miserable Creatures; and either of these Ways might do as well as the other, since it is equally surprizing to see one in perfect Health fall into such terrible Fits at the Sight of any one Person, as to*

D *see*

see another recover out of such Fits upon the bare Touch of a suspected Witch; both of them tending only to the Discovery of the Criminal. Thus Anne Thorn *fell into a Fit in Court, when she first saw the Witch, but recover'd at her coming near to her. Here also the Reader finds some strange Circumstances, as that of the Hail-stones falling upon* Mary Longdon, *her being remov'd up and down,* &c. *which are different from any related in the Case of* Anne Thorn. *But it cannot be expected, that all Witchcrafts should be alike; and that the Devil should be oblig'd to act always uniformly, is a very strange Postulatum, which yet some of our profound Arguers against Witchcraft very unreasonably demand.*

To go on with the Relation.

This *Mary Longdon* having clos'd up her Evidence, *Florence Newton* peep'd at her, as it were, between the Heads of the By-standers that interpos'd between her and the said *Mary*, and lifting up both her Hands together as they were manacl'd, cast them in an angry violent Kind of Motion (as was seen and observ'd by *W. Aston*) towards the said *Mary*, as if she intended to strike at her, if she could reach her, and said, *Now she is down.* Upon which, the Maid fell suddenly to the Ground like a Stone, and fell into a most violent Fit, that all the People that could come to lay Hands on her, could scarce hold her, she biting her own Arms, and shrieking out in a most hideous Manner, to the Amazement of all the Beholders. And continuing so for about a Quarter of an Hour, (the said *Florence Newton* sitting by herself all that while, pinching her own Hands and Arms, as was sworn by some that observ'd her) the Maid was order'd to be carry'd out of the Court, and taken into an House; whence several Persons after that brought Word, that the Maid was in a vomiting Fit, and they brought in several crooked Pins, and Straws, and Wooll, in white Foam like Spittle, in great abundance: Whereupon the Court having taken Notice that the Maid had said she had been very well when the said *Florence* was in Bolts, demanded of the Gaoler if she were in Bolts or no: To which he said she was not, but only manacl'd.

Upon which, Order was given to put on her Bolts; and upon putting them on, she cry'd out, she was kill'd, she was undone, she was spoil'd; why do you torment me thus?

thus? and so continu'd complaining grievously for about half a Quarter of an Hour; and then came in a Messenger from the Maid, and inform'd the Court the Maid was well. At which *Florence* immediately and cholerickly utter'd these Words, *She is not well yet*. And being demanded how she knew she was not well, she deny'd she said so, tho' many in Court heard her say the Words; and she said, if she did, she knew not what she said, being old, and distracted with her Sufferings. But the Maid being reasonably well come to herself, was, before the Court knew any Thing of it, sent out of the Town to *Youghall*, and so was no farther examin'd by the Court. This Fit of the Maid being urg'd by the Court with all the Circumstances of it, to have been a Continuance of her Devilish Practice, she deny'd it, and likewise the Motion of her Hands, or the saying, *Now she is down*; tho' the Court saw the first, and the Words were sworn by one *Roger Moor*. And *Thomas Harrison* swore, That he had observ'd the said *Florence* peep at her, and use that Motion with her Hands, and saw the Maid fall down immediately upon that Motion, and heard the Words, *Now she is down*, utter'd.

Observation.

In nothing more does Jane Wenham *resemble* Florence Newton, *than in her impudent Lying backwards and forwards, which was observ'd by all that talk'd with her while she was under Examination; and even since her Condemnation, she cannot leave it of, but it is every Day taken Notice of by all that come near her.*

But to go on with this Relation.

Nicholas Stout was next produc'd by Mr. Attorney-General, who being sworn and examin'd, said, That he had oft try'd her, having heard say that Witches could not say the Lord's Prayer, whither she could say that Prayer or not, and found she could not; whereupon she said she could say it, and had often said it; and the Court being desir'd by her to hear her say it, gave her Leave; and four times together after these Words, [*give us this Day our daily Bread*] she continually said, *As we forgive them*, leaving out the Words, [*And forgive us our Trespasses*] upon which the Court appointed one to teach her these Words she so left out: But she either could not, or would not say them, using only these or the like Words, *Aye, aye,*

Trespasses;

Trespasses; that's the Words. And being oft press'd to utter the Words as they were repeated to her, she did not: And being ask'd the Reason, she said she was old, and had a bad Memory; and being ask'd how her Memory serv'd her so well for other Parts of the Prayer, and only fail'd her for that, she said she knew not, neither could she help it.

Observation.

In the Account above refer'd to p. 10 and 12, the Reader will find that this was exactly the Case with Jane Wenham. *When she came to this very Petition, she could not repeat it; no, not after another w: o rehears'd it slowly to her. 'Tis true, this Experiment was not made in Court, the Judge thinking fit to wave it, altho' it was desir'd by Mrs.* Gardiner, *towards the End of the Tryal. Neither did Mother* Wenham *care for it herself, having so often found herself foil'd at this Petition, and that,* Lead us not into Temptation, &c. *tho' her Memory was as good as* Florence Newton's *as to the rest of the Prayer.*

To proceed with the Tryal of Florence.

John Pyne being likewise sworn and examin'd, said, That about *January* last *Mary Longdon*, being his Servant, was much troubl'd with little Stones that were thrown at her wherever she went, and that he hath seen them come as if they were thrown at her, others as if they dropp'd on her; and that he hath seen very great Quantities of them, and that they would, after they had hit her, fall on the Ground, and then vanish, so that none of them could be found. And farther, That the Maid once caught one of them, and he himself another, and one of them with a Hole in it, she ty'd to her Purse, but it vanish'd in a little Time, but the Knot of the Leather that ty'd it, remain'd unalter'd. That after the Stones had thus haunted her, she fell into most grievous Fits, wherein she was so violently distracted, that four Men would have very much to do to hold her; and that in the greatest of her Extremities, she would cry out of Gammar *Newton* for hurting and tormenting of her. That sometimes the Maid would be reading in a Bible, and on the sudden he hath seen the Bible struck out of her Hand into the middle of the Room, and she immediately was cast into a violent Fit. That in the Fits he hath seen two Bibles laid on her Breasts, and in the Twinkling of an Eye, they would be

cast

cast between the two Beds the Maid lay upon, sometimes thrown into the middle of the Room, and that *Nicholas Pyne* held the Bible in the Maid's Hand so fast, that it being suddenly snatch'd away, two of the Leaves were torn. That in many other Fits the Maid was remov'd strangely in the Twinkling of an Eye, out of the Bed, sometimes into the bottom of a Chest with Linnen, and the Linnen not at all disorder'd, sometimes betwixt the two Beds she lay on, sometimes under a Parcel of Wooll, sometimes betwixt his Bed and the Mat of it in another Room, and once she was laid on a small Deal Board which lay on the Top of an House betwixt two solar Beams, where he was forc'd to rear up Ladders to have her fetch'd down. That in her Fits she hath often vomited up Wooll, Pins, Horse-Nails, Stubs, Straw, Needles, and Moss, with a kind of white Foam or Spittle, and hath had several Pins stuck into her Arms and Hands, that sometimes a Man must pull three or four times before he could pull one of them out, and some have stuck between the Flesh and the Skin, where they might be perfectly seen, but not taken out, nor any Place seen where they were put in. That when the Witch was brought into the Room where she was, she would be in more violent and longer-lasting Fits than at other Times. That all the Time the Witch was at Liberty, the Maid was ill, and that as soon as she was committed and bolted, she recover'd and was well; and that when the Witch was remov'd to *Cork*, the Maid fell ill; and thereupon the Mayor of *Youghall* sent to see whether she was bolted or no, and to acquaint them the Maid was ill, and desire them, if the Witch were not bolted, they would bolt her. That she immediately recover'd, and was as well as ever; and when the Messenger came from *Cork*, and told them the Witch was bolted, it fell out to be the very Time the Maid amended at *Youghall*.

Nickolas Pyne being sworn, said, That the second Night that the Witch was in Prison, being the 24th of *March* last, he and *Joseph Thomson*, *Roger Hawkins*, and some others, went to speak with her concerning the Maid, and told her, that it was the general Opinion of the Town that she had bewitch'd her, and desir'd her to deal freely with them, whether she had bewitch'd her or no? She said she had not bewitch'd her, but it may be she had overlook'd her, and that there was a great deal of Difference

rence between bewitching and overlooking; and that she could not have done her any Harm, if she had not touch'd her, and therefore she had kiss'd her. And she said, that what Mischief she thought upon at that Time she kiss'd her, would fall upon her; and that she would not but confess, that she had wrong'd the Maid, and thereupon fell down on her Knees, and pray'd God to forgive her wronging the poor Maid. They wish'd that she might not be wholly destroy'd by her; to which she said it must be another that must help her, and not they that did the Harm. And then she said there were others, as Goody *Halfpenny* and Goody *Dod*, in Town, that could do these Things as well as she, and that it might be one of them that had done the Maid Wrong.

Observation.

All this last Paragraph (altering only the Names) is true of Jane Wenham. *She confess'd to several, that she had look'd upon* Anne Thorn; *which dark Expression, I must own, I was at a Loss to understand, 'till this very Passage explain'd it to me. I see now by it, that this is a Term of Art among the Witches, by which 'tis probable they mean some less Degree of mischievous enchanting; whereas, according to Mother* Newton, *the Word* Bewitching *seems to signify something still greater, perhaps hurting even to Death. Whatever be its Meaning, I declare that I very well remember* Jane Wenham's *saying that she had look'd upon* Anne Thorn. *The Conjecture of the Editor of this Edition of Mr.* Glanvill's *Book, in his Advertisement annex'd to this Relation, seems to be, that this overlooking, or (in* Jane Wenham's *Expression) looking upon, relates to* ’Οφθαλμὸς βάσκανος, *and that the Magical Venom came out at her Eyes when she kiss'd the Maid. And he leaves it to the Criticks in that black School, to determine whether this* ’Οφθαλμὸς βάσκανος *be not the first Sort of Witchcraft, distinct from that of bewitching People by* Images *made of* Wax; *and whether afterwards this Sort of bewitching by meer looking or touching, might not be call'd overlooking. To which I add, that it is a common Expression almost in every Body's Mouth, when they speak of a Person suppos'd to be bewitch'd, that he or she lies under an* ill Tongue; *and why they may not as well say under an* evil Eye, *as an* ill Tongue, *I do not see any Reason. However, I offer this only as Conjecture, and proceed farther to observe the Agreement of this whole Paragraph,*

ragraph, with the Case of Jane Wenham. *Mother* Newton here confesses, that she had done Wrong to the Maid. This also did Goody Wenham, and often would fall on her Knees, and pray to God to forgive her what she had done. *Mother* Wenham *was desir'd to help* Anne Thorn *if she could ; but she said she could not, for another was as deep in it as herself; and as* Florence Newton *nam'd two of her Neighbours, so did* Jane Wenham *also name three Women of* Walkerne, *as her Confederates, but could prove nothing upon 'em. I must needs say, when I first read this Story of* Florence Newton, *which was not 'till after* Jane Wenham's *being committed to Goal, I was not a little surpriz'd to find such almost exact Agreement between it, and those Passages to which I was an Eye and Ear Witness ; and it serv'd to me, as I doubt not but it will to the Reader, as a strong Argument of the Being of Witches. For how should two old Women, accus'd of a Crime merely imaginary, in distant Times and Nations, agree so exactly in a Term of Art, which is suppos'd peculiar to those who are guilty of that Crime ? How, I say, could this be, if there were no real Foundation for it, no Ground at all for this critical Distinction, between bewitching and overlooking.*

Let us now go on with the Relation.

Nicholas Pyne farther saith, That towards Evening the Door of the Prison shook, and she arose up hastily, and said, *What makest thou here at this Time of the Night?* And there was a very great Noise, as if Somebody with Bolts and Chains had been running up and down the Room. And they ask'd her what it was she spoke to? and what it was that made the Noise? She said she saw nothing, neither did she speak, and if she did, it was she knew not what. But the next Day she confess'd it was a Spirit and her Familiar, in the Shape of a Greyhound.

That he and Mr. *Edward Perry*, and others, took a Tile off the Prison next to the Place where the Witch lay, and carry'd it to the House where the Maid liv'd, and put it into the Fire 'till it was red-hot, and then dropt some of the Maid's Water upon it, and the Witch was then grievously tormented; and when the Water was consum'd, she was well again.

Observation.

The Reader will find, p. 20 of our Account, just such another Experiment made at Walkerne, *in which they also made use of the*

the Maid's Water, only instead of dropping it on a Tile, they put it into a Stone Bottle; and it was observ'd, that while it was over the Fire, the Witch seem'd in great Torture.

Nicholas Pyne *farther saith*,

That as to the Stones falling on, and cast at the Maid, as to the Maid's Fits, her Removal into the Chest, under the Wooll, betwixt the Feather Beds, on the Top of the Deal Board, betwixt two solar Beams, concerning the Bibles and their Remove, his holding one of them in the Maid's Hand 'till two Leaves were torn, concerning the Maid's vomiting, and her calling out against the Witch, he agreeth perfectly throughout with *John Pyne*, as before.

Edward Perry being likewise sworn, deposeth, That he, Mr. *Greatrix*, and Mr. *Blackwall*, went to the Maid, and Mr. *Greatrix* and he had read of a Way to discover a Witch, which he would put in Practice. And so they sent for the Witch, and set her on a Stool, and a Shoemaker, with a strong Awl, endeavour'd to stick it in the Stool, but could not 'till the third Time; and then they bad her come off the Stool, but she said she was very weary, and could not stir. Then two of them pull'd her off, and the Man went to pull out his Awl, and it dropt into his Hand with half an Inch broke off the Blade of it, and they all look'd to have found where it had been stuck, but could find no Place where any Entry had been made by it. Then they took another Awl, and put it into the Maid's Hand, and one of them took the Maid's Hand, and ran violently at the Witch's Hand with it, but could not enter it, tho' the Awl was so bent, that none of them could put it strait again. Then Mr. *Blackwall* took a Launce and launc'd one of her Hands an Inch and half long, and a quarter deep, but it bled not at all; then he launc'd the other Hand, and then they bled.

Observation.

Here again *Florence* Newton *and* Jane Wenham *agree in the Difficulty there was in fetching Blood of either of them. Page* 19 *of the Account, the Reader may see, that Mr.* Chauncy *stuck several Pins into* Jane Wenham's *Arms, and one up to the Head, yet no Blood follow'd, neither did she seem sensible of any Pain.*

Edward

Edward Perry farther faith, That after she was in Prison, he went with *Roger Hawkins*, and others, to discourse with the Witch about the Maid, and they ask'd what it was she spake to the Day before? and after some Denyal, she said it was a Greyhound, which was her Familiar, and went out at the Window; and then she said, *If I have done the Maid Hurt, I am sorry for it.* And being then ask'd whether she had done her any Hurt? she said she never did bewitch her, but confess'd she had overlook'd her, at the Time she kiss'd her, but that she could not now help her; for none could help that did the Mischief, but others. And farther the Deponent saith, That after at the Assize at *Cashal*, he meeting with one *William Lap*, and discoursing about these Passages with him, the said *Lap* told the Deponent, that if he would but take a Tile off the House near the Place where the Witch lay, and beat it red hot in the Fire, and then take some of the Maid's Water and drop upon it, that so long as this was doing, he should find the Witch grievously tormented. That afterwards he, *Edward Perry*, *Nicholas Pyne*, and others, put this in Practice, and found that the Witch was extreamly tormented and vex'd, and when the Experiment was over, she came to her self; and then they ask'd her how she came to hurt the Maid? and she said, That what Evil she thought against the Maid that Time she kiss'd her, that would fall upon her; and that she could not have hurt her, except she had touch'd her; and then she fell upon her Knees, and confess'd she had wrong'd the Maid, and desir'd God to forgive her. And then they put her upon saying the Lord's Prayer, but she could not say the Words, *And forgive us our Trespasses.*

Mr. *Wood*, a Minister, being likewise sworn and examin'd, deposeth, That having heard of the Stones dropt and thrown at the Maid, and of her Fits, and meeting with the Maid's Brother, he went along with him to the Maid, and found her in her Fit, crying out of Gammar *Newton*, that she prick'd her, and hurt her. And when she came to her self, he ask'd her what had troubl'd her? and she said, Gammar *Newton*. And the Deponent said, *Why? she was not there.* *Yes*, said she, *I saw her by my Bedside.* The Deponent then ask'd her the Original of all, which she related, from the Time of her begging the Beef, and after kissing her, and so to that Time. That then

they

they caus'd the Maid to be got up, and sent for *Florence Newton*, but she refus'd to come, pretending she was sick, tho' indeed it appear'd she was well. Then the Mayor of *Youghall* came in, and spoke with the Maid, and then sent again, and caus'd *Florence Newton* to be brought in, and immediately the Maid fell into her Fit far more violent, and three times as long as at any other Time; and all the Time the Witch was in the Chamber, the Maid cry'd out continually of being hurt here and there, but never nam'd the Witch, but as soon as she was remov'd, then she cry'd out against her by the Name of Gammar *Newton*, and this for several times. And still, when the Witch was out of the Room, the Maid would desire to go to Prayers, and he found good Affections in her in Time of Prayer; but when the Witch was brought in again, tho' never so privately, altho' she could not possibly, as the Deponent conceives, see her, she would be immediately senseless, and like to be strangl'd, and so would continue 'till the Witch was taken out; and then, tho' never so privately carry'd away, she would come again to her Senses. That afterwards Mr. *Greatrix*, Mr. *Blackwall*, and some others, who would needs satisfy themselves in the Influence of the Witch's Presence, try'd it, and found it several times, altho' it was done with all possible Privacy, and so as none could think it possible for the Maid to know either of the Witch's coming in, or going out.

Observation.

Here is, as in Wenham's *Tryal, a Clergy-man evidencing against the Prisoner, altho' I do not hear any Reflections made upon him for so doing; and there are two Things very remarkable in his Testimony, one, that he found good Affections in the Maid in Time of Prayer; the other, that there was a strange Alteration in her upon the Witch's coming into the Room. The first of these was always observ'd in* Anne Thorn, *who, as soon as recover'd out of her Fits, which was immediately upon their beginning to pray by her, always join'd in the Prayers with great Signs of Devotion and Trust in God, and in her Intervals, she was almost constantly reading or praying. There was also observ'd in her as great an Alteration upon Sight of the Witch, as in* Mary Longdon, *only it was for the better, which, as I have observ'd already, may be accounted for the same way as the others growing worse at the Presence of* Florence Newton.

The

The next Witness at the Tryal, was *Richard Magre*, Mayor of *Youghall*, who being sworn, saith, That about the 24th of *March* last, he sent for *Florence Newton*, and examin'd her about the Maid, and she at first deny'd it, and accus'd Goody *Halfpenny* and Goody *Dod*, but at Length, when he had caus'd a Boat to be provided, and had thought to have try'd the Water-Experiment on them all three, then *Florence Newton* confess'd, that she had overlook'd the Maid, and done her Wrong with a Kiss; for which she was heartily sorry, and pray'd God to forgive her. Then he likewise examin'd the other two Women, *Halfpenny* and *Dod*, but they utterly deny'd it, and were content to abide any Tryal; whereupon he caus'd *Dod*, *Halfpenny*, and *Florence* to be carry'd to the Maid; and he told her, these two Women, or one of them, were said by Gammar *Newton* to have done her Hurt. But she answer'd, *No, no, they are honest Women, but it is Gammar* Newton *that hurts me, and I believe she is not far off*. That then they afterwards brought in *Newton* privately, and then she fell into a most violent Fit, ready to be strangl'd, 'till the Witch was remov'd; and this for three several Times. He farther deposeth, That there were three Aldermen in *Youghall*, whose Children she had kiss'd, as he had heard them affirm, and that all the Children dy'd presently after; and as to the sending to *Cork* to have the Bolts put on, he swears as is formerly depos'd.

Observation.

Thus the Reader may find, p. 16 and 17 of the above-mention'd Account, that Jane Wenham *accus'd three Women of* Walkerne, *who were brought before Sir* Henry Chauncy; *and while he was examining* Jane Wenham *concerning them*, Anne Thorn *fell into a Fit, and every one of these three Women were brought to her, and touch'd her, but she seem'd not to perceive them in the least. Then* Jane Wenham *was privately brought to her, and touch'd her, and she sprung up immediately as usual; and afterwards she said she could not say any Thing against these Women, who were thereupon discharg'd. It is really very remarkable to see these two Cases agree in so many minute Circumstances, insomuch, that the one Story seems to be only an Imitation of the other: And yet I can say, to my certain Knowledge, that all these Things were done before this Tryal of* Florence Newton *was taken Notice of by any concern'd in the Prosecution of* Jane Wenham.

To proceed.

Joseph Thomson being sworn, said, That he went in *March* last with *Roger Hawkins*, *Nicholas Pyne*, and others, to the Prison, to confer with *Florence Newton* about the Maid, but she would confess nothing that Time: But towards Night there was a Noise at the Prison-Door, as if something had shook the Door, and *Florence* started up, and said, *What aileth thee to be here at this Time of the Night?* and there was much Noise. And they ask'd her what she spoke to? and what made the great Noise? But she deny'd that she spake, or that she knew of any Noise, and said, *If I spoke, I said I knew not what*. And they went their ways that Time, and went to her again the next Night, and ask'd her very seriously about the last Night's Passage, and the Noise. And then she confess'd to them, that it was a Greyhound that came to her, and that she had seen it formerly, and that it went out at the Window. And then she confess'd, that she had done the Maid wrong, for which she was sorry, and desir'd God to forgive her.

This was the most material Evidence against *Florence Newton*, for bewitching *Mary Longdon*. She was also indicted for bewitching to Death one *David Jones*, by kissing his Hand thro' the Prison-Gate; but this no way resembling *Wenham*'s Case, I refer the Reader to the Relation it self, at the End of Mr. *Glanvill*'s *Sadducismus Triumphatus*. One Thing only I shall take Notice of to him, that the Author of the Advertisement annex'd to it, saith, That he conceiveth this Relation to be taken out of a Copy of an authentick Record, every half Sheet having *W. Aston* writ in the Margent, and *W. Aston* at the End, whom he supposes to be some Publick Notary, or Record-Keeper. He adds this Witch of *Youghall* is so famous, that he hath heard Mr. *Greatrix* speak of her at my Lord *Conway*'s at *Ragley*. And for my own Part, I hope the surprizing Agreement of this Story with *Jane Wenham*'s, will sufficiently justify my inserting it here.

A short ANSWER *to the principal Objections made, first,* Against the Being and Power of Witches *in general: And secondly, The Case of* Jane Wenham *in particular.*

AFter a Relation of Matter of Fact so very strange, and yet so well attested, as the Account of the Sorceries and Enchantments of *Jane Wenham,* I thought fit, in order to satisfy some well-meaning Men, who have imbib'd a strong Prejudice against the Being of Witches, to set before them the principal Objections against it; and in as clear a Method as I can, to shew the Emptiness of those noisy Exceptions made against the Prosecutors of *Jane Wenham,* as if they attempted to take away a poor Woman's Life, for a Crime that she cannot, if she would, be guilty of. But before I do this, I must premise, that nothing here alledg'd, is intended to convince those that deny the Being of *Spirits in general,* and in Consequence the *Immateriality of Human Souls,* and the *Existence of a God.* I don't pretend, by this plain Narrative, to convince *Atheists,* but refer 'em to the many excellent Authors that have treated on those noble Subjects, and shall here suppose my Reader to believe both the Being of a God, and the Truth of the holy Scriptures; and such a one I desire only to attend with Impartiality, while I endeavour to remove his Scruples.

In order to which, it is necessary, in the first Place, to fix the Meaning of the Word *Witch*; by which I mean *One, who, by open or secret League, consenteth to use the Aid and Assistance of an evil Spirit, in working Wonders beyond the ordinary Power of Nature.* By Wonders I do not mean *Miracles,* which can only be done by divine Power; but *strange Things,* preter-natural, not super-natural. The *Hebrew* Word [*Mecasseph*] is translated by the *Septuagint* φαρμακόϛ, which signifies *Veneficus,* in the vulgar *Latin Maleficus,*

Maleficus, altho' Dr. *Moore* saith from *Aben Ezra*, That the proper Signification of that Word, is one *qui mutat & transformat Res naturales ad Aspectum Oculi*. Take it in either of these Significations, or in both, it comes within the Definition of a Witch just laid down, as do all those other Words for a Sorcerer, which you find put together in the 18th Chapter of *Deuteronomy*, Ver. 10, 11. *There shall not be found among you any one that useth Divination, or an Observer of Times, or an Enchantor, or a Witch, or a Charmer, or a Consulter with a familiar Spirit, or a Necromancer.* All these Words imply doing or telling something wonderful, by Virtue of a Confederacy with an evil Spirit. The Word φαρμακὸς does also imply the making Use of natural Means, such as Herbs, Ointments, &c. to do strange Things withal, by the Assistance of their confederate Spirit. All these, I say, are so many Names for a Witch, who may have several Properties more than any one of these Names intimates; for which Reason they seem to be put all together in this Command of God to his People, not to suffer any such Persons among them.

Having thus fix'd the Meaning of the Word, I come to the first general Objection made against the Being of Witches, which is this:

Obj. 1. That the Actions ascrib'd to Witches, are impossible in their own Nature to be done by Man, and very ridiculous.

Answ. That there are indeed many Circumstances in the Stories of Witches, very strange and unaccountable, I readily allow; and farther, that they are impossible to be perform'd by Man, without the Assistance of some other Power: But then this very Thing is a strong Argument, that there is really the Assistance of some Spirit actually employ'd in doing these Wonders. If I see, for Instance, as in the Case of *Anne Thorn*, a poor lame Creature, that the Minute before could scarce creep on the Ground; if I see her on the Sudden start up, and run with a most prodigious Swiftness, and nimbly vault over a Five-Bar Gate. When I see this, I say, I am ready enough to believe it could not ordinarily be done; but then, for that very Reason I ascribe it to the Power of the Devil; so that the seeming Impossibility of the Thing, proves it to be done by Witchcraft: And in such Cases all depends on the Strength and Credibility of the Evidence, as to Matter of Fact.

Fact. But certainly 'tis a very wild way of Arguing, to conclude, that because a Thing which is sworn by several and credible Eye-witnesses, is strange and unaccountable, nay, impossible to be perform'd by Man alone, that therefore it must be false, and never done at all. At this Rate no Man must believe his Senses, and consequently all the Testimony of Miracles to the Truth of the Gospel, falls to the Ground. Ought not rather every wise and discerning Man, at the Sight of such wonderful Things, immediately to apply himself to discover, whether the Thing may not, in its own Nature, imply no Contradiction, but be, altho' above the Power of Man, yet within that of some *other immaterial Agent*; and by other Circumstances to discover what that Agent is, whether a good Angel, or an evil Spirit?

We ought in these Cases carefully to distinguish between what is impossible in its own Nature, and consequently implies a Contradiction; and what may be done, altho' we cannot conceive the *Modus* of it; which shews indeed the Weakness of human Understanding, and the Imperfection and Short-sightedness of our Apprehensions; but is no more an Argument against the Reality of such Performances, than it is against the Truth of this Proposition, *The Fœtus is really form'd in the Womb of a Woman*, because we know not the Manner how it is so form'd. Methinks it savours too much of Pride and Conceitedness, for a Man to exalt his own Opinion above the clearest Testimony and plainest Demonstrations of Fact; and to chuse rather to give the Lie to all the World, than believe a Thing beyond the Reach of his narrow Conceptions.

As for Things of this Nature being ridiculous; if those who cannot understand, and therefore will not believe them, are resolv'd to turn 'em into Ridicule, who can help it? It neither detracts from the Truth nor Credibility of any Matter of Fact, that some, who are wise in their own Conceits, make a Jest of it. This only proceeds from a conceited Ignorance, the Censure or Applauses of which are equally below a wise Man's Regard. So that, in short, the Answer to this Objection, comes to this, That unless it can be prov'd that those Things are impossible to be done by any Power whatsoever, *that of Spirits not excepted*, this Objection can be of no Force against the Testimony of our Senses, or that of credible Eye-witnesses to *Matter of Fact*.

Obj.

Obj. 2. It is very improbable that a Spirit of such Wisdom and Power as the Devil, should stoop so low as to submit to be at the Command of a silly old Woman, and run up and down to execute her petty Revenge.

Answ. That there are Orders and Degrees of evil Spirits, is not at all improbable; and, upon this Supposition, it will not be absolutely necessary, to put the *Prince of Darkness himself* upon these little servile Employments; but we may well enough ascribe it to one of his inferior Agents. It is also the Opinion of some learned and ingenious Men, that the Familiars of Witches, may be the departed human Souls of some wicked and malicious Men, possess'd with an insatiable Thirst after Mischief, which by the *Laws* and *Capacity* of their *Condition*, they may not be capable of executing themselves; these may be employ'd in some of the meanest Services of the Kingdom of Hell. We know that, the Souls of good Men, in a separate State, are said to be ἰσάγγελοι, or in a like Condition with the blessed Angels; and why then may not the Souls of evil Men be also ἰσοδαίμονες, in the worst Sense of the World, in a Condition or State like that of the infernal Angels? And what if we should farther suppose many of these Witches Imps, to be the departed Souls of some that have been Witches themselves! I see nothing unreasonable in this Conjecture; which if allow'd, a still more probable Account may still be given of some of the most vile and mean Performances of such Spirits; altho' all the greater Wonders of Witchcraft, such as raising Storms and Tempests, and the like, are undoubtedly done by the Devil himself, that *God of this World*, and *Prince of the Power of the Air*. I urge farther, that supposing these Familiars to be really *Devils*, that is, such *Spirits* as had before their Fall been *Angels of Light*; yet still the only Difficulty here objected, comes to this, That the greatest Degree of Wickedness is also the most abject Baseness, and vilest Slavery. And how this can be of any Force against Matter of Fact, and the clearest Testimony, I leave to the Judgment of any sensible and impartial Reader. I come now to a more specious Objection.

Obj. 3. It is inconsistent with the Providence of God, to permit the Power of Witches to hurt the Innocent; such as Children, who are most subject to be bewitch'd.

Answ. Suppose I should bring an Argument against the Providence of Almighty God, from the *other* Dangers and Violences

Violences that Children are expos'd to, either from Accident, or Cruelty of their Neighbours; and upon Sight of a murder'd Child, should exclaim against the *Justice* of *Heaven*, for not miraculously protecting it against the Barbarity of its inhuman Butcher: Should I not immediately be reprimanded for murmuring against God, and forgetting the many and wonderful Preservations of others? Should I not be put in Mind, that considering the Weakness of that State, it is rather wonderful that there should be so *few* Instances of this Kind, than that there should be *any*? Just so it is in this Case, considering the Power, the Number, and implacable Malice of evil Spirits, it is only owing to the Care of Providence over us, that there are so *few* of us subject to their Power; and if some Witches are permitted to hurt now and then one of their innocent Neighbours, it is certainly for some wise and good End that they are so permitted; such as perhaps the Discovery of the Witches themselves, the convincing of an Unbeliever, or some other wise Reason, which lies hidden from our Sight among the unfathomable Depths and Mysteries of Providence; against the Being or Justice of which it is no more an Argument, than the unequal Distributions of Good and Evil in this Life, the Ignorance and Barbarity of the much greatest Part of the World, and the many Perils and Dangers we are all daily subject to. And if it be not a concluding Argument against the very Being of Providence, it cannot be sufficient to take away the Evidence of Sense in Matters of Fact.

Obj. 4. It is also objected, that the Strength of Melancholly, and Force of Imagination, ascribes any strange Event to Sorcery and Witchcraft, which is the more suspicious, because the Persons accus'd, are generally poor old Women; and those afflicted, are, for the most Part, either Children, or weak ignorant People, that are easily impos'd upon.

Answ. That the Power of Fancy is very great, may easily be acknowledg'd; and yet, I must needs say, it requires more *Credulity* to believe, that so many and so clear Circumstances of Fact, as, for Instance, the Conveyance of Pins through the Air into the Hands of a Person when they are ty'd down, or the finding of very curious and artificial Cakes of Feathers in a Pillow but a little before stuff'd with Down, and other the like strange Things, to

F be

be all but the Work of Fancy, and that forty or fifty Spectators should be all, just at the same Time, impos'd upon by the same *chimerical* Imaginations: This, I say, requires more Credulity to believe, than all the Stories of Witchcraft put together. At this Rate, no Man can tell when or how to believe what he sees or hears; and it puts an End to the Credit of all human Testimony whatsoever. As for the Reason, why *silly old Women* should generally enter into these Combinations with the Devil, it is probable, that the Devil takes Advantage of this their *Ignorance and Poverty*; especially, if accompany'd with a malicious Mind, and a Custom of invoking the Devil in Curses and Imprecations, as in the Case of *Jane Wenham*; and that thus he more effectually secures their Souls to him for ever, and puts them, as far as possible, from any Likelihood of making their Peace with God by Repentance. However, there is nothing more to be concluded from this Part of the Objection, than that the *Policy* of *Hell* is unknown to us, which cannot destroy the *clear Evidence of Matter of Fact*.

Obj. 5. Another Objection is, That since the Times of the Gospel, there can be no Witches, because our Saviour Christ *came to destroy the Works of the Devil*; and it is notorious, that he is driven from his Temples, and all his Oracles are struck dumb; from whence it is probable, that he has no longer the Power he once had to assist his Servants in working Wonders.

Answ. The Scriptures do more than once expresly mention *Witches and Sorcerers,* since the Time of our Saviour Christ, witness that noted Place in the 5th Chapter of the Epistle to the *Galatians,* Verse the 20th. Besides which, the Story of *Simon Magus* alone might sufficiently confute this Objection, who work'd such Wonders, that he deceiv'd many: *He,* says the Author of the *Acts of the Apostles,* c. 8. v. 9. us'd *Sorcery,* and *bewitch'd the People of Samaria*; and yet all the strange Things he did, were done by the assisting Power of the Devil; so that some Time after our Saviour's Ascension, this Power did remain to the great Deceiver; and I believe the Objectors will find it more difficult, than at first Sight it appears, to fix any Period of Time when this Power of Satan ceas'd. If they say it was, when he was driven from his Temples and his Altars, pray let 'em tell me when was that? Or are they
sure

sure that ever there was such a Time? Does not the Devil still retain such a Dominion over the Minds of whole Nations in *America*, and other Parts of the World, that they erect Temples to him, and fall down before him, worshipping him as a *God*? And why this Part only of the Devil's Power, which consists in making *Compacts*, and entering into Covenants with such wretched Creatures as *Witches* are, should be taken from him, and all the rest left intirely to him, I must profess my self not able to imagine.

Besides, there is one ugly Consequence from this Objection, which I believe few of those foresee that have it so often in their Mouths, which is this: If from the Silence of Oracles, and the Extirpation of Idolatry, it may be concluded, that the Devil is also forc'd to leave off all Communication and Correspondence with such vile profligate Persons as Witches; no Reason can be given, why from the same *Topicks* it may not as well be collected, that he is also put from his *nearer* Temples *within* us, and unable any longer by his Temptations to seduce Mankind to eternal Ruin. There is as great a Congruity of one Consequence with the Premises, as of the other; tho', I must needs say, they can neither of them be prov'd by any Logick I ever yet met with. I shall only urge farther against this Objection, two other Places in the New Testament, wherein Sorcerers are expresly *mention'd, and severely threaten'd*. The first is, Revel. 21. 8. *But the Fearful and Unbelieving, and the Abominable, and Murderers, and Whoremongers, and Sorcerers, and Idolaters, and all Lyars, shall have their Part in the Lake which burneth with Fire and Brimstone; which is the second Death.* The other is in the last Chapter of the *Revelations*, v. 15. *For without are Dogs, and Sorcerers, and Whore-mongers*, &c. Here you see no less than Fire and Brimstone in one Place, and perpetual *Exclusion* from the holy City, the New *Jerusalem*, in the other, expresly denounc'd against Sorcerers, who are reckon'd among the vilest Offenders, and most profligate Sinners, such as *Murderers* and *Idolaters*. Now, what a Jest is it to suppose the Scriptures all this while *fighting with a Shadow*, and threatening Damnation to those who shall be guilty of a Crime impossible to be committed? If this is not ridiculing the Word of God, I know not what is.

Obj. 6. I shall mention but one Objection more against the Being of Witches in general, which is such a one as I would willingly have omitted, on Account of its horrid Profaneness, were I not too well satisfy'd, that 'tis often made Use of among those who call themselves *Christians*; it is this: If we believe Witches can do Wonders by the Help of the Devil, how shall we know that the Miracles of our Saviour were not also the Effects of a *Diabolical Imposture*?

A. ſ. To this Objection, the best Answer will be in our Saviour's own Words to the unbelieving Pharisees, Matt. 12. 26. *If Satan cast out Satan, he is divided against himself, how then shall his Kingdom stand?* The Design of our Redeemer's coming into the World, was to destroy the Kingdom of Satan, to preach Repentance and Salvation to Sinners, and to shew us the Way to eternal Life; how then could the Miracles of Christ be attributed to the Power of Satan, which he came to pull down?

It ought farther to be consider'd, that the wonderful Works of the blessed Jesus were truly *Miracles*, that is, above the Power of any created Being (that of the Devil himself not excepted) to effect; such as raising one from the Dead, who had been really dead so long, that those of his Relations, who had bury'd him, suppos'd that *by this Time he stink'd*, Joh. 11. 39. And what was most wonderful of all, raising himself the third Day. Besides, the Miracles of Christ were all full of Love and Charity, such as healing the Sick, giving Sight to the Blind, Food to the Hungry in a Desart, &c. Whereas nothing but Spite, Envy, and Malice, appears in the strange Things done by these Confederates of Satan, the End and Design of them being to torment and hurt their Neighbours. The Miracles of our Saviour bear upon them the clearest Marks of the Finger of God of Mercy; whereas the Wonders done by Witches and Sorcerers, do plainly indicate a Hellish and Diabolical Malice. Those who are so forward to raise this Objection upon every Occasion, would do well seriously to consider what that Sin against the Holy Ghost is, *for which there is no Repentance.* This was, in the Opinion of the most learned Divines, nothing but the *attributing the Miracles of Christ to the Power of the Devil*; and let them have a Care lest they also come near the Commission of that *dreadful Sin.*

I have

I have now done with the principal of those Objections, that are commonly rais'd against the Being and Power of Witches in general; I come now very briefly to speak a Word or two to those which are more particularly urg'd against the Case of *Jane Wenham*.

And first, 'tis objected, that her Confession might be the Effect of Fear; or if it was not, she might accuse her self falsely, only to be out of the World: That there have been Instances of this Nature, where discontented Persons have confess'd themselves guilty of capital Crimes whereof they were innocent, only to be rid of their Troubles by Death.

I answer, as to the first Part of this Objection, That the Confession of *Jane Wenham* was free and unconstrain'd, no Force having been us'd to bring her to it; for the Truth of which, as I said before, p. 33. of the Account, &c. we appeal to Mr. *Archer* of *Sandon*, her near Kinsman, who was present, when she confess'd that she liv'd above sixteen Years in a Course of Witchcraft.

As for the other Suggestion, That possibly her Discontents might make her falsely accuse herself, to be out of the World, I allow, that in some Cases this Consideration may have its Weight. As for Instance; Suppose a Man who labours under very great Troubles and Afflictions, and is known to be discontented, and weary of his Life, should voluntarily come before a Magistrate, and accuse himself of a capital Crime, and desire that the Punishment of Death may be inflicted on him for it; and this, when there are no other Circumstances by which it may be thought probable that he did commit this Crime: In such a Case as this, a discontented Man's Confession alone, I must needs say, I think ought not to convict him. But this is quite another Case, and widely different from that of *Jane Wenham*. Here were very violent Presumptions against her, long before her Confession, which only serv'd the more strongly to prove what had been before alledg'd; and indeed so strong was the Evidence against her, that many have been convicted upon weaker Proofs, without any Confession at all; so that here is all the Reason in the World to believe her Confession. It is the Opinion of Mr. *Perkins*, in his Treatise of Witchcraft, p. 212. *That when Proceeding is made against a Man at first upon good Probabilities, and he is thereupon drawn to a free Confession, that which*

which he hath manifested thereby, *cannot but be a Truth*. So I am sure it is reckon'd in other Cases, as Murders, Thefts, and other such Crimes; and why it should not be so in the Case of *Witchcraft*, I can see no Manner of Reason. If there be a Robbery committed, and a Man taken up for it upon strong Suspicions, that Man, if he confesses, shall, by such a Confession, be more strongly convicted; and, by Parity of Reason, if a Woman, upon violent Presumptions, is accus'd of Witchcraft, her Confession ought to be taken as a strong Confirmation of the Evidence brought against her.

Obj. 2. It is also objected, That one Part of *Anne Thorn*'s Information, in which she says, that a Cat spoke to her, is very ridiculous and incredible.

Answ. Is it more ridiculous and incredible, that an evil Spirit should assume the Shape of a Cat, and in such a Shape speak so as to be heard and understood, than that the Devil should speak to *Eve* in the Shape of a Serpent? Which we are oblig'd to believe upon the Credit of Divine Revelation. 'Tis the Opinion of the pious and profoundly learn'd Mr. *Mede*, p. 223 and 224 of his Works, ' *That there is a Law in the Commerce of Spirits and Men,* ' *that a Spirit must present himself under the Shape of some* ' *visible Thing*: And he supposes farther, that s Spirits ' are to converse with Men under some visible Shape; *so* ' *there is a Law given them, that it must be under the Shape of* ' *some such Thing, as may more or less resemble their Condition*. From whence he concludes, that good Angels can take upon 'em no other Shape, but that of Man, the most excellent of all visible Creatures; and therefore he says an Angel is said to appear, in the Gospel, like a *young Man, his Countenance like Lightning, and his Rayment white as Snow,* as it were resembling Man in his glorious State before the Fall.

He supposes also, that while Man was in his Integrity, the Devil could not appear in an *human* Shape, but was forc'd to take up with that of a *Beast*, tho' the most *subtil* and *sagacious* one of all the Beasts of the Field. But now indeed the Case is alter'd, *Man* being also fallen, and one falling Star (says he) may resemble another; and therefore he sometimes appears in the Shape of *Man* in his Imperfection, like a *deform'd old* Man.

Now, upon the like Supposition, why may not a wretched Spirit appear in the Shape of one of the meanest of
the

the *Brute Beasts?* There is no Shape too base and vile to represent one of those miserable Spirits, fallen for ever from *God* and *Goodness,* and become one of the vilest Slaves in the *Regions* of *Darkness.* As for the Truth of the Matter of Fact, it is too well confirm'd by the unhappy Experience of the two poor Sufferers, *Anne Thorn* and *Anne Street,* who almost every Day continue to see and hear this evil Spirit tempting and tormenting them in the Shape of a Cat.

Having now answer'd the most material Objections against Witchcraft, and this Case in particular, I submit the whole to the Reader's impartial Judgment; and as for those who are resolv'd to remain Unbelievers, and therefore will be very ready to start frivolous Objections, and ask impertinent Questions, I shall take no Manner of Notice of them, unless they will first make it appear, that a rational Account can be given of the whole Course of *Anne Thorn*'s and *Anne Street*'s Disorder, without ascribing it to the Witchcrafts of *Jane Wenham.*

I shall conclude all, with producing the Judgment of the learned Arch-Bishop *Tillotson* upon the following Text; which, I hope, will have some Effect with those who ridiculously object it to be meant of *Witchcraft.*

"*The Son of God was manifested, that he might destroy,* ἵνα λύῃ, *that he might dissolve or demolish the Works of the Devil;* by which St. *John* does more especially mean *the idolatrous Worship of the Heathen,* which consisted in the Multitude of their Gods, and the bloody and barbarous Rites and Sacrifices, whereby they worshipp'd them; and likewise in the Multitude of their Mediators, between the Gods and Men, who were also esteem'd by them an inferior Sort of Deities. Both these Kinds of Idolatry had strangely prevail'd, and over-run the World, before the Appearance of our Lord and Saviour, who came on Purpose to deliver Mankind from the horrible Superstition and Slavery of the Worship of false Gods, to pull down this Kingdom of the Devil, and to demolish that Fabrick which he hath been so long a rearing, and so beat him out of those strong Holds, which he thought had been impregnable. *See Sermon* 17. *Posthum. Fol. Vol.* 1. *Pag.* 127.

F I N I S.